GW01455010

Accounting in the
Foreign Exchange Market

Accounting in the Foreign Exchange Market

Ian J. Martin BA, FCA

Finance Director, Baring Securities Ltd

London
Butterworths
1987

United Kingdom	Butterworth & Co (Publishers) Ltd, 88 Kingsway, LONDON WC2B 6AB and 61A North Castle Street, EDINBURGH EH2 3LJ
Australia	Butterworths Pty Ltd, SYDNEY, MELBOURNE, BRISBANE, ADELAIDE, PERTH, CANBERRA and HOBART
Canada	Butterworths. A division of Reed Inc., TORONTO and VANCOUVER
New Zealand	Butterworths of New Zealand Ltd, WELLINGTON and AUCKLAND
Singapore	Butterworth & Co (Asia) Pte Ltd, SINGAPORE
South Africa	Butterworth Publishers (Pty) Ltd, DURBAN and PRETORIA
USA	Butterworths Legal Publishers, ST PAUL, Minnesota, SEATTLE, Washington, BOSTON, Massachusetts, AUSTIN, Texas and D & S Publishers, CLEARWATER, Florida

British Library Cataloguing in Publication Data
Martin, Ian J.
   Accounting in the foreign exchange market.
   1. Foreign exchange — Accounting
   I. Title
   657'.48   HG3853.7

ISBN 0 406 50320 6

Typeset by Kerrypress Ltd, Luton, Beds

Printed and bound in Great Britain by Billings Bookplan, Worcester

To Kerensa

Preface

More than half the profits earned by Britain's top 100 companies are generated either overseas or from exports. The majority, if not all, of those companies would probably claim that they have an excellent understanding of their currency exposures, that there are staff in place to monitor group-wide flows of foreign currency and that they adopt a sophisticated 'risk averse' approach to hedging. Their shareholders could therefore be forgiven for being confused if they read in the annual report that the performance of their company has been adversely affected by exchange rate movements. Cynics would probably also note that it is far less common for a company to cite exchange rate movements as having been responsible for a more beneficial outcome than might otherwise have been expected.

Unfortunately, of course, it is not just the larger companies that are affected by foreign exchange rate movements and there is probably no economic activity in Britain today which is not affected in some way, either directly or indirectly, by the value of sterling. For some it might be a very direct exposure arising from an international trading relationship; with others the linkage may be more subtle and consist of indirect relationships such as the company's underlying cost base as compared with that of an overseas competitor.

The foreign exchange market is the largest market on earth and now accounts for something in excess of US $250 billion of transactions a day. Although much of that activity is represented by inter-bank trading on the 'spot' market, a growing volume is in the more esoteric and far less understood hedging products that have been developed over the last few years. Faced with a continual barrage of new instruments and yet lacking the experienced personnel required to choose between such products, many companies find themselves ill placed to cope with ever increasing fluctuations in exchange rates. Of even greater concern, perhaps, is the apparent lack of overall understanding of foreign exchange risk amongst senior management. Problems such as the recently discovered Volkswagen forex losses would be far less common if general management had a better grasp of the business implications and control requirements relating to foreign exchange exposure.

Many larger companies have been able to address these difficulties through the establishment of experienced treasury operations which are charged with the responsibility for managing the group's currency positions and, wherever possible, optimising the value of any foreign currency cashflows. Others have adopted a more pragmatic approach, arguing that the extent of their currency exposures is so great that it is virtually impossible to manage them realistically and that, on balance, the group probably wins on some exposures and loses on others. There are even a few large corporations which appear to have ignored the question altogether, and where the managing director may still be heard to say that acquiring a forward foreign exchange contract is essentially no more than currency speculation.

Because foreign exchange rate fluctuations have now become a fact of life, it is very easy to lose sight of the size of some of the currency swings now taking place. If one looks at the period from the, so-called, plaza accord (September 1985) through until the end of 1986, sterling fluctuated by between 20% and 30% against each of the yen, the Deutschmark, the Swiss franc and the French franc. The appreciation of the pound against the US dollar between March 1985 and March 1986 amounted to almost 40%. Even if Britain does eventually join the EMS, and assuming that this in itself does not cause major currency tensions within Europe, it will not stop sterling from suffering from fairly major fluctuations against the US dollar and the yen. There may also be the prospect of a long series of periodic re-alignments between sterling and other EMS currencies.

Accounting is central to the issue of foreign exchange exposure in that it provides the methodology for measuring and evaluating that exposure. The accounting profession has, however, suffered just as much as anyone else from the rapid development of the foreign exchange market, and general confusion and misunderstanding has sometimes been left to mix with fairly conservative accounting concepts to produce what has been, in retrospect, a meaningless result.

This book has been prepared for accountants with the objective of providing the reader with a fairly broad understanding of the foreign exchange market and the numerous hedging products now available to the corporate treasurer. It establishes a comprehensive approach to foreign exchange accounting which broadly accords with current professional guidance, whilst at the same time providing a realistic and commercially sensible result. Considerable emphasis is placed on the need to move progressively towards a more realistic accounting approach which better matches the underlying commercial activity. Although the book does not set out to be provocative, some of the concepts discussed herein are likely to be unfamiliar to many readers.

The first two chapters describe the development of the foreign exchange market as it exists today and discuss in some detail, its current structure and operation. Chapters 3 and 4 examine the nature of foreign currency exposure and the ways in which a corporation can manage that exposure on both a short-term and a long-term basis. Chapter 5 then reviews the financial reporting environment and the development of accounting standards in this area. The recommended approach to foreign exchange accounting is described in general terms in chapter 6, with the following three chapters then exploring the key elements of that approach in more detail. Chapter 7 covers transactions accounting, chapter 8 deals with the question of balance sheet translations and chapter 9 sets out the approach to consolidations. Finally, chapter 10 covers the subject of accounting systems and internal controls.

The final part of the book consists of a series of self-contained reference sections. The first of these contains a detailed description of many of the hedging products now available on the market — ranging from fairly standard forward transactions and currency futures through to currency swaps, options and the so-called 'third generation' products such as range forwards or swap options. The following three sections cover in turn each of the accounting aspects reviewed in chapters 7, 8 and 9. These sections provide a summary of the recommended accounting approach in each area and include examples, where appropriate, of some of the more complex accounting approaches required.

Finally, I would like to take this opportunity of thanking Roma Holmes, for her extraordinary typing efforts, Theresa Martin for her persistence and encouragement in helping me reach the end, and the commissioning staff at Butterworths for their patience and understanding.

Ian J Martin

June 1987
London

Contents

CHAPTER 1

Setting the scene

A BRIEF HISTORY

The era of fixed exchange rates
The Snake
The international marketplace
Increasing intervention
The future

A EUROPEAN PERSPECTIVE

Operation of the EMS
The ECU

A BRIEF HISTORY

Some might argue that history has no place in a book which sets out to be 'forward looking' or in a market which is driven by change. Without, however, considering the nature of the current market in the context of developments over the course of the last 40 years or so, it is difficult to appreciate the speed with which the market has moved and continues to move. It is sometimes difficult today to recall that as recently as the mid-1960s a simple division on a mechanical calculator took as long as 30 seconds, and that the use of electronic calculators was only introduced into the exams of the Institute of Chartered Accountants as recently as 1972. The computer-driven, 'high tech' dealing environment of today's foreign exchange markets is, in point of fact, still a fairly recent development.

The era of fixed exchange rates

The history of today's foreign exchange markets probably begins somewhere between the two World Wars when, certainly up until the Wall Street Crash, there was a system of fixed exchange rates linked to gold and silver. The currencies of many of the larger Western economies were 'convertible' to the extent that their governments stood ready to redeem them against one of those key metals. The market itself was, of course, extremely small by modern-day standards and those transactions which occurred were generally only for small amounts. International communication was by telegraph and settlement generally by airmail.

Although convertibility came to an end in the 1930s it was re-established after the Second World War as a result of the Bretton Woods agreement. The Bretton Woods conference in 1944 laid the foundations of what was to be the world's new international monetary system. It confirmed the post-war dominance of the US dollar by establishing par values for the convertibility of the dollar against gold, and provided for a series of fixed exchange rates between the US dollar and the other principal convertible currencies. Convertibility in a true sense, however, probably did not become a reality until about 14 years later, as the period of reconstruction of the Western economies was beginning to come to an end. By this time international trade had begun to grow and the telex had significantly enhanced the ability of international centres to communicate with each other.

The next ten years saw a period of fairly stable fixed rates of exchange where the only 'excitement' in the foreign exchange market tended to be the occasional rumour concerning a potential revaluation or devaluation. Markets remained extremely insular with, in particular, the New York and European markets rarely trading with each other. The US economy appeared to be immune from international developments and there was little or no concern in Europe as to the growing balance of payments deficits emerging on the other side of the Atlantic. By now many of the major currencies were emerging as either 'strong' or 'weak', depending upon their country's economic performance. The British pound was fast losing its status as a major reserve currency and the French franc was suffering as a result of France's economic and political instability, whereas the Deutschmark and the Swiss franc were becoming favourite alternative homes for capital.

The first major upheaval in the foreign exchange markets came in 1967 when the pound finally came under insurmountable pressure to devalue. Despite the Bank of England's sales of well over US$1 billion in support of the currency, the pressure was too great and a devaluation eventually took place during the weekend of 18 November. It was the first, but by no means the last, example of massive Central Bank intervention failing to prevent a currency adjustment which economic circumstances had made unavoidable. Meanwhile, in the US, the American involvement in Vietnam and the increasing deficits of the American economy had created such a drain on gold reserves that in early 1968 official international gold payments were suspended. Although international capital controls were quickly introduced, they could not prevent large capital outflows from France and inflows into Germany. The German authorities, reluctant to see their currency revalued at that time, found themselves having to absorb billions of dollars in order to keep down the value of the Deutschmark. Towards the end of 1969, the pressure became too great and there was a devaluation of the French franc and a subsequent revaluation of the Deutschmark.

This was the beginning of the end for Bretton Woods and its eventual demise was presaged in 1970 by the 'floating' of the Canadian dollar. By the end of 1970 the downward pressure on the US dollar fuelled by the ever-increasing US payments deficits and the corresponding upward pressure on the Deutschmark was beginning to completely 'seize up' flows of international finance. The situation deteriorated in 1971 and on one day alone in May of that year the Bundesbank took delivery of in excess of US$1 billion. The pressure was too great and in quick succession West Germany, the Netherlands, Switzerland and Japan all either formally revalued their currencies or allowed them to float upwards as the Canadians had in 1970.

The Snake

Throughout the troubles seen in Europe, the US government had consistently refused to accept that there was a 'dollar problem'. Their view had been that there might be a problem with the Deutschmark, but not with the dollar. After the events of early 1971, this became an untenable position, and during that summer President Nixon finally put an end to the convertibility of the dollar. No longer was there to be a fixed link between the US dollar and gold. By the end of 1971 the dollar had been formally devalued, certain other currencies had been realigned and the Bretton Woods system had been replaced by the so-called Smithsonian Agreement.

The Smithsonian Agreement involved the introduction of 'Central Rates' around which exchange rates were to be allowed to fluctuate. The so-called 'Snake' was in fact to have a relatively short history – in the Spring of 1972 the Germans introduced additional regulations to try and restrain the Deutschmark once again, and shortly afterwards the major European currencies created a mini-system within the main Snake. Massive intervention was required in mid-1972 to support the dollar at its pre-determined rate and, within Europe, some of the weaker currencies had difficulty in keeping pace with the stronger Deutschmark. The pound itself eventually left the Snake, but only after the UK had spent billions of dollars attempting to support it.

The situation deteriorated further in 1973, initially with Italy taking regulatory measures to support the lira, and then with Switzerland, flooded now like Germany with capital flows, allowing the Swiss franc to float upwards. Within a matter of weeks, both the German and Japanese central banks were refusing to purchase more dollars, eventually resulting in a formal 10% devaluation of the US dollar. To all intents and purposes the Smithsonian Agreement was now already a thing of the past.

The Snake did not completely disappear, as six European currencies continued its operation. It is also wrong to label the initial post-Smithsonian era as a period of truly floating exchange rates – it was more a case of a series of 'dirty floats', with the majority of central banks being committed to some form of intervention. The extent of that intervention, its objectives and the way in which it operated, varied substantially from country to country. This gave rise to considerable confusion in the foreign exchange markets; confusion which became far more serious as those active in the market slowly became aware of the knock-on implications of the 1973 Yom Kippur War. The subsequent quadrupling of oil prices, and the fact that oil still had to be paid for in US dollars, led to a sudden reversal in the decline of the US dollar to such an extent that those restrictions on capital flows previously instituted by the US and West Germany could eventually be abandoned.

Such gyrations in the currency markets resulted in substantial losses by some foreign exchange traders (the most notorious of which was probably the bankruptcy of the Herstatt Bank in Cologne). With the world's press focusing on the foreign exchange markets to an ever-increasing extent and with losses such as those of Herstatt and, closer to home, the difficulties of Lloyds Bank Branch in Lugano, bankers and corporates alike were forced to take far greater notice of what was already rapidly becoming a far more sophisticated market.

The international marketplace

Although technology and improved communications had resulted in a considerable increase in the volume of international foreign exchange trading, the majority of transactions in the early 1970s were still driven by the local marketplace, even if settlement took place in another location. Furthermore, for largely historic reasons, New York was still a far less sophisticated player in the currency markets than, for example, London. The introduction of SFAS 8 (see chapter 5) in 1975, however, required American companies with overseas operations to take account of current market rates when preparing their financial statements. American companies were forced to take far more notice of exchange rate fluctuations than previously, and the New York financial market responded by increasing its own involvement internationally. Most of the New York banks had already established sizeable operations overseas and it was simply a case of transferring the experience that those branches had acquired back to their head offices.

The other important development over the course of the 1970s was the emergence of the international currency broker. These brokers, with their direct links between the major centres, allowed an almost total integration of trading activities between these centres, and brought the pace of activity in New York up to that of centres such as London. By the end of the decade, the American markets had even abandoned their approach to quoting the price of another currency in dollars and substituted it for the 'European' approach of quoting currencies against the US dollar.

The second half of the 1970s witnessed a series of currency 'shocks' which generally originated from underlying economic pressures. From late 1974 through until the end of 1976, the pound was under fairly continual pressure against the dollar and this only abated when the dollar itself came under pressure in 1976. The traditional 'British problem' of high inflation and bad trade figures, together with the impact of capital flows out of countries which had been using sterling as a reserve currency, resulted in the pound falling to all-time lows against a number of key currencies, with the turning point only being reached in early 1977 after a substantial amount of help had been received from the IMF and other major countries.

After a brief respite in the second half of 1973, courtesy of the price of oil, the US dollar had continued something of a switch-back ride against the Deutschmark until 1977, when the increasing size of the US deficit again set it on a firmly downward path. The depreciation of the dollar accelerated in 1978, by which time the majority of western countries were becoming somewhat alarmed at its apparently unstoppable fall. The fear of a financial crisis resulted in fairly heavy intervention by all of the major central banks – most of it to no avail – with the dollar's 'free fall' only really being brought to an end by the 'Carter package' of November 1978. Pressure on the dollar continued, though at a reduced level, until 1980 when yet another change of sentiment led to the start of what was to become, over the next five years, an inexorable rise – particularly against the Deutschmark.

Increasing intervention

The Bundesbank had not, over the last decade or so, been slow to intervene in the foreign exchange markets on behalf of the Deutschmark, but over the course of the early 1980s, it became increasingly frustrated with the continued reluctance of the US government to take any action itself to stem what it now saw as an unacceptable rise in the level of the dollar. It was becoming increasingly clear, both to the German and most other central banks, that the increasing size of the foreign exchange markets was making it extremely difficult for any one country to have very much influence over the longer-term level of a particular rate of exchange. Whilst it was perhaps possible to 'influence' a trend, or to start a trend when the market appeared to be indifferent in terms of the direction it was taking, it was certainly not possible for any one central bank to reverse a trend which was not to its liking.

The central banks accordingly became more subtle in their approach, selecting their timing with care and attempting to move when the market was very shallow and/or when other indicators might support a change of direction. The best example perhaps, is the so-called 'Bloody Friday' in September 1984 when the Bundesbank launched a fairly blatant attempt to bolster the Deutschmark against the dollar by carrying out an extremely visible open market operation right under the nose of the Federal Reserve in New York. The Deutschmark purchases were carried out during the course of the London lunch-hour, when only a few early risers were active in the markets in New York. Apart from its timing, Bloody Friday was also seen as a direct protest by Germany against the inactivity of the Federal Reserve.

The pressure continued to mount on the Americans to do something to limit the rise in the dollar, particularly against the yen, culminating in a Group of Five meeting in January 1985 which announced the intention of the participating governments (the US, Japan, West Germany, France and the UK) to mount concerted efforts to influence foreign exchange markets as and when they considered it appropriate. The next month saw the first action taken under that accord when the central banks of those countries committed approximately US$11 billion to selling the dollar against a selection of other currencies. Despite initial views that even this level of activity was insufficient to move the market, within six weeks all of the major European currencies had strengthened against the dollar by between 10 and 15%. A similar operation took place in September and October of 1985, where intervention to the tune of another US$10 billion resulted in further substantial falls in the dollar against, in particular, the yen and the Deutschmark.

The difficult question to be addressed is the extent to which this intervention was successful due to the size of the operation itself, as opposed to the sentiment which underlies it. Many commentators find it surprising that a market now well in excess of US$200 billion per day can be swayed by an operation of only US$10 billion mounted by the central banks. What those observers perhaps fail to take into account, however, is the extent to which the current volume within the market comprises primarily inter-bank trading, rather than real 'third party' activity. Some estimates put the inter-trader element of the market as high as 99.5% of the total, suggesting a 'real world' activity of something closer to US$1 billion daily. The extent to which the dilution effect of the inter-bank volume can spread the impact of a concerted central bank operation is unknown, but it is reasonable to assume that a significant amount of the pressure created by the operation must flow through to the ultimate price- maker.

The future

The great problem with concerted central bank intervention is that, for it to be effective, it requires that those central banks involved in the operation all have, in broad terms, the same view as to the direction in which a particular exchange rate needs to move. During 1985 there was no question amongst key economists that the US dollar was grossly overvalued. The very fact that those countries were expressing those sentiments as well as backing them up with US dollar sales was more than enough to convince the markets that, come what may, there was going to be a fairly determined effort to 'push the dollar down'. The question was, of course, how far? It is accordingly not surprising that towards the end of 1986 and in early 1987 the consensus began to crumble. The US began to indicate that 'the right level' had been reached whilst some other countries involved let it be known publicly that they did not necessarily agree. It was necessary to resort to a compromise whereby the finance ministers of the major countries concerned began to speak of commitments to particular 'ranges' and to the general need for 'stability'. Intervention across the spectrum started to become more patchy, and the whole debate soon developed into another field day for economic commentators to provide their views as to the 'most appropriate' level for a particular exchange rate.

Another problem with trying to manage what are quite clearly freely floating exchange rates is the question of 'over-shooting'. This is the name provided to the now fairly common phenomenon whereby most markets, particularly those subject to a certain amount of speculation, tend to 'over-correct' when moving in a particular direction. The process of over-shooting introduces yet further instability into the exchange rate process, providing still more opportunity for speculators to move in and out of the markets.

Whilst accepting that, for the time being, intervention in the markets is certainly the order of the day, it is inconceivable that such intervention can continue to be effective other than for fairly short periods of time. The underlying economic objectives of the major Western economies are such that it is quite conceivable that they will be prepared to create a consensus in relation to a particular exchange rate for a while; but the period of that consensus can all too quickly come to an end as the exchange rate concerned reaches, or over-shoots the levels originally anticipated. Neither foreign exchange dealers nor central bankers have particularly good reputations for playing poker, and yet the environment in which we currently find ourselves is not so very dissimilar to that of a card game for exceedingly high stakes. One wonders which side has the best qualifications for such a game?

The future then is likely to be one permeated with periodic agreements by the major central banks to target particular levels for some of the more important exchange rates; sharp short-term fluctuations, sometimes within a long-term trend brought about through an economic readjustment; continuing demand for the nimblest of those currency dealers able to operate within such an environment; and of course increasing losses by those that are exposed to currency fluctuations and yet not sufficiently in control of their exposures.

A EUROPEAN PERSPECTIVE

No review of the foreign exchange market, however brief, would be complete without a short section on the European Monetary System (the EMS) and the European Currency Unit (or ECU). The EMS as we know it today was formed in 1979 out of the ashes of what had long become a very unmanageable currency Snake (see earlier comments) and attempts by most European countries at managing what very quickly became known as 'dirty floating'. The idea had first been muted in 1977 but it took a considerable amount of political will over the course of the next two years to make it a reality.

The EMS had ambitious objectives of leading to a zone of monetary stability in Europe through the convergence of economic and financial policies. In its original form many of its supporters had also envisaged it leading very quickly to a European currency and, ultimately, to full economic integration. These objectives have clearly not been achieved but generally speaking the EMS is seen by those within it and by many outside it as having been a broad success. There have been a fairly limited number of realignments over its life so far and it has kept exchange rates fairly stable in between those movements. If one allows for differential levels of inflation in the various countries concerned, there has in fact been a considerable amount of stability over the first seven years of its life.

Sterling has never been a member of the EMS but ever since its formation, the question of whether or not the UK should join has been a regular topic of political conversation. The arguments for and against membership are regularly aired by the Press on occasions such as the annual Tory Party Conference or the Budget. The government appears to have blown hot and cold on the issue throughout this period, probably quite simply because it is extremely difficult to determine whether or not it would be a 'good' or a 'bad' thing for the UK to become a full member. Arguments tend to centre around whether or not the pound has reached a stable level, the extent to which it would inhibit the government from freedom of action in either fiscal or monetary areas, the need for completing the 'long-term readjustment' of the UK's economy prior to embarking on such a linkage, etc etc.

Operation of the EMS

The countries currently participating in the EMS comprise Belgium, Denmark, France, Italy, The Netherlands, Ireland and West Germany. These countries have agreed central rates or 'par values' against each other's currencies and against the ECU. The ECU itself comprises a theoretical currency which is based upon a weighted average or 'basket' of the participating currencies. There is a 'band' around the central rate around which each currency is allowed to fluctuate against any other currency. Within this band the lowest permissible level is known as the 'floor' and the highest, as one would expect as the 'ceiling'. The rates are maintained within the bands by the participating central banks which, together, undertake to intervene in the market by buying or selling the appropriate currency to compensate for any undesirable pressures. Although the detailed way in which central banks must intervene is left very much to the discretion of the individual institutions, the points at which intervention is required are specified in the terms of the agreements. If a floor or a ceiling is in danger of being breached, the two central banks for the respective currencies which are reaching their intervention points are required to go into the market to counteract the pressures which have brought the rates close to the intervention points. The periodic (but far from frequent) changes in central rates are approved as and when necessary by all participants.

The ECU

The ECU was initially seen as very much a political statement by the newly formed EMS to provide, in the words of Michel Candessus, 'the international expression of our solidarity'. It has, however, long since broken out of its 'official' role and has become an active artificial currency in a number of important markets. The ECU's most noticeable achievement is probably its use as a Eurobond issuing currency. Total ECU issues in 1986 were in the order of the equivalent of US$10 billion. Total outstanding lending denominated in ECUs is probably now in the region of US$75 billion, giving it a share of around 10% of all non-US dollar Euromarket lending.

Foreign exchange turnover in the ECU has grown to an extraordinary extent, so much so that Kredietbank announced in March 1986 that its foreign exchange turnover in ECU was second only to its dollar trading, with an average daily volume in excess of ECU100 million and average daily deposit transactions in excess of ECU700 million. There are now ECU futures and options contracts being traded in Amsterdam, New York, Chicago and Philadelphia, with a contract in London shortly to be launched. It would be unfair to say that any of these contracts have proved particularly successful to date but there appears to be a general degree of optimism concerning future growth.

The composition of the ECU is based upon the relative internal EEC trade volumes of each of the community's members. It is supposed to be recalculated every five years, although the recent expansion of the Community has required more frequent adjustments. There are weightings of about 30% for Deutschmarks and between 10 and 20% for each of the main European currencies (the French franc, Italian lira, Dutch guilder and the pound). The remaining EEC currencies make up the balance.

An official exchange rate for the ECU is calculated each day by the EEC Commission, although there are now continuously available prices quoted in the foreign exchange market. The value can be calculated by multiplying the fixed amount of each European currency in the basket by its current exchange rate against, say, US dollars. The sum of those US dollar amounts then represents the rate (in US dollars) against the ECU.

There are numerous types of users of the ECU, both in terms of funding and by way of using the ECU currency markets for hedging. Many large internationals have found that their European operations broadly reflect the currency weightings used for the ECU, and have found it more convenient, for example, to hedge future sales through the use of ECU forward transactions than by effecting individual forward contracts in each of the underlying currencies concerned. Many European internationals have found that they can use the ECU for billing or financing as an alternative 'international currency' to the traditional US dollar. For most of them it is the currency least likely to fluctuate substantially in terms of their domestic currency.

CHAPTER 2

The foreign exchange market

THE INTER-BANK MARKET

Market participants
Technology
Market operation
Spot trading

THE FORWARD MARKETS

Relative interest rates
Nature of the forward market
Other forward markets

Although the foreign exchange market is by far the largest market in the world, it remains to many a phenomenon which is little understood. It is a market which today affects almost everyone in one way or another and impacts, either directly or indirectly, upon just about every area of economic activity.

A broad understanding of the world's foreign exchange markets is essential to a proper understanding of currency exposure and the way in which corporations are now able to use those markets to reduce or eliminate such exposure. It is also fundamental to a proper understanding of the accounting treatment to be employed for some of the more complex of those products referred to later in this book. The present chapter accordingly provides the reader with an introduction to the operation of the foreign exchange markets and reviews the fundamental relationship between forward foreign exchange rates and interest rates.

THE INTER-BANK MARKET

The foreign exchange market is a vast world-wide network of buyers and sellers of currencies, operating from approximately 12 major centres and countless minor ones. Participants range from giant banks and multinational companies with daily turnovers of several billion dollars, down to tourists who purchase small amounts of foreign banknotes. It is a market in which participants rarely meet and where the actual currency is rarely seen. Rather it is a world linked by telephone and telex lines with currency transfer being effected telegraphically from one account to another.

Since 1977, the Federal Reserve has conducted a detailed survey every three years to ascertain the volume of New York's foreign exchange turnover. The most recent of these was in March 1986 at which time the central banks in the UK and Tokyo carried out parallel exercises. The survey was conducted over the first two weeks of March and confirmed the size of the foreign exchange market in those three centres alone as being approximately US$200 billion per day. When the activities of other important centres are included, it seems unlikely that the total market can be less than US$250 billion per day. Volumes of this size are difficult to comprehend but can, at the very least, be thought of as the annual US current account deficit being turned over once every eight hours! When one translates the figures into annual volumes or into individual transactions the figures really become quite staggering.

The survey confirmed London as, by far, the leader in world foreign exchange markets, with a daily turnover of approximately US$90 billion. New York and Tokyo each accounted for a further US$50 billion approximately. Whereas nearly 60% of transactions in London were accounted for by £/$ and DM/$ transactions, the largest volumes in New York came from DM/$ and yen/$ activity. 73% of London's activity consisted of spot trading (63% in New York) and the majority of the remainder consisted of forwards. Perhaps surprisingly, less than 1% of total volumes were accounted for by options, futures and similar products. The survey also showed that approximately 9% of London's volume came from transactions involving a corporate counterparty – a figure that was substantially higher than the previous estimates which ranged from 0.5% to 2.5%. The figure of 9% for transactions involving a corporate counterparty naturally includes the 'trading' activities of many corporate treasury departments. An increasing proportion of this business, however, like the inter-bank activity, is carried out for the purposes of realising a short or longer-term trading profit rather than, necessarily, as a result of an underlying need by that corporate for a particular currency. This makes it virtually impossible to evaluate the 'real' currency market underlying the considerable volume of 'inter-trader' activity, although it would seem reasonable to conclude that this is probably, as previously estimated, closer to the 1% level.

Market participants

Of the approximately 350 banks included in the 1986 survey by the Bank of England, ten of the larger institutions accounted for approximately one-third of total foreign exchange volumes. A further 14 were responsible for originating in excess of 1% of total activity. This puts over half the volume in London within the hands of only 24 banks, with the remainder being spread around an extremely large group of banks and corporates. The corporates have, in particular, become substantial players over recent years – initially in response to a desire to obtain more preferential rates for what were, in many cases, very substantial transactions, and more recently in an effort to control more efficiently their overall currency exposures. This latter trend is examined more fully in chapter 4 but has resulted in many of the world's major international corporations becoming far larger players in the foreign exchange markets than the banks with which they used to deal. The oil majors were particularly early in recognising the need to manage better their requirements for US dollars, with Burmah Oil perhaps the best known 'trail blazer' in the early days. BP has long been thought to have a currency trading operation which exceeded, in volume terms, the Bank of England's own dealing department, and an increasing number of companies (such as, for example, VAG) have become recognised as market makers in their domestic currencies. These corporate participants operate in the markets in exactly the same way as the international banks – mixing their 'real world' needs with the intra-day trading activities of their dealers. Their exposure management systems are nearly always as good as, and sometimes much better than, those employed by many of the world's medium-sized banks and the dealers they employ frequently move between the two sectors.

The other major group of participants in the currency markets are the international money brokers which now operate in most of the world's major financial centres. The brokers have performed a very important function in the inter-bank market, bringing together buyers and sellers in a far more efficient manner than direct linkages between all of the individual players in those markets could ever achieve. Broking operations have grown with the markets, particularly in the late 1970s as they began to establish direct overseas links. The New York market would never have expanded as much as it has done over recent years without those international broking links.

Broking houses themselves vary from relatively small offices with a handful of brokers, to major organisations involving many hundreds of staff. There are still relatively few international foreign exchange brokers and the majority of the larger participants originated in London. These are large organisations specifically designed to service the more significant of the market's participants with a considerable amount of technology assisting in the process. The majority of modern-day dealing rooms will have direct lines to all major broking operations within the locality as well as to a selected number of key market-making principals and overseas branches, etc.

The final group of participants that we must consider are, of course, the 'clients'. These range from individuals and companies through to national governments or international organisations. Some banks operating in the market choose to nurture client business whereas others may decide to avoid it, due to their small client-base or to other reasons. Many of the world's central banks or monetary authorities engage in active dealing to a greater or lesser extent – either to fund the needs of the local government or simply to attempt to bring a greater degree of discipline to the currency under their control. Most corporate clients of the inter-bank market tend to operate their business through one or more of the banks active in the market, although the larger operations with their own foreign exchange trading activities naturally use brokers in the same way as the banks.

Technology

It has been technological advances which have enabled the foreign exchange market to reach its current state of development as quickly as it has. The markets in the international centres around the world are now largely indistinguishable from each other – except perhaps in terms of the depth of the market at certain times in the 24-hour dealing day when the larger centres for a particular currency are closed. Most of the larger banking groups and, indeed, some of the world's major international corporates are now making markets on a 24-hour basis from three or more centres around the globe.

All the foreign exchange trader strictly needs is a telephone. Today's dealer, however, generally requires a minimum of two VDU screens, a bank of telephones, squawk boxes linking him to the brokers and a keyboard. One screen is likely to be displaying market prices and the other the most recent news items via a Reuters link or the equivalent. His telephone board will provide him with direct lines into the dealing rooms of other banks, most local currency brokers and perhaps one or two of the bank's more important corporate customers. He uses the keyboard to update his own prices on the screen and to change the page numbers displayed on his Reuters screen.

Although many dealing rooms still utilise dealing tickets to initiate the processing of a transaction through the back office, increasingly today the dealer is responsible himself for inputting a transaction directly into the computer. That entry adjusts the dealer's position, sends out a confirmation to the counterparty and ultimately, generally after further checks, automatically results in the settlement payment being made to the counterparty through one of the local clearing networks. The dealer might also utilise a micro computer in order to assist him with complex arbitrage calculations, and the most sophisticated dealing rooms now combine all of these functions in anything up to half a dozen VDU screens, one or more of which will be 'touch operated', perhaps eliminating the need for a keyboard.

As with most of the other international markets now developing in equities, government securities and corporate debt, there has been some debate over recent years as to whether or not there would be a move towards some centres being operational for 24 hours of the day. Although in both technical and legal terms, it is now possible for most major financial centres to be operational for 24 hours (this has recently even become possible in Tokyo), the trend appears to be towards the reliance on sophisticated technological links between individual trading centres, with those centres taking direct responsibility for trading during their own particular time zones. The markets in Tokyo, Hong Kong and Singapore tend to stay active well into Europe's 'early morning', with most of London's foreign exchange dealing rooms now being active from 7.30 or 8.00 a m. From the early afternoon, New York joins the London activity, often working fairly late into the night until the Far Eastern centres re-open. It was at one time envisaged that Los Angeles would fill the critical gap between the New York and Japanese trading days although, in practice, this has not really happened. Although Los Angeles is still an important trading centre, it has nowhere near the volume of the other major locations.

Market operation

Currencies can be grouped into three general categories: convertible, semi-convertible, and non-convertible. Convertible currencies are actively dealt in the inter-bank markets, generally on a global basis. Semi-convertible currencies are also traded internationally but to a far more limited extent. Trading takes place on a case-by-case basis at predetermined rates of exchange with ultimate settlement always taking place through the local central bank for the currency concerned. A large number of Third World currencies fall into this category. Finally, non-convertible currencies are those where circulation is tightly controlled by the local authorities with a rate of exchange frequently pegged at a level considerably out of line with the 'free market' rate. The majority of Eastern European countries have non-convertible currencies. There tends to be little real trading in non-convertible currencies, although a certain amount of black-market activity often does take place.

There has been a slow but steady relaxation in foreign exchange controls since the economic summit at Rambouillet in 1975. Some countries, however, still operate controls, even where the currencies are, to all intents and purposes, treated as being fully convertible. At the time of writing, for example, there are still controls in certain Western countries, such as in France, where local companies have only been permitted to maintain foreign currency bank accounts since May 1987. There are still constraints over the amount of foreign currency that can be held and individuals are still barred from opening currency accounts. Controls in some centres prohibit or restrict outward or inward investment through the application of foreign exchange controls – typically by using a two-tiered currency system.

In excess of 95% of world-wide currency trading is now against the US dollar with most of the remainder being either against sterling, Deutschmarks or yen. The pre-eminence of the dollar is now total – largely because of the sheer magnitude of the dollar financial markets (there are more dollars in the world than all other currencies put together) and the extensive use of the dollar for pricing international transactions. The US dollar is now by far the greatest component of foreign currency reserves held by the world's major central banks. Sterling remains an important trading currency, largely for historic reasons, whereas the Deutschmark and the yen are both important due to the economic strength of their respective countries, and the increased proportion of international trade with which they are now involved. German and Japanese stocks and bonds have now also become an important part of international portfolios.

There is a second group of convertible currencies which are heavily dealt in certain centres but which sometimes lack liquidity in other locations. These include the Swiss franc, French franc, Dutch guilder, Italian lira and the Canadian dollar. Other convertible currencies such as those of Australia, New Zealand, Hong Kong, Singapore, Portugal, Spain, Belgium, Austria, Mexico and the Scandinavian countries, are all dealt extensively on a local basis, and internationally where local commercial reasons necessitate. The extent to which a currency is, or is not, traded outside of its country of origin is generally determined by the extent to which that country is involved in international trade. Third World countries, where investment has traditionally been 'inward', tend to see currencies traded almost exclusively on a local basis.

In each of the major financial centres there is one or more 'market makers' for each of the main convertible currencies referred to above. A market maker is a bank which is prepared to provide prices on demand to either purchase or sell the currency concerned. They make prices both to other banks and through brokers to the market in general and, subject to the counterparty being acceptable to the market maker in terms of its current credit lines, they are generally committed to deal at the prices being quoted.

Market makers tend to convey their prices to the market via 'indication rates' on the screen services offered by agencies such as Reuters. The indication rates are just that, they do not necessarily represent the rates at which the organisation would be prepared to deal – those being quoted in response to a specific request at a particular point in time. The rate quoted will then be adhered to by the market maker, for either a purchase or a sale of the currency concerned, on the assumption that it is against dollars and for an acceptable round sum amount. Quoted rates are likely to be amended somewhat for either odd or small amounts of currency. Rates are invariably quoted against dollars unless otherwise requested. Whereas some of the world's larger banks may be prepared to make markets in a number of currencies, it is generally unusual for a bank to make markets in more than, say, its home currency and the local currency. In some cases there are geographical alignments (such as the Nordic countries) where a bank might be prepared to make markets in a number of currencies with which it was familiar, but this tends to be the exception rather than the rule.

A trend over the last year or so in the inter-bank market has been the almost imperceptible shift away from market making by all banks other than the very largest organisations. This has almost certainly been caused by the extreme volatility of the markets and the growing realisation that quoting on both sides on a continual basis can be an extremely expensive activity if one does not have the proper resources to manage it. The shift has, however, been made very quietly, and insofar as their corporate customers are concerned, most banks are prepared to 'make a price' for just about any currency obtainable. In real terms, however, the number of market makers in, say, sterling in London is probably around a dozen, and those active in most other currencies substantially less. Even some of the world's major banks are now shifting almost imperceptibly towards more of a 'niche' operation than previously – specialising in those markets where they perceive themselves as having the greater expertise.

Spot trading

About three-quarters of London's foreign exchange trading volume and almost two-thirds of New York's activity consists of 'plain vanilla' spot foreign exchange trading. This is very much the motor house of the foreign exchange market with, as we shall see subsequently, other trading activity generally riding on the back of the spot market.

Because of the traditional difficulty in effecting 'immediate' delivery of foreign exchange, the market has developed around the idea of a standard 'two-day settlement' rule. Spot foreign exchange trading is accordingly based on the assumption that the transaction will be settled in two business days' time. Next-day or even same-day settlement is possible but such transactions do not constitute 'standard' spot foreign exchange trades as such. The end-of-day 'spot' foreign exchange rate is not (as some observers might suspect) the theoretical rate at which currencies could be purchased or sold as of that date. It is, in fact, the rate for settlement two days forward. The rate for a same-day settlement would be slightly different.

The spot rate of exchange quoted by any market maker is in fact a dual price – the first representing the bid price, being that at which the dealer is prepared to purchase the currency concerned, and the second being the offer price, being that at which he is prepared to sell it. The presumption is always that the currency in question is being quoted against the US dollar. The difference between the buy and sell rate is, of course, the dealer's 'spread' or margin. The size of the spread varies depending upon market conditions and the currency in question. For spot dollar/sterling transactions the spread is typically ten 'pips' or 'points'. The bid and offer rates will apply to 'standard size' transactions for delivery in two days' time. Where the amounts are small, non-standard or larger than normal, the spread is likely to be increased to allow for the greater exposure taken by the dealer in handling the position he is taking on. Non-standard amounts traditionally originate from the corporate sector and are 'bundled' or 'unbundled', as appropriate, into standard transaction sizes before being passed on to the market.

Market terminology

The language of the foreign exchange dealer is as colourful and unpredictable as many of the dealers themselves. Whilst the following does not pretend to be a comprehensive summary of 'dealerees' it does cover much of the technical vocabulary used both by the dealers and their back offices.

Arbitrage. This is the process by which the dealer can take advantage of a disequilibrium between two markets. It might be possible to arbitrage between the forward currency markets and the money markets.

Basis point. This is a term for describing one-hundredth of a unit and, in the foreign exchange market, can be thought of as representing one-hundredth of 1p or 1 cent, etc. In the money market, one basis point is one-hundredth of 1%. Foreign exchange dealers typically refer to 'pips' or 'points' to avoid confusion with the use of basis points in the money markets.

Bid rate. This is the price at which the dealer is prepared to purchase foreign currency.

Cable. This refers to the trading of sterling against the US dollar. It originates from the days in which settlement was made by cable transfer.

Contract rate. This is the exchange rate embodied in the contract – whether a spot or forward transaction.

Delivery date. This is the maturity date for a foreign exchange contract and is the date on which the actual exchange of currencies takes place. It is also known as the 'value date'.

Discount. A currency is said to be at a discount against the dollar if its forward rate is cheaper than the spot rate.

Euro-currency. Any currency domiciled outside its country of origin is referred to as Euro-currency.

Fixed dates. These are the monthly calendar dates used in the forward market for one-month, three-month, etc transactions. They comprise the next business day if the one-month forward date is a non-working day, with the exception that if the spot date falls on a month-end, the fixed dates for forward transactions will also be the last business days of each month. The measurement of fixed dates takes place from the spot delivery date as opposed to the deal date.

Forward outright. This term is used to describe a forward foreign exchange contract that has been entered into on a 'one-off' basis.

Forward rate. This is the rate embodied in a forward contract.

Hit. A bid rate is said to be 'hit' if the counterparty agrees to undertake the transaction at the quoted rate.

Indication rates. These are rates issued by a market maker to indicate the rates at which he is likely to be dealing. The market maker is not obliged to deal at these rates.

Market making. Market makers in any currency hold themselves out as being prepared to make a bid and offer quotation on the currency concerned.

Middle rate. This is the mid-point between the bid and offer rates quoted by a market maker.

Odd date. This is any delivery date which does not comprise either a spot or a 'fixed date'.

Offer rate. The rate at which a dealer is prepared to sell a foreign currency.

Position. A dealer's net position is his overall position (spot and forward) against his base currency. If the position is 'flat' or 'square' it is approximately zero. Alternatively, it might be 'long' (more currency bought than sold) or 'short' (more currency sold than bought).

Premium. A currency is at a premium to the dollar when its forward rate is dearer than the spot rate.

Rollover. A foreign exchange dealer's rollover is a form of 'overnight swap' involving a purchase/sale – typically between the next business day and the following business day. It should be differentiated from the rollover transactions available to corporate customers (see Reference Section A.5).

Spot bid. The price of purchasing the currency for spot delivery. Spot delivery will always take place two business days after the deal date.

Spot next. An overnight swap from the spot date to the following day.

Spot offer. The price of selling the currency concerned for spot delivery.

Spot one week. This is a one-week swap from the spot date and is sometimes referred to as a spot-a-week.

Spot rate. The price of one currency against another expressed as a ratio and for delivery in two business days' time. There is a discussion of quoting methods in the main text.

Spread. The difference between a bid and an offer price.

Straight dates. See 'Fixed dates'.

Swap. The simultaneous purchase and sale of the same amount of a given currency for two different dates. This should not be confused with the capital market swaps discussed in Reference Section A.7.

Swap price. The swap price is the price differential between the two dates of a swap. The text describes how forward rates are linked to the spot rate through a number of 'swap points'.

Taken. This is the phrase used when a dealer's offer has been accepted by a counterparty.

Value date. See 'Delivery date'.

Bid and offer prices (also known as a two-way price) are quoted on a continual basis by recognised market makers in the currency concerned, and from time to time by others in the market. The price is quoted as a linked set of numbers which, in the case of the Deutschmark, might be for example: 1.8330 – 1.8340. Although this is the way in which the closing spot rate is generally reported in the financial press each day, the abbreviated way of indicating the same price is to quote 1.8330 – 40. During the course of the trading day, all participants in the market will be aware that the spot rate is a little over 1.83 and individual dealers accordingly limit their quotes to stating 30-40. A typical market maker's quote might accordingly be 'dollar/mark 30-40 on five'. This would suggest that the bid offer rate quoted was being restricted to round amounts of US$5 million with a buying rate of 1.8330 and a selling rate of 1.8340. The market quote remains valid until a dealer indicates 'change', 'cancel' or 'out'.

When quoting a spot rate, the two currencies ('dollar/mark' in the example above) are placed such that the rate represents the number of units of the second currency per unit of the first one. All currencies are traditionally quoted 'against' the dollar, with the exception of sterling which, once again for historical reasons, is traditionally quoted as the base currency. A 'cable' quotation might accordingly be 1.5255-1.5265, indicating the number of dollars per sterling unit. Two-way prices are always quoted with the bid price first and the offer price second. Some participants in the market may choose to make a one-way price where they only wish to buy or sell. This can either be done by imposing an unrealistic spread on the transaction with a resulting 'out of market' rate to one side of the two-way price or, more reasonably, simply by making a one-way price such as, using the dollar/mark example above, 'I pay 30' or 'I offer 5 at 40'.

A quotation such as that used for sterling/dollars is known as a 'indirect quote' because it expresses the number of units of foreign currency acquired for one unit of the home currency (ie sterling). Such a quotation in New York would be referred to as a 'direct quote' because the home currency is, of course, US dollars. The normal method of quoting European currencies in their home country is to use the direct quote – such as in the dollar/mark example above. Although New York originally used a direct quote for European currencies (as it still does for sterling) it switched to using an indirect quote some years ago in order to ensure that rates were consistent with those used in Europe. It is interesting to note that when dealing with a domestic counterparty, many New York banks still use the direct quote.

Sterling is not the only currency to employ an indirect quote: certain other currencies such as the Irish punt, and the Australian and New Zealand dollar, are also generally quoted in terms of the number of US dollars per unit of currency. There are also individual rules applied in some of the world's futures exchange such as, for example, the IMM in Chicago.

Although the glossary of market terminology covers most of the technical jargon in the market it does not cover the actual language of the dealer. This tends to develop very much like rhyming cockney slang, with abbreviations for individual currencies and the use of terms such as pit, slammed, banged, hit hard, etc. Currencies are sometimes said to 'go north' or 'go south' when they move either higher or lower and the actual conversation between two dealers, or between a dealer and a broker, is often extremely difficult for the untrained to decipher. A typical exchange between a dealer and a broker, for example, might go as follows:

'What is Swissie?'
'I pay 49.'
'I give you 3, can do 5.'
'5 done, can do more.'
'5 I sell.'
'Thank you, nothing there.'

There are numerous possible variations on the above exchange with, as one would expect, variations between individual locations.

In London, when dealing through a broker, the name of the counterparty is never disclosed until the end of the transaction, at which point the contracting parties have the ability to withdraw from the deal if they have no credit lines available with the counterparty in question. This is not a regular occurrence as dealers tend to indicate to the brokers in advance any lines which are already fully used, and it is in their own interests not to renege on a transaction unless it is absolutely essential. If a bank does so frequently, it can rapidly obtain a bad name in the market.

THE FORWARD MARKETS

Although forward markets first developed in Europe in the inter-war years, they were fairly unsophisticated and rather small. There was virtually no demand at all for forward cover from the corporate sector and when a forward transaction was entered into it was generally very difficult to price it, due to the absence of any generally recognised interest rate standard (see below).

The demise of the fixed-rate currency system in the early 1970s coincided with the growth of the Euromarkets which, in themselves, provided an ideal market for evaluating interest rate differentials. With the ever-growing gyrations in spot exchange rates and the growing awareness of the corporate sector of the risks arising from foreign currency exposure, the concept of forward currency hedging became more prevalent. Banks themselves became far more aware of the way in which they could make money from arbitraging between the forward foreign exchange market and their money market activity, and the considerable growth in spot trading provided an ideal training ground for forward foreign exchange dealers.

The present section reviews the overall structure of the forward markets and the way in which they currently operate. The discussion focuses primarily on the more traditional forward foreign exchange contract but also provides an introduction to currency futures and currency options. These products, together with the multiplicity of more exotic derivatives now available, are examined in greater detail in the Reference Section.

Relative interest rates

It is still only fairly recently that politicians have stopped referring to forward exchange rates as being an indication of the market's expectations of future currency movements. Although there is now a general understanding that a forward exchange rate is a function of the spot rate of exchange and the interest rate differentials between the two currencies concerned, there is still frequently little perception as to why this is the case and why, in any event, the forward rate might not indicate future currency trends.

If one approaches the issue from an economic standpoint it is possible to construct a theoretical model of the economy where there are very direct linkages between forward premiums and discounts, interest rate differentials, expectations of movements in spot rates and expected differential rates of inflation. When a state of equilibrium is reached in such a theoretical economy the forward premium or discount between any two currencies would indeed equate to the expected movement in the spot rate. Such a state of equilibrium does not, of course, exist in practice – and current expectations accordingly diverge from the mathematically derived forward exchange rate.

The easiest way to demonstrate the calculation of a forward exchange rate is probably to consider how a bank could lay-off the exposure created by entering into a forward contract with a corporate customer. If, for example, a customer wishes to dispose of US dollars against sterling 12 months forward, then the bank will be asked to enter into a contract to buy forward US dollars. It can eliminate the exposure so created by doing a similar transaction in the forward foreign exchange market or, alternatively, by using the cash markets to achieve the same effect. For simplicity, let us assume that the approach to be adopted in the latter case would involve using the inter-bank money markets. The process would entail borrowing dollars for 12 months, selling them on the spot market and depositing the sterling proceeds for a similar period. For the purposes of illustration let us assume that the forward US dollar position of the bank created as a result of its deal with the corporate, amounts to $1 million; that the current spot rate of exchange is 1.5; and that 12-month Euro-currency rates for dollars and sterling are 7% and 11% respectively. In order to 'fully hedge' the forward position, the bank would need to proceed as follows:

(a) borrow $934,579 at 7% for 12 months;
(b) sell at 1.5 to yield £1,401,868;
(c) deposit £1,401,868 at 11% for 12 months.

By the end of 12 months the interest on the dollar borrowing would have amounted to $65,421, resulting in a total dollar liability of $1,000,000. This would then be repaid by using the dollar funds received at that date from the corporate.

In the meantime, the sterling deposit would have accrued interest of £154,205, resulting in a total receipt of £1,556,073. These funds would then be available to pay the corporate for the dollars received.

Assuming that the bank makes no profit from the overall transaction, the effective forward rate able to be quoted to the corporate is 1.5561 (comprising 1,556,073 divided by 1,000,000).

In reality, of course, a bank entering into a forward foreign exchange contract with a corporate would expect to make some sort of profit out of hedging the transaction. However, with the inter-bank interest rate and foreign exchange markets being as near to perfect (in an economic sense) as one can probably ever achieve, the profits to be made between a bank entering into a forward exchange transaction and then hedging out that position in the money markets is extremely small. Where a bank enters into a forward transaction with another participant in the inter-bank market and hedges it out in the way described above, it is said to have entered into a 'deposit swap'. Such transactions can also be thought of in terms of the bank deciding to fund a particular lending opportunity in another currency because relative interest rates and forward foreign exchange rates are such that it is slightly cheaper than funding in the actual currency of the loan. Such a series of transactions is, accordingly, also referred to as cross currency funding.

The forward currency market has long been driven by the availability of swap arbitrage possibilities within the inter-bank market. Recently, the corporate sector has also woken up to the fact that it is possible to carry out cross currency fundings - particularly when a currency position emerges which is in effect no more than a timing gap between the receipt and payment of funds in a particular currency. It can sometimes be far cheaper for the corporate to arrange a swap to cover the gap than to try to hedge out each of the positions independently or to borrow currency funds to cover the temporary shortfall.

Because of the direct linkage between the forward foreign exchange markets and the liquid inter-bank money market, it is hardly surprising that, until fairly recently, it has been difficult to obtain forward foreign exchange quotes for much in excess of one year. The forward market is also restricted to fewer currencies than the spot markets for the same reason. Today, however, it is fairly easy to arrange long-dated forward foreign exchange contracts (see Reference Section A.4) going out to five or even ten years - largely due to the increase in sophistication of the capital markets in general. With far greater liquidity in long-dated, fixed-rate money it becomes increasingly meaningful to quote long-dated foreign exchange rates.

Long term currency exchange agreements (see Reference Section A.8) have led the way in demonstrating the ease with which it is now possible to arrange a long-term forward contract, at least in most of the major currencies. Indeed, because of arbitrage possibilities, many long-dated foreign exchange transactions are possibly even serving to increase liquidity in the long-term deposit markets – something which is perhaps easier to see when one looks at generally illiquid currencies such as the South African rand and the Australian dollar. A final point to note on long-dated foreign exchange transactions is that the pricing of such transactions needs to take account of the compounding impact of annual interest flows on the theoretical underlying loans and deposits. With a large number of theoretical underlying interest rate instruments, there are now a number of different ways of pricing long-dated foreign exchange transactions.

Nature of the forward market

The difference between the forward rate of exchange and the spot rate of exchange is known as either a premium or a discount. Where a currency is quoted against the dollar and its forward rate is dearer than the spot rate, it is said to be at a premium to the dollar, or conversely that the dollar itself is at a discount. In the earlier example we calculated that the one-year forward sterling rate was 1.5561, as compared with a spot rate of 1.5. It will be recalled, however, that these are in effect dollar/sterling rates – expressing the number of units of dollars against a single unit of sterling. The fact that the forward rate is more expensive than the spot rate, means that the dollar is at a premium to sterling or that sterling is at a discount to the dollar. Forward rates are rarely, if ever, quoted in the market but are, instead, expressed as an adjustment to the spot rate. The adjustment, commonly known as the 'swap rate', is expressed in terms of the number of points adjustment required. In the earlier example, the 12-month swap rate would have been 561.

Spreads are applied to forward transactions in exactly the same way as to spot transactions with the bid price being lower than the offer price. Forward spreads are, however, almost always somewhat wider than those applied to spot rates of exchange, and this therefore has to be embodied in the forward quote. Both the forward points and the spread to be applied to the bid-offer relationship increase as one moves further into the future. If we return to the earlier example of the Deutschmark spot rate of 1.8330-40, then, with the Deutschmark at a premium against the dollar, the one-month and three-month forward swap rates might be quoted as 34-31 and 108-103 respectively. When taken together with the spot rate, the true forward rates can be calculated as follows:

	Bid	Offer
Spot rate	1.8330	1.8340
1-month swap adjustment	.0034	.0031
1-month forward rate	1.8296	1.8309

Spot rate	1.8330	1.8340
3-month swap adjustment	.0108	.0103
3-month forward rate	1.8222	1.8237

In the above example the swap rate has been subtracted in each case because the dollar is at a discount. Had the dollar been at a premium to the Deutschmark, the swap rate would have been added. We added the swap rate in the earlier case of sterling because we were dealing with a rate expressed in dollar/sterling terms rather than sterling/dollar and the dollar was at a premium to sterling. Had we expressed that exchange rate in the reciprocal (ie the sterling/dollar rate) we would have had to subtract the swap rate to obtain the forward rate. In the Deutschmark example it will be noted that spreads have increased from 10 points using the spot rate to 13 at the one-month forward position and 15 using the three-month forward rates. This is a fairly normal increase in spreads over these periods.

When a market maker is asked to furnish forward prices he will normally do so by quoting a sequence of swap rates covering the 'straight dates' at one week, one month, two months, three months, six months and twelve months. He may be prepared to quote other dates on request. For each maturity period there will be a bid-offer quote along the lines already discussed which indicates, in effect, the points differential at which the bank is prepared to sell the near date and buy the far date and/or to buy the near date and sell the far date as appropriate.

Before leaving the question of forward foreign exchange pricing it is worth returning again to the question of premiums and discounts. Those unfamiliar with the market frequently find that determining whether or not the currency is at a premium or a discount is the first major stumbling block to understanding the nature of a forward foreign exchange transaction. Another way of looking at the question is to consider the relative yields in the underlying Euro-currencies. If one ignores any question of exchange risk, it is clear that the currency with the higher yield constitutes the more attractive investment. In terms of the pricing of forward foreign exchange contracts, a positive interest differential translates itself into the pricing of a forward foreign exchange contract by reducing the forward rate as compared with the spot rate. It is, in other words, more advantageous for the buyer of forward currency. Conversely, the currency with the lesser yield, will be less advantageous for the forward buyer since the opportunity cost of retaining the higher yielding currency until the forward date will be positive. In other words, the currency with the higher yield will be at a discount on a forward basis against the currency with the lesser yield. Conversely, the currency with the lower yield will be at a premium to the currency with the higher yield.

Although forward exchange rates are inextricably linked to spot rates, the operation of the forward exchange market is much more akin to running an interest book. Taking a position in the forward markets generally means creating a mismatch in the forward maturity ladder of the book (ie creating a prospective mismatch in future flows of the foreign currency concerned). Such gap positions represent an exposure to movements in interest rate differentials rather than an exposure to movements in the spot rate of exchange. In reality, because of the way in which forward prices are calculated, a movement in the spot rate of exchange does have a small impact on forward premiums or discounts, but this is not the 'accepted wisdom' of the relationship and it is generally ignored in terms of evaluating risk.

Chapter 3 explores the nature of net and gap positions and chapter 4 reviews a number of approaches to exposure management. Recognising the fundamental difference between net and forward exposures is essential to a proper understanding of the way in which one should monitor and account for foreign exchange exposures. The fact that it is interest rates, rather than foreign exchange rates, which are the primary determinant of gains or losses arising from a gap position is central to the whole question of the most appropriate accounting treatment.

Other forward markets

Although the traditional forward foreign exchange contract is still by far the favourite methodology for effecting a non-cash hedge of a foreign exchange position, there are a number of other important markets which have developed over the past few years. The oldest of these is the futures market, where the International Monetary Market (IMM) in Chicago started trading in 1972. Futures markets now exist in the majority of major international financial centres, including the London market which opened under the aegis of the London International Financial Futures Exchange (LIFFE) in 1982.

These financial futures markets have largely developed out of the international commodity markets, and their primary role in recent years has been in the trading of interest rate futures. The general efficiency of the forward foreign exchange market has meant that currency futures have not been traded as extensively as they otherwise might have been. The markets operate within a physical exchange with membership of the exchange being limited by a combination of financial resources, a membership fee, and frequently a total cap on the number of members. Contracts are traded by open outcry between members on the floor of the exchange with the exchange or a clearing house operating a margining system in relation to all consummated deals. Delivery rarely, if ever, takes place with an 'alternative settlement' process usually occurring at the maturity date of the transaction. There is normally an original margin payable for each contract opened, with a variation margin payable, usually on a net basis, at the end of each day. A variation margin is always paid in relation to any open losses but the treatment of unrealised profits varies between exchanges. Non-members of the market may gain access to it by either trading with a member or trading 'through' a member acting in the role of broker. In both cases it is likely that the non-member will be margined in the same way as the member.

Unlike the forward exchange markets, futures markets deal in predetermined amounts of currency for delivery at predetermined dates. It is accordingly extremely easy to match buyers and sellers, but frequently more difficult to arrange an effective hedge. The credit risk when dealing in futures is all but eliminated through the guarantee of the exchange and/or the clearing house.

The majority of users of currency futures tend to be those who use the financial futures markets in other ways. This includes commodity traders and those banks which are heavy users of interest rate futures. In the US there is also a significant amount of retail interest — largely for speculative purposes. A more recent form of currency future is the 'index future' whereby it is possible to hedge in terms of, for example, the US$ Index. This allows a dollar-based entity with a large number of different currency exposures to hedge those exposures in general terms by using the weighted average US$ Index of that currency's value against a basket of other major currencies. Index futures are potentially of particular use to major international investment funds which might wish to avoid having to hedge on a case-by-case basis.

An important difference between currency futures and forward foreign exchange contracts is the extent to which the former allow banking participants in the foreign exchange markets to manage their currency exposures on a dynamic basis without, necessarily, increasing their overall credit exposure and, as a consequence, their use of capital. If a bank creates a forward currency position using a forward transaction and then closes out that position in the same way, it will generally, under current arrangements, have created two separate exposures – both of which will potentially bear a credit risk and both of which will be subject to capital adequacy requirements if they extend beyond a particular maturity. If the same series of transactions were carried out using currency futures, it would have been possible to close out the initial position by, in effect, liquidating it. Both positions could, accordingly, be removed from the bank's books. With the recent focus by the regulatory authorities on the capital implications of longer dated forward foreign exchange deals, it is likely that the currency futures markets will witness a considerable growth in interest from the banking sector - at least insofar as those longer dated periods are concerned.

Currency futures are discussed in more detail in Reference Section A.6 which also includes a summary of most of the traded futures contracts available at the time of writing.

The other major group of forward currency transactions are the various types of option contract now available. Options closely resemble insurance policies in terms of their effect and are priced on the basis of both the underlying value of the currency in question and its past and expected volatility. There are now a large number of derivative option products specifically designed to better address customer needs.

The more traditional form of option contract gives the holder of the option the right, but not the obligation, to buy (in the case of a call option), or to sell (in the case of a put option), a predetermined amount of currency at a predetermined price (known as the strike price) on or before a specified maturity date. The 'writer' or 'issuer' of the option receives a premium at the point of issuance and is then obliged to complete on the transaction at the 'holder's' or 'purchaser's' option. An option holder's potential loss is accordingly restricted to the size of the premium paid whereas his potential gain is theoretically unlimited.

Option contracts tend to be used either as a hedge against uncertain future currency flows, or to enable the purchaser to maintain an upwards speculative position whilst eliminating the majority of any downside exposure.

Short-dated currency options are actively traded on a number of futures exchanges around the world and a number of the major banks make an active two-way market in over-the-counter currency options. The latter are generally specifically designed to meet particular customer needs. Longer dated currency options are still fairly uncommon, however, with relatively few extending beyond one year. As the market becomes more liquid, more and more banks are becoming involved.

Exchange traded options are either options on the underlying currency futures contract – where, as previously mentioned, settlement rarely takes place, or are options on the physical delivery of the currency itself – in which case settlement is far more common. Over-the-counter options, when exercised, generally result in physical settlement of the currency concerned.

A particular confusion with currency options is the terminology involved. A 'put' option on Swiss francs means that the buyer, or holder, has the right to put Swiss francs to the seller in exchange for US dollars at the predetermined exchange rate. A 'call' option gives the holder the right to require the issuer to provide Swiss francs in exchange for US dollars. Currency options and their various derivatives are discussed in more detail in the Reference Section and Section A.11, in particular, includes a comprehensive listing of exchange traded options available at the time of writing.

CHAPTER 3

Foreign currency exposure

ORIGIN OF CURRENCY EXPOSURE

Transaction exposure
Translation exposure
Economic exposure

ASPECTS OF RISK

Foreign exchange positions
Positions and risk
Transaction and translation exposure
Economic exposure
The long-term view

THE IMPACT OF TAXATION

The complex interaction of trading and international capital flows between the major Western economies has resulted in virtually every area of economic activity in those economies now being influenced, in one way or another, by fluctuations in exchange rates. The impact of currency movements, however, is felt in many different ways. Whilst the exposure flowing from the acquisition of overseas inventory might be all too apparent, that relating to a company's market position in relation to an overseas competitor may be far more obscure.

The effective management of foreign currency exposure is now a central objective of most major companies, and the recent introduction of numerous alternative hedging products has resulted in that overall process now becoming a fairly complex art. Chapter 4 reviews the alternative organisational structures and approaches to exposure management and discusses some of the pitfalls frequently encountered.

To understand the need for exposure management, however, and to appreciate fully the likely scope of that activity, it is initially necessary to explore the underlying nature of currency exposure. The present chapter accordingly reviews the origins of currency exposure and the particular risks which flow from it.

ORIGIN OF CURRENCY EXPOSURE

Over recent years there have been a number of attempts better to define the nature of currency exposure, and to develop a more definitive way of considering it. Discussion has generally been summarised under three broad headings: trading or transaction exposure; translation or balance sheet exposure; and finally, operational, cashflow, economic or strategic exposure. The terminology has often been used inconsistently and attempts at clarification have sometimes simply created more confusion.

Foreign exchange exposure can be defined quite simply as being an exposure to future movements in exchange rates, and in the final analysis it is either direct – originating from a foreign currency transaction – or indirect – such as that which flows from, for example, a particular competitive position. The direct exposure flowing from a foreign currency transaction can be conveniently sub-divided into the exposure which exists due to a future transaction being denominated in some way in a foreign currency; and second, the exposure which arises as a result of having actually carried out the transaction.

This chapter accordingly considers currency exposure under three separate headings: transaction exposure, which is defined as that which originates from the fact that a future transaction is denominated in a foreign currency; translation exposure, which flows from having to aggregate foreign currency assets, liabilities and commitments into a single reporting currency; and economic exposure which is the indirect exposure which exists as a result of current economic relationships. The term structural exposure is used in the context of an economic scenario which results in a continuing future exposure to a flow of foreign currency transactions over a period of time.

Transaction exposure

A company is potentially exposed to foreign exchange risk whenever it enters into a cross-currency transaction. Such transactions range from the relatively straightforward act of purchasing US dollar travellers cheques for the sales director's marketing trip to Europe, through to extremely complex currency trigger provisions in the pricing sections of certain long-term construction contracts. Some transaction exposures are, by their nature, frequently difficult to identify, and any resulting currency gains or losses can become hidden in, for example, sales or cost of sales.

In general terms, transaction exposure arises whenever the local currency value of a company's future foreign currency receipts and/or payments is liable to fluctuate as a result of movements in foreign exchange rates. Typical examples of transaction exposure include the following:

(a)Inventory transactions. The purchase or sale of inventory where settlement is required, or expected, in an overseas currency.

(b)Product pricing. The pricing of a product in one currency whilst issuing invoices in another (unless the pricing arrangements are totally disregarded in assessing profitability or future cashflows).

(c)Billing arrangements. The invoicing of sales in one currency whilst accepting settlement in another – unless the foreign exchange effect is subsequently 're-invoiced' to the purchaser.

(d)Suppliers' billings. A corresponding situation exists in relation to suppliers where a currency exposure arises whenever a supplier bills in a currency other than that used for settlement.

(e)Long-term contracts. A 'fixed-price contract' with the pricing denominated in a foreign currency will result in a currency exposure unless there are suitable currency 'trigger' clauses in the contract.

(f)Sale of an overseas asset. Any disposal of an asset located overseas (and valued in terms of an overseas currency) can result in a transaction gain or loss at the point of sale.

(g)Dividends, etc. Dividend income, royalty payments, management charges and similar flows between two currency areas.

(h)Debt related transactions. The drawing down of loans, etc denominated in a foreign currency.

Transaction exposure relates to future cashflows denominated in a foreign currency. Such flows may be either trade related, such as the acquisition of inventory, or capital related, such as the drawing down of debt.

Certain transaction exposures are pervasive in that they are an integral part of a group's operations. For example, any profitable overseas operation which results in a continual long-term flow of profits to a parent company will, in effect, give rise to a long-term position in the currency concerned. Similar 'structural' relationships arise where there is a permanent mismatch between costs and revenues as a result of the locations of, for example, a manufacturing plant or a main export market. Such structural exposures are, by their very nature, an ongoing feature of the company concerned and give rise to particular difficulties of exposure management.

Structural exposures are sometimes of such fundamental significance to the organisation that they can have a major external influence on the perception of the organisation's operations as viewed by, for example, the stock market on which the company is quoted. The proper recognition of such circumstances is fundamental in deciding the nature of the exposure management required.

Translation exposure

Translation exposure derives from the accounting convention whereby assets, liabilities and operating results are converted into the local currency for the purposes of financial reporting. Such exposure arises whenever there is a mismatch between assets and liabilities or, for that matter, between offsetting forward commitments. It is, perhaps, the most easily identifiable form of foreign currency exposure and is often the one which is best understood by general management or financial commentators.

Translation exposures may be either transitory, such as in the case of cash held in a foreign currency bank account pending its sale into the local currency, or more permanent, such as where an overseas investment has been funded in the local currency. The latter can also be seen as a form of structural exposure, which the company may have decided to enter into, or to maintain, for particular commercial reasons.

The transitory form of translation exposure is essentially no more than the impact of a time delay on a transaction exposure. In other words, it originates from a cashflow timing difference and exists at the balance sheet date due to a delay in completing the ultimate cash settlement. The exposure originating from the acquisition of inventory denominated in a foreign currency, for example, is only eliminated once the foreign currency has been acquired to satisfy the billing of the overseas supplier. If one prepares a balance sheet between the date of the inventory being supplied and the date on which the company acquires the foreign currency to pay the related billing, there will be an exposure in the foreign currency concerned, represented by the amount payable in currency then included in the accounts.

The longer-term form of translation exposure is a somewhat more difficult concept in that it does not relate to any immediate foreign currency cashflow. Whether the exposure originates from a long-term transaction exposure or from a form of structural exposure such as a long-term investment, it will have little relevance to short-term cashflows. It is this particular anomaly which has given rise to the phrase 'accounting exposure'.

Because of the need to consolidate all foreign currency assets, liabilities and operating results into the local currency for financial reporting purposes, and the fact that this also involves translating any long-term or semi-permanent exposures into that currency, translation exposure has often been seen as an 'artificial' exposure in the eyes of general management. Because there are no immediate cashflows in the foreign currency concerned, it is frequently left as an unhedged exposure.

A particular form of translation 'exposure' is often perceived to originate from the need to translate foreign currency income statements into the local currency for consolidated reporting purposes. This is a particular problem which originates from the approach generally adopted to consolidating the results of overseas operations and does indeed, in a mathematical sense, produce a foreign currency gain or loss whenever a different rate is used for converting transactions occurring during an accounting period to the rate which is used at the end of the period. In order to agree consolidated retained earnings in the parent company, a foreign currency gain or loss will arise in the consolidated accounts.

Economic exposure

The most difficult currency exposure to evaluate and monitor is the economic exposure arising from the complex interaction of the company's business and foreign exchange rates in a more general sense. A simple example of where economic exposure can reverse the apparent impact of a straightforward translation exposure is where a company has manufacturing assets based overseas in a location which is subject to a devaluation against sterling. Although the balance sheet carrying value of those assets might reduce and, on the face of it, the flow of revenues from the manufacturing operation in question would suffer a corresponding reduction in sterling terms, it may well be that the effect of the devaluation on the competitive position of that overseas manufacturing operation is such that (particularly where most of the output is exported) there is a more than compensating increase in sales volume. In such a situation the apparent negative impact of the devaluation against sterling is in fact more than compensated for by the increased stream of revenues from the manufacturing assets concerned.

Another example of economic exposure is where a domestic single product manufacturer selling entirely within the local market has, as its chief competitor, an overseas manufacturer exporting an identical product into that market. In such a situation a strengthening of the local currency may enable the overseas manufacturer to reduce his local currency based prices and thereby increase market share — at the expense of the domestic manufacturer who has no direct benefit from the revaluation of his currency. Although he appears to have no obvious currency exposures, it is possible that the most important influence over the profitability of the domestic manufacturer is, in effect, the foreign exchange rate between the domestic currency and that of the overseas competitor. The domestic manufacturer is, in economic terms, seriously exposed to a revaluation of the local currency.

Failure to recognise economic exposure can, of course, result in incorrect hedging decisions being made and, in the extreme, may lead to a situation where an apparently sound hedging strategy is in fact increasing the net overall exposure of a company to particular currency movements. This might exist, for example, where a domestic manufacturer is contemplating a capital expenditure in the currency of a particularly significant competitor which is, at the time, a lower cost producer, benefiting from a temporary devaluation of its own currency. This temporary advantage may have allowed the overseas competitor to increase market share by reducing prices below those that might otherwise be charged by the local company. Although the local manufacturer might be inclined to hedge his projected capital expenditure in order to protect it against an appreciation in the overseas currency, any such appreciation might have a more than compensating impact on its ability to compete with the overseas competitor. In such a situation the company is, in commercial terms, already hedged against such an appreciation, and any attempt to effect a separate hedge against the future capital expenditure will result in an even greater exposure to the possibility of a further depreciation of the overseas currency.

Such economic exposures as these do not, of course, traditionally feature in a company's financial statements in an accounting sense. Their impact is felt over a period of time through the overall competitiveness of the company within the markets in which it operates. In those situations where a translation, or transaction, exposure has effectively been hedged by an economic exposure, there could be a situation where the gain or loss on the former will be clearly identifiable in the financial statements whereas the compensating 'hedge' created by the economic exposure will be hidden in the underlying future profitability or otherwise of the business concerned. An interesting accounting question which we return to in subsequent chapters is the extent to which one should attempt to try and identify separately the effect of what is, after all, simply an alternative form of hedging arrangement.

ASPECTS OF RISK

The identification of foreign exchange exposure does not, in itself, provide an indication of the likely risk which might flow from that exposure. A proper understanding of the underlying risks is, however, fundamental to the whole process of exposure management. There are a large number of operational or organisational risks associated with any form of foreign exchange activity, but these will be reviewed in chapter 10. The present chapter confines itself to an examination of the business and accounting risks arising as a result of the existence of foreign currency exposure.

Foreign exchange positions

Currency exposure is traditionally discussed in terms of the 'position' that the company may hold in a particular foreign currency. A currency position arises whenever there is a difference between the assets and liabilities denominated in a particular foreign currency or where there is a mismatch between the future anticipated cashflows of that currency. There is a need to differentiate between the overall 'net' or 'open' position of a particular currency and any 'gap' positions created by the mismatch between future anticipated cashflows in that currency.

The concept underlying a 'net' or 'open' currency position is that it measures the extent to which the company concerned is exposed to future movements in exchange rates between its own local currency and that of the currency concerned. Unfortunately, of course, most companies have little idea as to the extent of their future foreign currency transactions and it accordingly becomes necessary to define the net position in terms of either all transactions already entered into or, alternatively, those transactions currently entered into together with those which, at the present time, it is expected the group will enter into over a predetermined period of time. Many companies accordingly attempt to define an open position over, for example, a six or twelve month time horizon, whereas others might choose to consider it in terms of simply those transactions already entered into or committed. The position should, at a minimum, cover all current committed foreign currency transactions, and wherever possible should also include prospective transactions over a reasonable future period.

Although the open position is defined as the net of currency assets, liabilities and commitments and any future currency cashflows, it takes no account of mismatches in the timing of cashflows. A 'gap' position exits in a currency whenever there is a projected timing mismatch in underlying future cashflows. It is not uncommon for a company to find itself with a fairly small open position and yet very large offsetting gap positions in certain future periods. Whereas an open position can be defined in terms of an absolute amount of the currency concerned, a gap position needs to be defined in terms of both the amount of the mismatch and the initiation and termination of the projected gap.

A 'spot' position is generally defined as the net of the company's currency assets and liabilities together with its projected cashflows in that currency over the next few days. Some companies use a 'three-day' rule to coincide with the operation of the spot foreign exchange market, whereas others treat any projected cash movements occurring within the next seven days as being a part of the spot position.

Liquidity ladders

The spot, open and any gap positions in a particular currency can best be viewed by considering future projected cashflows in that currency. This will often entail constructing a liquidity ladder such as the following:

	$000
Spot position	
Dollar current account	55
Amounts due in dollars	(30)
Outstanding spot purchases of dollars	100
Spot position (1 January)	125
Gap positions	
Contracted settlement of dollar asset purchases (31 March)	(350)
Forward purchase of dollars (30 June)	200
Open position	(25)

The spot position in the above example is a long position of $125,000, whereas the open position is a short one of $25,000. The gap positions can best be seen by considering the cumulative currency cashflows over the six-month period:

	$000	Cumulative £000
Spot	125	125
31 March	(350)	(225)
30 June	200	(25)
	(25)	

There is accordingly a $125,000 gap between 1 January and 31 March and then a $225,000 gap between 31 March and 30 June.

Positions and risk

The risk arising from a net position in a foreign currency is fundamentally different to the risk that arises from a gap exposure in that currency. A mismatch in forward anticipated currency flows represents a potential exposure to the need to either deposit or borrow currency funds for the duration of the 'gap'. During that period, the company will have a mismatch between the local and foreign currencies, although the mismatch will disappear again at the end of that period. Whereas an overall net position can be closed out by way of a cash transaction in the spot foreign exchange market, a future gap position can only be effectively hedged through the use of forward foreign exchange contracts or their equivalent. The closing out of a future gap exposure through the use of two forward contracts has nothing to do with managing the net position, as it is simply a question of managing future cashflows in the currency concerned.

Closing the gaps

If we reconsider the liquidity ladder set out on p 36 above, we see that it would have been possible to close out the various exposures as follows:

(a) spot sale of $125,000;
(b) forward purchase (value 31 March) of $350,000;
(c) forward sale (value 30 June) of $200,000.

This series of transactions can, perhaps, be better viewed as follows:

(a) spot purchase of $25,000 to close out open position;
(b) spot against three-month swap of $150,000;
(c) three-month against six-month swap of $200,000.

We can then represent these transactions and the underlying projected cashflows as follows:

	Previous	*Spot purchase*	*Swaps*		*Net*
	$000	*$000*	*$000*		*$000*
Spot	125	25	(150)		—
31 March	(350)		150	200	—
30 June	200			(200)	—
	(25)	25	—	—	—

Chapter 2 demonstrated that the primary determinant of forward exchange rates will always be relative interest rates and that movements in forward premiums or discounts originate solely from movements in interest rate differentials. It is for this reason that gap exposures must not be confused with the exposure flowing from a net position. By way of example, let us consider a UK company which is planning to import an asset with a fixed foreign currency cost. Let us assume that the asset will cost DM100,000 and that it is anticipated that delivery and settlement will take place in 90 days' time. In the absence of any other transactions in the foreign currency concerned, the company would be said to have a 'short' position of DM100,000 in that currency.

Let us now assume that the company has just received DM100,000 in connection with another transaction and decides to keep it on deposit for 90 days (and then use it for the purchase of the asset) rather than converting it into sterling and then having to re-convert it in three months' time. In such a situation the company will have a 'square' net position in Deutschmarks, with the DM100,000 deposit in effect offsetting the commitment to spend DM100,000 in 90 days. Although the foreign currency deposit is, of course, yielding interest over the three- month period, it may be doing so at a significantly different rate to that which would be earned in sterling. If the funds are, for example, left on seven-day deposit, the company is exposed to fluctuations in relative interest rates between sterling and the foreign currency. It would, of course, be possible to eliminate the uncertainty element by placing the funds on three-month deposit so that they would become available at the same time as they were required for the purchase of the overseas asset. If the company decides to put the DM100,000 on seven-day deposit, the overall effect will be as follows:

(a)   The company will be square in net overall terms in the foreign currency.
(b)   The company's spot position will be either zero or DM100,000, depending on the particular definition adopted by the company for 'spot'.
(c)   Its seven-day forward position will in any case be long by DM100,000.
(d)   The 90-day forward position will be short by DM100,000.
(e)   The combined effects of (c) and (d) above are a gap position of 83 days of DM100,000.

We have already noted how the gap position is, in effect, an interest rate exposure. It is possible to 'close out' this position either by way of a treasury operation (depositing the funds for the full 90-day period) or through a pair of matching foreign exchange contracts.

To close out the above gap position using two foreign exchange contracts it would be necessary to effect a sale of the foreign currency either spot or seven-day forward with a corresponding re-purchase 90-day forward. This would eliminate any remaining exposure of the company to fluctuations in relative interest rates, without affecting its overall net position. It is important to remember that the gap position represents no more than an exposure to movements in the relative levels of interest rates between the local and foreign currencies, rather than anything to do with movements in the underlying foreign exchange rate. The movements in the relative interest rates will, of course, be reflected through movements in forward premiums or discounts quoted for the foreign currency concerned.

One final form of currency position which should be mentioned at this stage is the 'contingent position' created as a result of having entered into a transaction involving a contingent foreign currency exposure. Such transactions include long-term construction tenders, fixed-rate overseas supply agreements where the purchaser has an option on the amount and timing of the supply, conditional fee arrangements denominated in a foreign currency, and, of course, legal contingencies where there is a foreign currency element. Contingent exposures can be either potentially long or potentially short, depending on the circumstances, but should, generally, be segregated from committed forward positions, with the risks associated therewith being separately monitored. The contingent exposures themselves will be dependent upon the outcome of certain outside factors, one of which might, in certain cases, be the actual level of foreign exchange rates themselves. For example, a company that decides to 'write' a foreign currency option, creates a contingency which is dependent upon the future movements in the exchange rate concerned (see Reference Section A.11).

Transaction and translation exposure

Transaction exposure originates, as discussed earlier, from the decision to enter into a foreign currency transaction. The exposure arises because of the transaction being at least partly denominated in a foreign currency, with the consequence that the local currency equivalent of the item will be determined by future rates of exchange. Once a transaction has been carried out there will in many cases be a delay in cash settlement and it is that delay in settlement which we have identified as giving rise to translation exposure.

Once the company has decided to enter into a foreign currency transaction it has, in effect, created an open position in the currency concerned. That open position might have already been 'closed out' as a result of the settlement arrangements relating to the transaction but, in the event of settlement being required in the foreign currency concerned, and no particular hedging arrangements having been made, the company will need to acquire sufficient foreign currency in order to effect the ultimate settlement of the foreign currency transaction.

The separation of the transaction exposure from the translation exposure is fundamental to the accounting approach discussed in subsequent chapters. It is built around the concept of the transaction date being critical in terms of the point at which the exposure becomes fixed in an accounting sense: a concept which is consistent with most other areas of historic cost accounting. Once the local currency equivalent of the foreign currency transaction has become fixed, the company is subject to translation exposure to the extent that it chooses not to hedge the subsequent settlement.

The 'value' of any foreign currency position, be it an outright position or a gap position, can be evaluated at any point in time by effecting a revaluation of that position in such a way as to determine the net gain or loss that would arise if one were to eliminate the exposure entirely using foreign exchange contracts. This entails performing a 'forward revaluation' of any exposed forward positions as well as a spot evaluation of the spot position. It assumes, in effect, that the company goes into the foreign exchange market and undertakes currency transactions in such a way as to match all outstanding exposures in the currency concerned.

The resulting 'value' of those positions is a cumulative currency gain or loss which will increase or decrease in relation to future shifts in foreign exchange rates. It is this 'value' which is exposed as a result of the currency positions.

The process of valuing the spot and forward currency positions and, in particular, the way in which forward foreign exchange rates are used to revalue the forward positions, means that any movement in value on a gap position can be attributed solely to movements in forward premiums or discounts. The value of such gap positions, in other words, is a function of interest rate differentials rather than the underlying spot rate of exchange.

It will accordingly be seen that it is only the net position that can ever be impacted by movements in the spot rate of exchange and it is this, in an economic sense, which represents the exposure of the company to future exchange rate movements. The existence of a gap position gives rise to exposure to future movements in interest rate differentials and any such gap position does, of course, need to be included in the overall calculation of the net position.

Returning to the concept of transaction exposure, it can be seen that it is the transaction itself, rather than the timing of any cash settlement, etc which will give rise to the foreign exchange risk. Once the company has hedged any settlement obligations, it will have eliminated any translation exposure arising as a result of the transaction. Whether the hedging is carried out by way of a cash market transaction or a forward foreign exchange contract will not affect the fact that the open position has been eliminated. Although there could be a fairly large timing difference between the expected date of settlement and the value date of the hedge or the acquisition of foreign currency funds, this will simply give rise to a gap position in the currency concerned which, as discussed above, will not be exposed to future movements in exchange rates. The mismatch is more to do with the overall financing of the transaction and the way in which management chooses to utilise its available financial resources. This concept is examined in detail in chapter 7 where the differentiation between exchange rate and interest rate exposure is developed into a comprehensive accounting approach.

The discussion so far has dealt primarily with transaction exposure or the 'transitional form' of translation exposure. The risks arising from such exposures are fairly easy to identify and manage. The position can, however, become somewhat more complex in the case of longer-term 'structural' exposures which may generate a series of transaction exposures over time.

Let us consider the case, for example, of a company which is projecting an image (or already has an image) of carrying a particular exposure to a foreign currency on an ongoing basis. Such a structural exposure is, of course, accounted for in exactly the same way for a company that has no such image. For example, a UK insurance broker which is known to have a structural flow of US dollar brokerage and an inherent overhead cost base in sterling may be perceived by the stock market and others to be permanently 'long' in US dollar revenue. On the assumption that the company has no long-term hedging policy (or at least does not have one that is communicated to the outside world) the market will perceive the company as having a long-term exposure to US dollars. In the event of the dollar appreciating against sterling, the market will accordingly assume that brokerage income will rise by somewhat more than would otherwise have been the case. In such a situation it is important for management to balance the currency risk arising from the long-term structural exposure, against the risk that an elimination of that exposure could cause the company to not perform in the way in which the outside world expects it to.

Economic exposure

In discussing the origin of economic exposure we have already touched upon the kinds of risk that can flow from it. It is important to recognise that there are a large number of extraneous factors that can determine the precise form of risk arising from a particular economic exposure. It is, for example, often more sensible to examine the inflation adjusted exchange rate for a particular foreign currency when attempting to evaluate the impact over time of a shift in that rate. The obvious linkage, in macroeconomic terms, between inflation and foreign exchange rates can mean that looking at nominal rates (as opposed to 'real' rates) can provide a misleading picture as to what has actually occurred.

It is usually extremely complex to ascertain the degree of real economic risk arising from economic exposure to currency fluctuations. Two companies with identical prospective cashflows in a particular foreign currency can have very different real levels of economic risk, depending for example on the competitive position of the two companies concerned. Questions such as dominance, market size, product substitution, etc all play a part in determining the overall economic exposure of a company, and most of these factors are dynamic, with the economic exposure at one particular point in time possibly changing in the future as economic relationships develop.

Because of the difficulty in assessing economic risk on a comprehensive basis, it is often easier to consider it over a more limited time horizon. We shall accordingly see in the following chapter that currency management techniques often involve an attempt to evaluate economic exposures over say the next 12 months, and ignore the future beyond that time-frame. There are, of course, no prizes for being able to evaluate a company's economic exposures five years after the event!

The long-term view

Any student of economics will appreciate the long-term theoretical relationship between expected movements in exchange rates and expected differentials in inflation rates. Some commentators accordingly argue that any mismatch in the long-term structural currency position of a company should, over time, be compensated for by differential rates of inflation in the individual economies concerned. For example, if we consider a company which is importing goods from an overseas country and is therefore exposed, in foreign currency terms, to the exchange rate of the foreign currency concerned, it might be argued that such exposure is offset, in the long term, by differential rates of inflation in the two countries. In other words, if there is a devaluation of the foreign currency over time, with a consequential reduction in the local currency cost of imported goods, then that reduction will, eventually, be offset by an increased level of inflation in the foreign country.

Although the economic theory is perfectly sound, it does only apply in the 'long term' and with most economic markets being in a permanent state of disequilibrium, one does not necessarily make a great deal of money out of trading on the long term. Any form of structural exposure, be it a translation exposure or an economic exposure, can be ignored if one wishes to adopt the 'long-term approach'.

Perhaps the more important issue is the extent to which these kinds of exposure are perceived by, for example, the investor in the company concerned. If one argues that a central objective of the company is to perform in a way expected by investors, certain of these exposures should, indeed, properly be ignored by management on the basis that they are 'expected' by the shareholders. One is prompted to ask, however, whether any apparent lack of stock market recognition of such exposures has more to do with a lack of understanding rather than a degree of ambivalence. If management's role is to maximise profit and, wherever possible, to minimise risks, it is proper that they should take account of known short-term economic exposures and structural currency flows in assessing the management of their currency positions.

There is a strong argument in favour of taking account of translation exposure only to the extent that it can be measured within the particular planning horizon in question. For example, if a company chooses to assess economic exposure over a 12-month forward time-frame, and to manage its exposures within that time-frame, then perhaps translation exposure should also be taken into account only to the extent that it might impact results over the next 12 months. If one is going to ignore the long term for strategic economic planning purposes, perhaps one should also ignore it for the purposes of translation exposure?

THE IMPACT OF TAXATION

Whenever considering the risks which flow from a foreign currency exposure it is important to understand the taxation implications of any gains or losses which might arise. The true commercial risk to a company from an exposure is, after all, the 'after tax' result of that exposure. The impact of taxation is important for transaction exposure, translation exposure and economic exposure, although the precise impact is, of course, somewhat different in each case.

The particular matter to be addressed in considering the impact of taxation in this area is generally the way in which currency gains or losses are taxable (or not taxable) in particular fiscal jurisdictions. Such an approach is fundamental to determining an effective approach to exposure management and may well determine where an exposure hedge is to be booked.

This book does not attempt to consider the fairly complex issues surrounding the UK taxation of foreign exchange gains and losses. There are a number of useful texts in this area including Jill C Pagan *Taxation Aspects of Currency Fluctuations* (Butterworths). A major issue concerns the distinction between 'capital' and 'revenue'. This distinction, which is central to the determination of trading profit in the UK, can give rise to differing treatments in tax terms for two sides of a 'square' currency transaction. For example, if a UK company match funds an overseas investment by borrowing the foreign currency concerned long-term to match the anticipated duration of the investment, then any determination of the capital gain, or loss, arising on disposal would be based on the sterling cost and proceeds at the time of acquisition and sale, without any account being taken of the funding mechanism. It is accordingly possible for a company to make a sterling gain on an overseas investment purely due to currency fluctuations and to find that this would be taxed as a capital gain with no allowance being made for the 'loss' on the currency funding.

The other main area of contention concerns situations where one half of a commercially matched transaction may be classified as revenue and the other half as capital. When capital gains are taxed at an effective lower rate than trading income, it is possible to have a situation where a gain may be chargeable to corporation tax and a loss at the lower percentage rate of capital gains tax. The capital loss itself may be of no particular use to the company in question. There are also situations where a profit may be taxable but a related currency loss might be disallowed.

CHAPTER 4

Exposure management

THE GROUP TREASURY

A decentralised approach
The centralised treasury

EXPOSURE MANAGEMENT

Exposure identification
Management policy
Constraints over exposure management

APPROACHES TO HEDGING

Hedging costs
Internal hedging techniques
External hedging techniques
Selective hedging
Interest rate exposure

EXTERNAL SERVICES

Major participants
Forecasting services
Netting services

Although most company chairmen would claim that they and their companies are fully aware of the likely impact of foreign currency exposure on their operations, and that they are carefully managing those exposures and optimising the opportunities arising from them, it is those same chairmen who stand up in front of their shareholders and the press to announce that their results have been adversely impacted by movements in foreign exchange rates. Does this mean that they are not actually controlling their currency exposures as well as they would have us believe, or is it more to do with the fact that there are certain exposures that they are actually unable to control? Perhaps it suggests that such corporates are managing their exposures, but getting the market the wrong way round, or that their spokesmen are simply using currency swings as a convenient excuse for results which might otherwise be difficult to explain? On the basis that exchange rate movements tend to be fairly democratic and impact on everyone alike, and bearing in mind that in such a situation there are likely to be some winners and some losers, it is perhaps surprising that we are not having our attention drawn just as frequently to unexpected gains!

The truth of the matter is, of course, somewhere in between the possible explanations of inadequate control, poor understanding, unexpected exposures, getting the market wrong, etc. Many international bankers would be astonished at the size of the open positions that some corporate treasury operations are allowed to run, and the reluctance with which some corporates make use of available hedging products can be as shortsighted as committing their entire stocks of inventory to a game of roulette.

This is not to say, of course, that some corporate treasury operations are not extremely well run and controlled, and that some companies have not invested a considerable amount of resources in ensuring that they are fully aware of their currency exposures. There are, however, a very large number that are still struggling with the concept, and some where, even though management may have a broad understanding of the problem, there are inadequate controls or insufficient information to enable any sensible management of currency exposures to take place. The present chapter reviews alternative ways of structuring the exposure control function within a corporate group, and examines, in particular, what can be done to identify the exposures that exist. It then looks at alternative ways of managing those exposures through the mechanism of hedging and briefly reviews the available 'external' services now on the market to assist corporates in this area.

THE GROUP TREASURY

The role of the group treasurer has changed dramatically over recent years as corporates have woken up to the fact that significant costs can be saved, and indeed that revenues can be earned, by a proper management of the group's financial resources. Whatever the role of the group treasury in terms of funding or the management of surplus resources, it is essential for the function to become closely involved in the management of the group's currency exposures.

The corporate treasuries of major international corporates now range from fairly small and unsophisticated advisory roles through to major self-contained financing operations, sometimes now already established as 'in-house' banks in every sense of the word. Their objectives, in terms of currency management, are probably similar, but their approach to the problem and the resources available to them are sometimes worlds apart.

A decentralised approach

One way of structuring a group treasury role is to limit it to a largely advisory activity, with responsibility for the setting of overall currency objectives, and establishing limits for individual operating locations. In such a scenario there is likely to be little or no foreign exchange trading carried out by the central treasury: the majority of transactions being entered into individually by the operating units incurring the currency exposure. Little attempt will be made to identify potential 'netting' opportunities around the group, although there is likely to be some use made of cash management systems. Some corporates take the view that it is cheaper to utilise an external banking cash management network to ensure that they can optimise the management of financial resources, and a number of American banks, in particular, have been extremely keen to market these services.

The management of a group's currency positions in a 'decentralised' environment is likely to be fairly crude in that the majority of decisions will be delegated down to the operating units. Those units will be allowed to run open positions (and almost certainly gap positions) within what will often be fairly broad limits established by the group treasury.

Moving away from a completely decentralised approach, it is possible to arrange for all major (however defined) exposures to be either discussed with, or handled by, the group treasury. The establishment of carefully-defined, inter-company billing arrangements can often reduce the number of locations with significant currency exposures. A common solution, for example, is to try and retain as many exposures as possible in the largest manufacturing location in each currency area. This can be achieved by ensuring that billings out of that area (for example to a downstream sales company) are made in the currency of the purchasing company, rather than that of the key manufacturer. Arrangements such as these can significantly reduce the number of world-wide locations where the group treasurer needs to focus his attention. Under such an arrangement, it becomes extremely important to ensure that the pricing used for inter-company billing does not provide the wrong commercial signals to, for example, the downstream retail operations. (This is, of course, simply one small part of the larger problem of costing inter-unit transfers of products or services.) Some companies opt for the use of predetermined, internally-set exchange rates, whereas others use day-to-day market prices. Even in the latter case, however, there are generally discussions as to whether or not it should be the spot or the forward rate of exchange prevailing on a particular transaction date which should be used.

The centralised treasury

The extent to which a group's treasury functions are centralised will be determined by a consideration of all of its areas of responsibility, including its probable funding, corporate advisory and planning roles. In terms of the group's foreign exchange operations, however, the most satisfactory arrangement is usually a wholly-centralised group treasury which is responsible for absorbing, monitoring and managing all currency positions arising around the group. The benefits of centralisation may be summarised as follows:

Policy decisions

It is far easier to ensure that consistent policies are followed throughout the group. A decentralised arrangement is extremely hard to control and frequently gives rise to communication difficulties. A centralised approach does not necessarily eliminate all of the communication difficulties, but it does at least provide for a consistent policy over the longer term.

Matching / netting

Most large corporates are likely to have offsetting currency flows around the globe which, if centralised into a central treasury, can then be offset. This naturally reduces the number of outside foreign exchange contracts which need to be entered into.

Dealing volumes

The larger dealing volume of a centralised treasury should ensure that more competitive rates are obtained and that the corporate's leverage vis-à-vis its bankers is maximised. It can enhance the corporate's standing with its bankers and provide access to more sophisticated hedging arrangements.

Cash management

The management of currency exposures is inextricably linked to the management of the group's liquidity in each currency. The centralisation of currency exposures usually also allows for the centralisation of key currency bank accounts and, as a result, to a far more efficient approach to cash management.

Controls

The improved systems necessary for a centralised group treasury will almost certainly provide a greater degree of control than the local systems which would have to be used in individual operating companies. This is just as true for the back office settlement and processing functions as it is for the front office dealing role.

Resources

A decentralised approach to currency management will generally result in a fairly poor level of foreign exchange expertise being present in individual operating companies. Centralising resources into one area allows for a considerable upgrade in those resources and for enhanced internal education around the group of the dangers and opportunities arising from currency exposure.

Centralising currency management in the group treasury function ensures that individual operating units are free to concentrate on the business that they are experienced in. They can use the group treasury not only to absorb their day-to-day trading exposures but also to take on committed or contingent forward exposures of which they become aware. That is not to say, however, that centralisation is necessarily advantageous in all circumstances.

Some companies are so diversified that the centralisation of foreign exchange becomes too complex or impractical, whereas others find that centralising the external control of exposures leads to a reduced appreciation by local managers of the importance of such exposures. Centralisation has most benefit within the context of a group having a fairly consistent corporate 'culture' and management philosophy throughout its operations. Finally there is the question of costs: the establishment of a centralised treasury function will generally require additional highly-paid personnel as well as an investment in new dealing, settlement and accounting systems. The benefits of centralisation must be weighed up against such costs.

There are a number of ways in which a group can structure its internal activities to ensure that all currency exposures are absorbed by the group treasury. Approaches adopted include the assignment of currency receivables and payables to the group treasury in return for local currency funds at then current rates of exchange. An alternative is the transfer of receivables, through a re-invoicing process, and of payables through the operation of an international accounts payable centre linked to the group treasury. In either of these cases, the treasury ends up settling all currency receivables and payables on behalf of the operating units, at the same time effectively relieving them of any exposure in relation to same.

By far the most satisfactory way of handling a centralised group treasury, however, is to treat it very much as an in-house banking operation and have individual operating units carry out foreign exchange transactions with it as and when required. Such transactions are then arranged by the operating units in accordance with the group's laid-down policy, which might, for example, envisage the closing out of all known expected exposures over, say, the next 12 months. The group treasury would accordingly become the internal counterparty to the resulting hedging transactions of the operating units and would absorb them into its own position prior to deciding what approach to take as regards laying the exposures off in the market, and/or netting them against other internal exposures.

An advantage of the 'centralised in-house bank' approach is that it leaves primary responsibility for the identification and elimination of exposures at the operating level, whilst providing a structure within which the various benefits of centralisation can be realised. The more sophisticated arrangements such as these have significant systems implications, both for the group treasury and for the individual operating units. These are further examined in chapter 10.

There are a variety of examples of how a centralised treasury has benefited a group's performance through the improved management of its currency exposure. One of the better-documented of these concerns the case of Polysar, the large Canadian petro-chemicals company which is the world's largest producer of synthetic rubber and rubber latex. The group has locations in 15 different countries and sells its products in just about every country on earth. About 75% of its revenues originate in foreign currency. In 1981, Polysar lost approximately Canadian $17 million as a result of foreign exchange. The company set about establishing a comprehensive hedging programme and reduced its losses to Canadian $4 million in 1982 and Canadian $2 million in 1983. 1984 and 1985 both showed small currency gains.

The change of fortune for Polysar was brought about not as a result of more favourable currency trends or shifts in their underlying activity, but as a result of a concerted effort to identify and then hedge currency exposures. This was a fairly complex 'two-pronged' attack involving the establishment of a hedging operation between the US and Canadian dollar as well as between US dollars and all other currencies. Their foreign exchange management is now handled from their group headquarters in Ontario and, to a lesser extent, a financial management location in Switzerland. It adopts a 12-month time horizon in terms of its hedging posture, on the basis that it finds it difficult to identify exposures much beyond one year. Now, as well as actively managing its exposures, it also attempts to 'play' the currency markets to a limited extent to maximise perceived trends in exchange rates.

EXPOSURE MANAGEMENT

There is nothing particularly magical about the management of a group's foreign exchange exposures. The process often commences with a period of education: ensuring that senior management is properly aware of the risks of currency exposure and, in broad terms, the ways in which such exposure can be reduced. This is frequently a far more complex process than it might at first appear, largely due to the reluctance of senior corporate managers to accept that this is an aspect of their business that they do not perhaps understand particularly well.

The next step is to identify the nature and extent of the organisation's currency exposures, both current and prospective. It is only then that one can address the question of whether or not such exposures are going to be managed (and in some cases the conclusion may be that they are either too complex to manage realistically or too small to justify the allocation of suitable resources) and if so, how that process should be structured.

Exposure identification

Whatever the structure of the group treasury function, one of its first activities should be to carry out a comprehensive exposures audit. The proper identification of all currency exposures is essential if the group is to be able to manage those exposures properly and evaluate the performance of the group treasury function.

The first stage in the process is to complete a group-wide search for all possible exposures, both the obvious and the more obscure. This should encapsulate transaction, translation and economic exposures and should ensure that all operating units are properly investigated for those 'hidden' exposures which traditionally only become apparent when a significant loss arises. It is important to ascertain, for example, whether a supplier is billing in one currency but operating a pricing structure based in another, or whether there are, perhaps, 'special billing arrangements' in certain sales operations, the effect of which might be for invoices to be effectively denominated in a different currency to that in which they are issued. These are some of the ways in which currency gains and losses can become lost in net operating income. The search process should review all forms of long-term contract in order to identify potential currency exposures, even if there appear to be none at first sight.

Once the initial review of exposures is complete it is necessary to ascertain what information will be required on a regular ongoing basis. If, for example, a decision is made to monitor exposures on a rolling three-month basis, the group treasurer will need to have a methodology for accumulating data showing future currency flows over that time frame. If a decision is taken to manage certain economic exposures actively, the information requirements can, in some cases, be quite extraordinary – involving regular reports on marginal costs and competitor activity, etc. The next stage is to establish appropriate data capture systems and to introduce communication channels to ensure that all information is flowing to the group treasury on a timely basis. Certain of these areas are discussed further in chapter 10.

Management policy

Having established a structure for the corporate treasury function and, hopefully, the extent of its role, and having completed the initial attempt at identifying the majority of the group's currency exposures, it is then necessary to define the policy framework within which exposure management will take place.

An important preliminary at this stage, however, is to be absolutely sure that responsibility for monitoring or managing each identified exposure has been properly documented and agreed. If, for example, one decides to adopt a fairly decentralised approach to exposure management, it is essential for the managers of local operating units to understand how they are going to be evaluated (ie in post-hedged terms for example) and the precise extent of their responsibilities. An exposure without anybody specifically responsible for it is almost guaranteed to go unmonitored and unmanaged until such time as it results in a noticeable loss!

Then there is the question of education. Although one now rarely hears the dealer's favourite after-dinner joke that 'many corporates still believe that forward contracts are bad because they represent speculation', there are still some senior corporate managers who are extremely reluctant to adopt anything but the mildest of approaches to currency management. Options are a particular instance where the corporate sector appears to have been extremely reluctant to bear what they see as an unacceptable cost for the insurance that they provide. The important thing to remember is that hedging and speculation are essentially the same: the difference is simply the starting position.

One of the more difficult policy decisions is generally related to the extent to which the corporate is prepared to use its natural foreign currency flows (ie those originating from any structural positions it may have) actively to 'play' the currency market. Many corporates are ideally placed to use the currency markets to effect arbitrage transactions, perhaps on an international scale, between the currency and interest rate markets.

Whatever the decision as regards the group's approach to exposure management, it is essential that clear policies are set out well in advance. If a treasurer is expected to protect the group from currency risk whilst simultaneously making profits from swings in exchange rates, the company is probably suffering from a lack of clear management guidance. The group treasurer must be clear as to whether or not his primary role is to protect the group from exposure or to act as a self-contained currency dealing centre attempting to make profits on currency movements. The two objectives are not incompatible but it is useful if the primary objective is clearly defined. The exposure management policies should cover the point at which an exposure is to be identified, the percentage of any exposure which is to be covered at any one time (if less than 100%), the maximum position which can be taken in each currency at any one time and, as already mentioned, the individual responsibility for managing each particular exposure. Special arrangements should be made for contingent or uncommitted cashflows as appropriate.

Constraints over exposure management

There are a variety of factors which limit or restrict the extent to which a currency exposure can be managed or hedged. Such restrictions may, in some cases, actually determine the nature of the hedge eventually entered into. It is appropriate briefly to examine here the more significant of these.

(a)Exchange controls. There is at present no exchange control in the UK, but the overseas subsidiaries of UK companies may, in some cases, be constrained in their dealings in other than their local currency. In some countries it is still necessary, for example, for forward transactions to be tied to specific sales and purchases and there is no possibility of 'leading and lagging' (see below).

(b)Availability of funding. Gearing requirements may prohibit the short-term borrowing and investment approach as a means of hedging future currency exposures (see below). In such situations it may be necessary to revert to the use of a forward foreign currency transaction.

(c)Information systems. As discussed in chapter 10, a critical aspect of an active treasury operation is increasingly a comprehensive dealing accounting and processing system to ensure that all known exposures are properly identified and evaluated.

(d)Staffing requirements. Depending upon the size of the company there will be a requirement for people to monitor currency positions on a daily basis and take the necessary decisions in respect of hedging, etc. It must be recognised that the process of exposure management is essentially an active one whereby the 'total picture' must be reviewed on at least a daily basis. Once a company reaches a certain critical size, it frequently becomes essential to employ foreign exchange traders who will deal directly with the dealing rooms of major banks, thereby keeping in close touch with the market and being able to obtain finer prices for the exchange transactions actually entered into. The cost of dealing room support required at this stage (including Reuters screens, extra telephone lines and back office support) can be considerable.

(e)Management involvement. The importance of management involvement cannot be overemphasised, and inadequate involvement by the key people responsible (from the boardroom down) can lead to misunderstandings and costly mistakes. Those involved need to have a proper understanding of the nature of the group's foreign currency exposures and associated risks, and there

is frequently a need for either elementary or sophisticated training of certain key individuals.

APPROACHES TO HEDGING

There are a variety of ways in which management can decide to approach a particular exposure. In addition to understanding its nature and monitoring its size, it is necessary to consider the extent to which it should be hedged. The options available to management are essentially as follows:

(a) not to hedge at all;
(b) a full hedging approach attempting to match as much exposure as is possible over the defined time horizon;
(c) selective hedging, where a decision to hedge a particular exposure is made based upon a value judgment applied to the individual transaction or exposure concerned;
(d) insurance of the exposure, essentially through the use of currency options or the equivalent; or
(e) a progressive hedging approach: hedging on a consolidated basis but only entering into hedging transactions on a progressive scale as predetermined 'trigger rates' are reached. The effect of such a strategy is not dissimilar to taking out a foreign currency option, although the complexity of the operation is increased and the risk cannot be entirely eliminated.

As already noted, there is still something of a misconception within British industry that entering into currency options, futures or even forwards is an essentially speculative activity. Some fairly large companies in the UK still take a view that they are 'not here to play at being bankers' and that management's attitude to foreign currency activity should be essentially passive, involving the conversion of currency flows into sterling as, and when, required. The truth of course is very different in that any foreign currency exposure gives rise to the risk of loss in the event of exchange rates moving in a particular direction. In such a situation the 'do nothing' approach is, of course, the least prudent course of action available to the company.

Hedging costs

A frequent misunderstanding when considering the whole question of currency hedging concerns the idea of the 'hedging cost'. Although it is true to say that there is, in effect, a cash cost of entering into many hedging transactions, it is not sensible to treat that cost as anything other than the consequential result of having created the currency exposure in the first place. It should, accordingly, be more correctly considered as, perhaps, part of the original transaction giving rise to the currency exposure. The only real question to be addressed in considering whether or not to hedge a transaction (in terms of the hedge costs) is the extent to which one is prepared to 'pay the premium' in order to reduce or eliminate the doubt or uncertainty existing as a result of the unhedged currency exposure. The extent to which this is a 'cost effective' approach is accordingly linked to a subjective judgment as to the price the company is prepared to pay to eliminate the uncertainty inherent in the exposure. Does the concept of hedging costs, however, have a role to play in evaluating the relative efficiencies of two or more alternative hedging approaches?

Hedging cost is often cited as being a means of determining the most efficient way of hedging a particular exposure. As one is again talking about the subjective question of uncertainty, however, it is only possible to effect such a comparison between two forms of hedging which give identical results: for example, the total elimination of the exposure in question. As there are few instances where exactly the same result can be achieved in more than one way, any attempt to use hedging cost in determining the most appropriate hedging strategy may well to be doomed to failure.

Internal hedging techniques

There are a variety of in-house options available to management when considering a suitable means of hedging a particular exposure. Such techniques tend to be closely allied with the underlying exposure that they are attempting to protect. These are some of the more common approaches:

(a) Matching techniques. This involves a process of attempting to match currency flows in such a way as to minimise the costs of buying/selling currency as well as eliminating (or reducing) any resultant gap exposures. It is generally a technique that can be employed either in long-term contract work, where currency flows can be determined well in advance, or where the activity is tied in with the management of the group's creditors, so that it is used as a major determinant in the timing of creditor settlement.

(b) Pricing considerations. There are a variety of means by which one can address those exposures originating from mismatched pricing and invoicing. An obvious technique is to invoice in the currency in which the majority of input cost is incurred: something which may not be possible where the majority of output is designed for export. An alternative approach, which is particularly appropriate in large one-off contracts, is to include currency protection clauses under which ultimate prices are adjusted if a particular exchange rate moves outside an agreed range. An alternative, although essentially similar approach, is to include cost or margin clauses to ensure that any increase in overall costs arising from currency movements can be passed on to the ultimate buyer, thereby preserving the sellers' predetermined profit margin.

(c) Inter-company netting systems. There are a number of degrees of sophistication that can be employed in ensuring that a large international group optimises its management of foreign currency resources around the world. Such arrangements may be linked to the banking facilities now available with most of the larger banking groups whereby multicurrency asset and liability management is provided through the world-wide consolidation of overdrafts and deposit facilities on very low spreads.

(d) Asset/liability management. With some currencies now generally recognised as being 'hard' and others as being 'soft', there are sometimes occasions where it is possible to ensure that the majority of assets and revenues arise in hard currencies with the majority of cash outflows and liabilities being denominated in soft currencies. Although such an approach may do little to reduce the

overall exposure of the company to foreign exchange rate movements, the inherent risk may in reality be reduced as a result of the greater general certainty over the direction of future exchange rate movements relating to the hard and soft currencies.

External hedging techniques

There are now an enormous number of methods available to the corporate treasurer better to enable him to hedge identified currency exposures. Many of the hedging products now available, together with a number of their more recent derivatives, are discussed in the Reference Section at the end of this book.

(a)Borrow, swap, invest. One of the oldest forms of hedging a future foreign exchange requirement has been to borrow local funds, convert them into the ultimate currency required and then invest them on the money markets on a fixed-term basis until such time as they will be required to meet the foreign currency commitment. The effect in economic terms should be similar to that achieved when entering into a matching forward foreign exchange deal.

(b)Forward or future transactions. The purchase of forward foreign exchange contracts or currency futures is one of the most straightforward ways of hedging a future currency commitment (see Reference Sections A.3, A.4 and A.6).

(c)Rollovers, etc. There are a variety of ways in which an anticipated settlement date can be extended into the future. The precise nature of the transaction depends upon the way in which it is structured and the circumstances surrounding the need for an extension (see Reference Section A.5).

(d)Advance collection. Gap positions can be reduced or eliminated through the discounting of foreign currency bills or the factoring of currency receivables with a financial organisation. Such an approach is, of course, also a means of funding so that the 'interest cost' implicit in the transaction can, if necessary, be thought of as being part currency hedge and part funding cost.

(e)Government guarantees. It is possible to acquire trade-related exchange rate guarantees from the governments of certain countries. In the UK, these are issued by the Export Credit Guarantee Department.

(f)Insurance type contracts. There are now a wide range of currency option contracts available. These range from straightforward derivatives of currency futures through to far more exotic products designed to address particular hedging opportunities (see Reference Sections A.11 through A.22).

Selective hedging

The idea behind selective hedging is that one enters into a hedge only when there is evidence to suggest that the risk of an exchange rate loss is greater than some 'trigger level'. It is a fairly easy concept to adopt when a particular currency is looking rather weak, but becomes extremely complex to manage on a day-to-day basis in a company involved in a large number of currencies.

Approaches range from the use of sophisticated options hedging models designed for the banking market through to the wholesale use of a consultancy firm specialising in exposure management.

Many companies adopt less formal forms of selective hedging whereby the finance director (or treasurer) is responsible for performing a fairly broad review of exposures within the context of the acknowledged structural exposures of the group. Although such an approach may be useful in identifying obvious exposures which need to be addressed and may still allow the group to respond to general market movements when they become evident, it is a long way from the more formal comprehensive hedging policies now adopted by the larger and more sophisticated international corporates.

One particular form of selective hedging is the concept of 'leading and lagging' whereby currency payments may be made before the due date or currency receipts may be delayed beyond their due dates, applying an in-house view as to likely movements in the relevant exchange rates over the intervening periods.

Selective hedging requires a fairly active monitoring of currency exposures. Sometimes a company may decide whether or not to hedge an exposure at the time that it is first recognised and then leave the position at that. More frequently those companies with easily forecastable cashflows may tend to cover routinely projected flows 'up to a certain period' (perhaps one month) with a parallel periodic review for 'unusual' exposures beyond this time frame.

Interest rate exposure

A final point to make in connection with currency hedging is the interaction with interest rate exposure and the resultant need to ensure that both exposures are managed together whenever appropriate. In the same way that it is possible to use the debt markets to hedge a foreign currency position it is, of course, possible to utilise the foreign exchange market to hedge certain interest exposures.

EXTERNAL SERVICES

Mention has already been made of the international netting services now available from some of the international banks, and the way in which some companies now use the services of a specialised exposure management consultant when practising a selective hedging approach. There are now, in fact, a wide range of foreign exchange consulting and forecasting consultancies in existence, using techniques ranging from fundamental economic analysis to extremely technical forms of chart analysis. This section examines some of the external services which are available in more detail.

Major participants

Traditionally it was possible to divide expertise on currency rates and the foreign exchange market between the 'academic' contingent, which tended to be based primarily in the universities or government forecasting centres, and the 'trading side', comprising the dealing rooms of the major banks. Those two poles of knowledge have, over the last ten years or so, moved closer together, with a large number of consultancy services growing up somewhere in between, using skills from both sides. Most banks now have a fairly sophisticated in-house economics department which, amongst other things, will perform a certain amount of 'fundamental analysis' in relation to future exchange rate trends. Although most of that analysis will be used in the management of the banks' own dealing positions, it is sometimes available to corporate customers either by way of a special service or simply via their contacts with the banks' dealers over the telephone.

Dealers themselves have become far more alert to general economic developments, and it is now comments by the US Secretary of State or the Director of the Japanese Ministry of Finance which tend to be used by dealers as an indication as to where markets might be moving over the next few hours. The basic division, however, between the longer-term view provided by econometricians and the short-term dealing perspective flowing from the banks, still exists either to a greater or lesser extent.

The investment banking community, relatively late entrants to the foreign exchange markets in any volume, are currently waking up to the possibility of providing a more rounded service to their corporate customers than has perhaps traditionally been available from the commercial banks. Whether this will develop into a broader service actually being available on a wider scale has yet to be seen. The other newcomers in the market have been the major management consultancy operations where interest was initially focused on the provision of treasury systems but where, in a few cases, it has now been recognised that there are ready pickings to be made from a much more active day-to-day role in advising many of their medium-sized clients on the management of their currency exposures.

The currency consulting services themselves tend to divide into those sponsored by, or supported by, the large banks, those which originate as a result of government or non-commercial funding, and those which have been developed purely in response to the corporate demand for such services in the private sector. The latter tend to range from fairly large sophisticated groups employing a large number of people, down to small specialised organisations, sometimes established with only a handful of clients in mind. Appendix 2 contains a listing of some of the more well-known consultancy services currently in existence.

Forecasting services

The main source of customers for the various currency forecasting consultancies is probably the large number of corporates which now practise some form of selective hedging. In any case where a company does not automatically cover its currency exposures, it needs to take a decision, subjective or otherwise, as to when to hedge a particular position or when to run with it. Forecasting services are also used for the purposes of budgeting and planning. Currency forecasting tends to fall under two headings: 'fundamental' or 'economic' analysis; and 'technical' analysis. Most consultancies tend to offer one or both of these.

The assumption underlying fundamental analysis is that movements in exchange rates derive from economic variables. Although this is certainly true in the longer term, it is clearly less so in relation to short-term fluctuations. There are broadly two approaches to fundamental analysis: an econometric approach, using computer models and applying predetermined macro-economic variables in different countries to derive forecast rates; and a more judgmental approach, probably using econometrics as only a guideline to the general direction in which rates are likely to be moving. It is worth noting that the record of forecasts based on economic analysis has generally been rather poor, and whilst it is not difficult to understand why this has been the case, it is perhaps surprising that so many commentators still place considerable store by it today. Whilst fundamental analysis might be of use in terms of long-term budgeting, etc, it is scarcely the tool for day-to-day or even month-to-month currency management.

In recognition of the deficiencies of an economic-based approach, most forecasting services now utilise some form of technical analysis. The majority of commodity and financial markets have, over time, been found to exhibit certain characteristic pricing patterns which, if analysed and monitored, can provide indications as to likely future movements. This is the 'pure' approach to technical analysis, using chart analysis in one of its many varied forms.

There are many forms of currency chart analysis but they generally use a combination of daily, weekly and monthly charts, documenting highs and lows over the periods in question and identifying the way in which the rate moved in between. Chartists consider various factors in their analysis, including observed volatility, cyclical trends, apparent resistance or support levels (perhaps evidencing central bank involvement), perceived 'equilibrium levels' and ranges within which a rate typically trades.

Proponents of technical analysis argue that it is extremely useful in terms of short-term management of currency positions and there are, indeed, a large number of corporate treasurers now using the results of such research material. Many financial commentators now believe that we are close to the point where the foreign exchange markets may begin to exhibit the properties of certain other commodity markets, whereby when a particular technical level is reached in the market, the market will move simply because of the large number of participants who are using technical analysis to manage their positions. There is a limited amount of evidence to suggest that over the course of 1986 and early 1987 certain movements in the US dollar were generated as a result of major movements of capital deriving from forms of technical analysis.

The sheer size of the foreign exchange markets and the increasing influence of external events (such as statements from political or regulatory sources) must surely mean that it is unlikely that technical analysis will ever become as important as it has done in some commodity markets. The very large number of participants in the market, the fact that the individual foreign exchange dealer is still the primary 'mover' of prices and the determination of the major central banks to 'control' certain currencies, will surely work against any tendency for technical analysis to become the driving force behind those markets. That is not to say, however, that it should be ignored and, for the selective hedger, some form of technical judgment is essential if the process is not to become entirely subjective. The proper use of technical analysis, supported by an understanding of the markets and the day-to-day influences upon them, can accordingly be a suitable way of proceeding with a selective hedging strategy.

Netting services

Automated netting systems are now offered by a number of international banks and enable international corporates better to manage mismatches in their flows of foreign currency. It is important to recognise that most netting systems do not, in themselves, assist with exposure management: they are merely a methodology for reducing the cost of currency mismatches when they do occur.

Netting systems are generally established for the world-wide management of a group's financial resources. It is unlikely that they would be set up purely for the purposes of reducing the cost of currency trading. They do, however, greatly assist in the management of the group's liquidity in each currency and can significantly impact the net financing costs of mismatches in currency flows. Netting systems should minimise the number of inter-company receipts and payments through the international banking network and should ensure that funds are, at the end of each day, utilised in the most efficient way possible.

Netting systems can either be developed in-house by the international corporate or can be purchased as a package from one of the major banking groups. The purchased packages range from sophisticated on-line cash management systems involving the linking up of a large number of microcomputer applications around the world, both in the corporate and in the bank responsible, down to much less sophisticated 'clearing arrangements' between a multinational and its main bankers. The preferred solution for any particular corporate will naturally depend on its individual circumstances.

One of the more useful aspects of world-wide netting systems, particularly in relation to currency management, tends to be the facility which enables cross-currency pooling of funds. Rather surprisingly perhaps, this is currently only available from two or three American banks, most of their competitors choosing to restrict pooling arrangements to individual currencies. Some banks even restrict the number of currencies for which the international netting service is available.

Although the concept of a comprehensive international netting arrangement between a multinational and its bankers is, perhaps, fairly straightforward, it seems to have presented innumerable technological problems in practice. The need, for example, to ensure that there are data lines between the corporate treasury locations within the multinational as well as within the bank, has often led to considerable delays in the installation of systems which, conceptually at least, do not appear to be unduly complex.

Netting systems have been used extensively in the US and are now growing in use in the UK; their success has been mainly on the domestic front, however, rather than internationally, and to some extent their benefit in a global sense has still to be proven. The banks have sometimes been reluctant to sell netting systems as a product because they see it damaging their own profitability, whereas the corporates have often been scared away by the sheer complexity of the task, and the potential costs in terms of computer consultancy time. It is likely that, for the foreseeable future, a far more efficient way of managing global resources is likely to be the proper organisation of a group treasury function with suitable internal flows of data within the corporate which will enable the group treasurer to operate in the most efficient way possible.

CHAPTER 5

The financial reporting environment

UNDERLYING BOOKKEEPING OBJECTIVES

Consolidated information
Currency information
Control aspects

ACCOUNTING GUIDELINES

Fundamental accounting concepts
Some key accounting issues
Development of accounting standards
Other guidelines

A SUMMARY OF SSAP 20 – THE INDIVIDUAL COMPANY

Introduction
Individual transactions
Balance sheet translation
Currency gains and losses

A SUMMARY OF SSAP 20 – CONSOLIDATED ACCOUNTS

The closing rate/net investment method
The temporal method
Equity investments financed by foreign borrowings
Financial statement disclosure

This chapter reviews the theoretical background to foreign exchange accounting (both in the UK and internationally) and summarises the various guidelines which have been developed over the last decade or so in this area. It attempts to place this theoretical discussion within the context of the bookkeeping objectives underlying them. The latter part of the chapter includes a detailed review of SSAP 20, the current UK accounting standard for foreign currency translation.

Foreign exchange accounting is, perhaps, one of the more complex areas of accounting theory, and is one which until the early 1970s many accounting practitioners chose either to ignore or rationalise away. As the world found itself moving away from fixed exchange rates, however, the profession began to realise that perpetually fluctuating rates, combined with the increasing internationalisation of world trade, could play havoc with any attempts to maintain consistency in other areas of accounting. As the foreign exchange market itself has become more sophisticated and complex, and as the attitude of corporations towards their foreign exchange exposure has become more understanding and realistic, the accounting profession has found it extremely difficult to maintain a comprehensive framework of agreed accounting policies.

The result is an accounting environment consisting of a number of fairly broad conceptual guidelines; certain prescribed, but frequently flexible, accounting standards in some of the more straightforward areas; little regulatory or statutory guidance in terms of a required accounting approach and, in general, a very diverse range of practical treatments actually adopted, both internally in preparing management accounts, and externally for the purposes of financial reporting. This environment has resulted in a considerable amount of flexibility in the more sophisticated areas of foreign exchange accounting: an attribute which is both a weakness and a potential strength in terms of developing consistent and realistic accounting approaches.

The lack of clear accounting guidelines in this area allows companies, should they so wish, to account for transactions in such a way as to provide the user of financial statements with a misleading impression of the company's financial position or results of operations. It can also result in erroneous accounting for management purposes, thereby increasing the risk of incorrect business decisions being taken, or inadequate attention being paid to, for example, significant foreign currency exposures. The flexibility can, however, also provide those preparing management or financial accounts with a valuable opportunity for ensuring that both are prepared in as realistic (ie commercial) a way as possible. An underlying purpose in preparing this book has been to encourage those in the position of determining a company's accounting policies to move towards a more realistic accounting approach by using the opportunities provided by the current gaps in the predefined accounting rules.

UNDERLYING BOOKKEEPING OBJECTIVES

Before examining the rules and guidelines currently applied in accounting for foreign exchange it is useful to review briefly the underlying objectives of both financial and management accounting in this area. Although the prime objectives of any accounting system are reasonably well understood, the following is a brief description of the specific requirements within a multicurrency accounting environment. For convenience these are examined under the following three headings:

Consolidated information.
Currency information.
Control aspects.

Consolidated information

A central difficulty in accounting for foreign currency transactions is that it is generally necessary for an accounting entity to present information, both internally and externally, on a consolidated basis across all currencies. It accordingly becomes necessary to effect a translation of any foreign currency amounts (whether on the balance sheet or the income statement) into the 'reporting currency'. The way in which accounting policies are applied will, amongst other things, determine the point at which that translation takes place and, in particular, whether it is at the date of the transaction, the date of settlement, an arbitrary date such as the month-end, or the date on which the actual reporting requirement falls.

The most obvious need for consolidated information is, perhaps, for the purposes of periodic financial reporting. There are very few corporate shareholders who would welcome, or even understand, data concerning the company's assets, liabilities, income and expenses if it were provided in the underlying currencies. There is also the conceptual difficulty of actually understanding what is meant by a particular item being 'denominated' in one currency or another. To avoid such problems, corporates naturally tend to report to their shareholders in a single currency, which may or may not be the currency of the country in which the company is domiciled.

Other major users of consolidated financial information are various regulatory authorities, many of which frequently require the same sort of underlying information as is necessary for the preparation of periodic financial statements. Some regulatory authorities may, however, require far more detailed information than that appearing in the published accounts on, perhaps, both a consolidated and 'underlying currency' basis. Consolidated information is also required internally by the general management of the company in order to evaluate and monitor, for example, customer exposures, country or industry outstandings, sales analyses, profitability assessments, global cashflow projections, etc. etc.

In some cases an overseas subsidiary might be required to adopt different foreign currency accounting methods for local financial reporting, or regulatory purposes, to those employed by the parent company for its own internal management accounting and/or financial reporting purposes. In such a situation it may be necessary for the subsidiary to account for foreign exchange in two completely different ways – as well as having to report in two or more currencies.

The nature of the company's operations, its relationship with its shareholders or holding company, and the various reporting requirements to which it is subjected, can accordingly have a profound influence on the underlying requirements of any accounting system.

Currency information

Chapter 3 explored how exposure to currency risk is a function of the positions maintained in each currency at any point in time. A careful monitoring of such currency positions is accordingly an essential part of management's overall control of the business. Chapter 3 also introduced the concept of economic exposure, and it was noted that as such economic exposures are generally unlikely to be reflected in the published financial statements, the exposure shown by the company's accounts might have little bearing on the overall economic risks faced by the company to movements in exchange rates. The accounting system must be able to provide details of currency exposure for both financial and management accounting purposes. In the case of the latter it is highly desirable that any identified economic exposures are, in some way, also included.

Earlier chapters also referred to the importance of monitoring gap positions in each currency in order to be able to control the interest rate risk implicit therein. To this extent it is necessary for the accounting system to draw a distinction between spot and forward positions in each currency and to provide what is, in effect, a maturity ladder in respect of those forward positions. The detailed accounting requirements in this area are, as will be seen from subsequent chapters, extremely complex and, to the extent that foreign currency monetary assets and liabilities exist, may also need to provide sophisticated information in respect of implicit interest yields, etc.

In a rapidly changing foreign exchange market the careful monitoring of currency risk is essential if management is to have the ability properly to control the operations of the company. The amount of currency information needed may accordingly be substantially more detailed than would be required by the normal monitoring/control/reporting requirements of most accounting systems. It is also likely that such information will be needed on a far more timely basis than that relating to other areas of the company's operations.

Control aspects

The accounting system has long been a central part of the way in which management controls the operations of a company. This is no less true in a multicurrency accounting environment and detailed requirements in relation to internal controls are reviewed in chapter 10. Some foreign exchange accounting systems have become exceedingly complex as a result of attempts by management to try and mirror underlying economic reality in the accounting records. Although this is, of course, a highly desirable objective, the fairly complex accounting systems which sometimes emerge may result in excessive burdens on the accounting function and a consequential reduction in internal control. A relatively straightforward accounting system which is understood by the accountants and all users of the information is generally preferable in those situations where the economic activities of the company are not, in themselves, overly complex.

A particular problem with multicurrency accounting is that it is not uncommon for corporate management to be fairly poorly educated on the implications of foreign exchange risk. Such situations can result in a significant weakening in internal control due to the inability of senior management to comprehend fully the currency gains and losses which may arise. It accordingly becomes essential for the accounting system to be able to analyse the impact of foreign exchange movements to whatever extent is necessary for management to be able to rationalise operating results on a regular basis. Many accounting systems are designed primarily with the objective of day-to-day control in mind, sometimes at the expense of the equally necessary need for longer-term investigation and evaluation of operating results on an 'after the event' basis.

ACCOUNTING GUIDELINES

In order to understand the ideas underlying current accounting standards on foreign exchange and, in particular, some of the deficiencies that have been grappled with over recent years, it is useful to review briefly the development of standards in this area and the conceptual background against which they have evolved. It is interesting to note that the most recent pronouncements on foreign exchange accounting in the UK and the US were probably just about the first time that there had been some measurable degree of detailed co-operation between the accounting professions in the two countries. That co-operation was brought about largely as a result of a number of earlier inadequate or misdirected attempts to deal with the problem, and the recognition that the issue itself was both complex and extremely important.

Fundamental accounting concepts

Modern-day accounting guidelines have been developed over time from four fundamental accounting concepts and it is worth reviewing these briefly in order to understand fully some of the difficulties faced by the accounting profession in grappling with the problem of foreign exchange accounting.

Going concern basis. Financial accounting has traditionally been based on the concept that the financial entity being reported upon would continue in business for the foreseeable future. Although accounting standards have now been developed to deal with certain situations where a company is no longer a going concern, the majority of accounting guidelines are based on the assumption that the entity in question will not be ceasing business within the near future.

Consistency. The concept of consistency requires that any accounting method adopted by a company should thereafter be applied consistently from one period to the next. There are, once again, now a number of guidelines to assist the preparer of financial accounts in dealing with situations where accounting methods are changed, but the overriding assumption of most accounting standards is that there will be a consistent application of any accounting policies adopted from one period to the next.

Accrual. The accruals concept involves the recognition of revenues and costs as they arise rather than as, and when, they result in cash movements. The concept implies a 'matching' of costs and revenues and is generally fundamental to the recognition of economic transactions in a commercially sensible way.

Prudence. The prudence concept requires that revenues should not be recorded before their ultimate realisation is reasonably certain. It further requires that provision is made for all known costs as, and when, they become identifiable.

The above concepts are necessarily applied somewhat differently in individual countries, with prudence in particular being interpreted far more strictly in a number of European countries than it is in the UK or the US.

There has traditionally always been something of a conflict between the prudence and accruals concepts and it is perhaps the financial services sector which has suffered most from this dilemma. The accruals concept, for example, surely requires a commodity trader to recognise unrealised profits on his trading portfolio; whereas in practice in the UK (as opposed to the US) it is still permissible, and in fact common practice, for commodity traders to value their trading inventory at the lower of cost and market value. Similar problems exist in the insurance industry where it is only recently that casualty companies have begun to admit that it may be more realistic to present their insurance liabilities on a discounted basis, thereby reflecting the fact that these liabilities will, in effect, be partly funded from future investment earnings on the related assets.

Some key accounting issues

One of the more obvious examples of where the concepts of prudence and accruals come into conflict is in the recognition of unrealised profits arising on the revaluation of foreign currency positions. Whilst some have deplored any recognition of currency gains until they have been converted into the reporting or 'base' currency, others have argued that unrealised profits should be recognised as long as they at least exist in 'cash' terms, whether or not the cash itself has actually been converted into the base currency. The majority of those active in the foreign exchange markets in the UK now regularly mark most of their spot and forward foreign currency positions to market, although even here there are a number of different approaches being adopted. Few, if any companies currently take account of their economic exposures when contemplating a revaluation of their currency positions.

The recognition of unrealised currency gains is, however, only one issue where there is a considerable diversity in the accounting policies adopted by UK companies. It is interesting to note that the report *Financial Reporting 1982/1983* identified approximately 20 different ways of treating foreign exchange in the UK.

The biggest divergence in approaches adopted has probably been in the translation of foreign currency balances, both as regards the most appropriate rate to use, and the treatment of any gains or losses arising on revaluation. The choice of the most appropriate rate of exchange to use in translating foreign currency balances has long posed a problem which has exercised accountants and businessmen alike. Alternatives include the historical (or actual) rate, the balance sheet 'closing' rate, a hedged or contracted rate or, in the case of income or expense items, an average rate, computed on any one of a number of different bases. A related issue has traditionally been whether or not items of a different nature (eg monetary versus non-monetary items; current versus fixed assets) should be treated in a different way. Both of these issues have now been substantially clarified by SSAP 20.

Other issues that have long been of concern in this area include the extent to which gains and losses from different sources might be offset against each other; whether, and if so how, inflation in the overseas country should be taken into account; whether unrealised foreign exchange gains are 'distributable' in the context of the UK Companies Acts; and whether the change in a subsidiary's net worth arising from its measurement in an investor's currency should be taken to income or shown as a movement on reserves.

Development of accounting standards

Discussion of the most appropriate accounting treatment for foreign exchange has been a long and protracted affair both in the UK and overseas. The discussion often became extremely emotive and at times there were a number of 'changes of direction' by those professional bodies endeavouring to standardise accounting practices.

SSAP 6 (*Extraordinary Items and Prior Year Adjustments*), issued in 1974, together with the limited amendment thereto, ED 16, published in 1975, both considered how foreign exchange gains or losses should be dealt with in published financial statements. They did not, however, attempt to set out a definitive method of foreign exchange accounting. These guidelines were drawn up in the context of fixed exchange rates and periodic major realignments between currencies which could easily be dealt with as extraordinary items as they arose. Although the era of fixed exchange rates was already long over, the profession had not yet faced up to the inevitable.

With the progressive abandonment of fixed exchange rates and, in particular, the weakness of sterling against other currencies, UK companies were forced to reconsider their accounting policies for foreign exchange. The traditional use of the 'historical rate' method, under which fixed assets were translated at original or historic rates of exchange and current assets, current liabilities and loans at the 'closing' rate of exchange, sometimes gave rise to significant foreign exchange differences which seemed to have little or no commercial meaning. In particular, where a foreign subsidiary was largely financed by borrowings in its own currency, the use of different rates of exchange for translating different elements of the financial statements resulted in extremely misleading results when the company was consolidated into the accounts of its parent. It was, after all, often in order to protect the parent against possible exchange losses that companies would raise foreign currency borrowings in the first place. During the 1970s the overwhelming majority of UK companies accordingly began to use closing rates for translating foreign currency balances when preparing their financial statements. Some companies also started to experiment with taking all foreign exchange gains or losses directly to reserves rather than to the profit and loss account.

The UK accounting profession's initial attempt at drafting a standard for foreign currency translation dates from an exposure draft (ED 21) issued in September 1977. It reflected the considerable diversity of theory and practice then existing, both nationally and internationally, by permitting the use of either the 'closing rate' method or the so-called 'temporal' method in respect of balance sheet translation. Within the 'closing rate' method the exposure draft advocated a concept under which exchange differences on certain loans denominated in foreign currencies could be offset against the compensating exchange differences arising on any fixed assets funded by those loans.

The ideas underlying ED 21 were expanded and clarified in ED 27, issued in October 1980. That exposure draft came down heavily in favour of the 'closing rate' method in the majority of cases, and also supported the idea of reserve accounting for exchange differences in certain carefully-defined circumstances. ED 27 also addressed the specific question of translating the income statement of a foreign subsidiary.

The position in the US was not dissimilar, although a definitive statement, SFAS 8, had been issued somewhat earlier, and advocated the use of the temporal method rather than the diversity of practices then in use. When that Statement was introduced the approach that it advocated was, in any event, probably already used by about half the major US corporates. SFAS 8 proved an acceptable accounting approach within the US throughout much of the 1970s during which time the US dollar remained fairly strong. It appeared to fit in well with the American approach of not allowing revaluations of fixed assets to be recognised in the financial statements, and the gains on exchange typically produced were not perceived as being an unreasonable reflection of the underlying economic reality. The US position changed during the latter part of the 1970s, and in 1979 the Financial Accounting Standards Board announced its intention of revising SFAS 8. An exposure draft was issued in August 1980 and, as this had been after lengthy discussions between the US and UK accounting professions, it was hardly surprising that it was broadly consistent with the ideas enshrined in ED 27.

The US exposure draft was revised and re-issued in June 1981, with a final Standard, SFAS 52, being released in December of that year. The UK's definitive Standard, SSAP 20, was eventually issued in April 1983. Although they are broadly consistent, the American Standard is far more comprehensive than SSAP 20. They each follow the broad concepts established by the earlier exposure drafts, but also set out ways of dealing with certain special circumstances which do not fit into the standard approach. An international accounting standard, IAS 21, was published in July 1983 and was, as one would expect, consistent with both the UK and the US Standards. Compliance with either SSAP 20 or SFAS 52 automatically results in compliance with IAS 21.

Other guidelines

Reference has already been made to the considerable amount of flexibility currently existing in foreign exchange accounting. Much of this comes from the fact that current accounting guidelines, such as SSAP 20, have been directed primarily towards the question of how one should produce consolidated accounts where one of the subsidiary operations is based in an overseas country. Although both SSAP 20 and SFAS 52 also address the question of foreign exchange transactions they are in no sense comprehensive in this regard. Neither of the statements address the more complex products now available in the market for hedging foreign exchange positions, and SSAP 20 even fails to deal particularly well with forward foreign exchange contracts.

In determining appropriate accounting policies in the UK one is, of course, able to draw on SFAS 52 or more recent US accounting pronouncements, such as SFAS 80 which deals with financial futures. There is, however, comparatively little in the way of other UK guidance or authoritative literature on the subject.

There are certain statutory provisions which need to be borne in mind when considering how to account for foreign exchange. These include the concepts of realised and distributable profits, now enshrined in the UK Companies Acts as a result of the enactment of the EEC's second and fourth company directives. Although it is essentially a legal question, most accounting authorities now agree that realised, and most unrealised, currency gains taken to the income statement are generally available for distribution by way of dividend. It is perceived that this is not necessarily the case for gains which have been taken direct to reserves, and some argue that unrealised gains on certain long-term monetary items should also be excluded. There is general agreement that, in the interests of prudence, all unrealised losses, whether taken to reserves or to income, should be taken into account when calculating distributable reserves.

There are a number of other statutory provisions which can influence the way in which foreign currency balances are accounted for in certain circumstances. The most obvious example is perhaps the prohibition of balance sheet set-offs. This issue has particular relevance when considering certain arbitrage or hedging techniques such as currency swaps, back-to-back loans and related arrangements. The Companies Acts now include a general prohibition of balance sheet netting unless there are legally enforceable rights of set-off between the parties concerned.

There are various other accounting standards of relevance to foreign exchange accounting, some of which provide a degree of guidance in this area. SSAP 18, accounting for contingencies, needs to be considered when dealing with foreign exchange options, whereas Technical Release 603 (window-dressing and post-balance sheet events), is of relevance in connection with certain hedging and arbitraging techniques.

Most of the aforementioned standards and guidelines are fairly straightforward and encourage the adoption of an accounting approach which properly reflects economic reality. Although there are numerous gaps in current standards, the flexibility that this provides can be beneficially applied in ensuring that the accounting policies that are ultimately adopted properly reflect the underlying commercial activity of the company.

A SUMMARY OF SSAP 20 – THE INDIVIDUAL COMPANY

SSAP 20 is clearly very central to any discussion of foreign exchange accounting in the UK, and it figures prominently in the chapters which follow. The remainder of this chapter reviews the scope and content of that Standard, notes some of the key areas not covered, and identifies those areas of flexibility which it expressly provides for. The full text of SSAP 20 has been included as Appendix 1.

Introduction

SSAP 20 sets out the overall objectives of currency translation as follows:

'The translation of foreign currency transactions and financial statements should produce results which are generally compatible with the effects of rate changes on a company's cashflows and its equity and should ensure that the financial statements present a true and fair view of the results of management actions. Consolidated statements should reflect the financial results and relationships as measured in the foreign currency financial statements prior to translation.'

These objectives embody the concept of a 'true and fair view' and, in dealing with transactions, refer to the importance of the impact of rate changes on cashflow and equity. In reality, the impact on cashflow and equity might well not be the same, and the actual recommendations of the Statement are not always compatible with the idea of wishing to reflect the impact of rate changes on cashflow. The use of actual exchange rates to translate, for example, the acquisition of inventory, often has little or no relevance to the rate which might be prevailing at the time when the company acquires the foreign currency required to satisfy the liability created by the inventory purchase. This is largely a question of semantics, however, and in broad terms the standard provides a fairly realistic basis on which to work.

SSAP 20 differentiates between the approach to be adopted in accounting for individual transactions within a company and the process by which a subsidiary or branch operation established overseas is consolidated into the accounts of the parent. In the latter case an attempt is made to take account of the way in which the overseas company is financed and managed, as well as trying to address the basic objective that the financial statements should reflect the 'results and relationships' as measured in the overseas financial statements prior to translation. The question of consolidations is separately considered in the following section.

Individual transactions

SSAP 20 deals initially with the question of how one translates the foreign currency transactions of an entity into its 'local currency'. Its general approach is to require that individual transactions be translated using the exchange rate in operation on the date on which the transaction occurred. It allows the use of average rates where major fluctuations do not occur, and states that contracted rates should be used when the transactions are to be settled in accordance with predetermined criteria. It is assumed that the latter refers to situations where the applicable exchange rate is referred to, for example, in a contractual agreement relating to the transaction itself, although it can obviously be perceived to have much wider relevance in the context of certain forms of hedging arrangement.

In those cases where a trading transaction is covered by a related or matching forward contract, the Statement allows the rate of exchange specified in that forward contract to be used in accounting for the trading transaction itself. It should be noted that the Statement does not *require* the use of the forward rate of exchange, simply *allowing* it to be used should the company so wish.

Balance sheet translation

When considering the question of assets or liabilities denominated in a foreign currency, SSAP 20 differentiates between monetary and non-monetary items. It recommends that once non-monetary items have been translated and recorded in the local currency, they be carried in the financial statements at the resultant local currency cost. Such an approach is totally consistent with the 'historic cost' accounting approach generally adopted, and usually means that assets such as plant and machinery or equity investments are carried in the balance sheet at values which do not fluctuate with exchange rate movements.

Monetary assets and liabilities existing at a balance sheet date are required by the standard to be translated at the closing rate or, if appropriate, at the rate specified in a related contract. The use of a forward foreign exchange rate embodied in a hedging forward contract is also permitted. This approach is consistent with that adopted for the translation of transactions and should generally mean that gains or losses on monetary assets and liabilities will only arise where there is a movement in the exchange rate between the date of the transaction (or previous balance sheet date) and the current balance sheet date.

Under certain circumstances, where a company has financed or hedged a foreign equity investment by way of a foreign currency borrowing, both the borrowing *and* the equity investment are revalued at the balance sheet date. Under such circumstances the Statement requires that the equity investment be denominated in the appropriate foreign currency, with any gains or losses on revaluation of both the equity investment and the related borrowing being taken to reserves.

Currency gains and losses

Exchange gains or losses arise during an accounting period where a business transaction is settled at an exchange rate which differs from that used when the transaction was initially recorded or, where appropriate, that used at the last balance sheet date. Exchange gains and losses also arise on unsettled transactions where the rate of exchange used at the balance sheet date differs from that used previously. The Statement requires that exchange gains and losses should be generally recognised in the profit and loss account for the period as arising from the ordinary activities of the company – unless they arise from activities which themselves would fall to be treated as extraordinary items, in which case they should be included as part of those items.

One exception to this general rule is where foreign currency borrowings have been used to finance (or hedge) foreign equity investments. Subject to the conditions set out below, the Statement requires the foreign exchange impact of revaluing both the investment and the currency borrowings at current rates, to be offset against each other in reserves. The required conditions are:

1. that in any accounting period, exchange gains or losses arising on the related borrowing be offset only to the extent that there are corresponding (and offsetting) gains and losses on the equity investment;
2. that the total amount of foreign currency borrowings used for the purposes of this offset is no greater than, in the aggregate, the total amount of cash that the equity investments are expected to be able to generate, either by way of future profits or otherwise; and
3. that the accounting treatment adopted be applied consistently from one period to the next.

It should be noted that where the hedge effectively covers all of the investment, the offsetting of gains and corresponding losses in reserves should provide a result similar to taking both sides of the hedged position to income. This may not, of course, be the case if the funding (or hedging) currency is not actually the same as the investment currency. The extent to which the gain or loss on a foreign currency borrowing exceeds the corresponding gain on the equity investment should, presumably, be taken to income in the normal way. The unhedged element of any equity investment would then be treated in exactly the same way as if the investment had not been hedged – in other words being translated at the historic rate of exchange rather than the hedged rate.

The Statement also refers to situations where long-term monetary items may result in exchange gains which might normally be recognised in the income statement but which, due to difficulties concerning the convertibility or marketability of the foreign currency concerned, might more appropriately be disregarded in preparing the accounts. The Statement provides for the non-recognition of currency gains on long-term monetary items where there are identifiable problems of recoverability. There is, of course, conceptually no difference in the application of prudence between a situation involving a long-term monetary item and one involving a short-term item; but one presumes that the Standard is simply trying to address what would clearly be a greater degree of uncertainty in the case of a long-term item.

Where a gain is not recognised in the income statement as a result of problems of recoverability the amount of the gain, or the amount by which exchange gains exceed past losses on the same item, is according to some authorities, required by the Standard to be taken to reserves. It is unclear whether or not this is the objective of the relevant paragraph in the Standard itself and such treatment would, in fact, appear to be incorrect. The question is examined in greater detail in chapter 8.

A SUMMARY OF SSAP 20 – CONSOLIDATED ACCOUNTS

The most vexed subject of discussion in the area of foreign exchange accounting has been the whole question of how to prepare consolidated financial statements where one of the companies is either based overseas or uses a different currency for financial accounting purposes. The theoretical arguments have largely revolved around the question of whether or not a subsidiary should be treated as 'an extension' of the parent company, and whether an attempt should be made to take account of the currency exposure of the parent to its 'net investment' in the subsidiary.

The closing rate/net investment method

SSAP 20 argues that the method used to translate financial statements for consolidation purposes should reflect the financial and other operational relationships which exist between an investing company and its foreign enterprise. The favoured method to be applied in most circumstances, is the closing rate/net investment method which recognises that the investment of a company is in the net worth of the foreign enterprise, rather than a direct investment in its individual assets and liabilities. The Statement recognises that, in this context, a foreign enterprise could be an overseas company, a branch or simply a separate operation identifiable by the fact that its activities are primarily within another currency.

Under the closing rate method the amounts in the balance sheet of a foreign enterprise are translated into the currency of the investing company using the rate of exchange ruling at the balance sheet date. The Standard requires that amounts in the profit and loss account of the foreign enterprise be translated at either the closing rate or at some average rate for the accounting period in question. The Statement does not rule out either of the latter alternatives on the basis that the use of a closing rate better achieves the objective of reflecting the financial results and relationships as measured in the foreign currency financial statements prior to translation, whereas the use of an average rate more closely reflects the profits or losses in cashflows as they accrue to the group throughout the accounting period. The Statement provides no real guidance as to when a closing rate should be used in preference to an average rate.

SSAP 20 argues that if exchange differences arising from the retranslation of a company's net investment in a foreign enterprise are introduced into the profit and loss account, the results from trading operations as shown in the consolidated financial statements would be distorted. The Statement therefore recommends that such gains or losses be not regarded as profits or losses in the normal sense, and that they be dealt with as adjustments to reserves. In the same way, where an average rate is used to translate the profit and loss account of the foreign enterprise, the difference between that average rate and the balance sheet closing rate used to translate retained earnings should also be dealt with through reserves.

Some authorities argue that reserve accounting for gains or losses arising in a company's net investment in a foreign enterprise is misleading. They point out that the overall performance of the parent company as regards an overseas investment comprises a combination of the underlying operating results and any currency gain or loss arising on the investment itself. Such authorities would argue that the entire results of translation should be reflected in the income statement for the period, rather than a portion going to reserves.

The temporal method

The Statement recognises that some foreign operations are essentially 'extensions' of the parent company whereby the affairs of the foreign enterprise are so closely linked to those of the investing company that its results can be regarded as more dependent upon the economic environment of the investing company's currency than that of the local currency. In such cases the Statement allows for the translation of the foreign enterprise's financial statements using the so-called temporal method.

The temporal method is essentially the method applied by a company, under SSAP 20, in translating the individual transactions in its financial statements. It would not normally result in any entries to reserves and differentiates between monetary and non-monetary items. The rationale for using the temporal method is that if the overseas operation is an 'extension' of the parent, there is essentially no need to differentiate between the translation of transactions recorded in the parent company's own financial statements, and those recorded in the books of the overseas subsidiary.

The Statement identifies a number of factors which it suggests should be taken into account in determining whether or not to use the temporal or the closing rate/net investment method. In particular, the following factors are identified as being of significance:

1. the extent to which cashflows of the enterprise have a direct impact upon those of the investing company;
2. the extent to which the functioning of the enterprise is dependent directly upon the investing company;
3. the currency in which the majority of the trading transactions are denominated; and
4. the major currency to which the operation is exposed in its financing structure.

The Statement does not accept that a foreign branch is automatically an extension of its parent for this purpose and requires that exactly the same criteria be applied to a foreign branch as to a foreign subsidiary.

Some authorities argue that there is little or no distinction between those companies where the overseas operation is an 'extension' of the parent, and those where it is (in currency terms) an independent operation. Such criticism tends to revolve around the difficulty in evaluating the independence of the operation and the way in which such operations are likely to be managed, rather than considering the underlying economic difference between the two concepts A more rational criticism of the differential approach being applied to the two situations is that the primary impetus for investment in an overseas country is, perhaps, the potential benefit which may accrue to the shareholders of the parent company. It seems reasonable to accept that such a rationale probably exists whether the overseas operation is being established as an 'extension' of the parent, or as a separately financed local operation. In that context it can, in some cases, appear unrealistic to use a different method of translation for the two situations.

Equity investments financed by foreign borrowings

SSAP 20 recognises that certain equity investments may be 'hedged' through the use of foreign currency borrowings. It accepts that in such cases it would be inappropriate to record an accounting profit or loss on the borrowing whilst flowing the corresponding impact on the equity investment into reserves. It accordingly allows for the offsetting of the two impacts in reserves both in a 'company only' situation and in the consolidation process. It should be noted that this is, once again, not a *required* treatment, and that the company is simply *allowed* to adopt the approach should it so wish.

Financial statement disclosure

Before completing our review of SSAP 20 it is important to note that it requires a number of disclosures relating to a company's foreign exchange activities. These may be summarised as follows:

1. the net amount of foreign exchange gains and losses on foreign currency borrowings less deposits, separately identifying:
   (a) the amount offset in reserves; and
   (b) the amount charged/credited to profit and loss; and
2. the net movement on reserves arising from foreign exchange movements and/or differences.

   It should be noted that certain banks and other corporations are in fact excluded from the first of the above disclosure requirements by virtue of the Companies Acts.

CHAPTER 6

An accounting overview

GENERAL CONCEPTS

Base currency
Monetary and non-monetary items

TRANSACTION ACCOUNTING

The standard approach
Exceptions to the rule
Translation into base currency

BALANCE SHEET TRANSLATION

The standard approach
Hedging
Non-monetary items
Off-balance-sheet exposures

CONSOLIDATIONS

Background
The key issues

DISCLOSURES

Economic exposure
Positional disclosure

A central purpose of this book is to establish some comprehensive accounting policies in the area of foreign exchange which, when taken together, will provide a rational framework within which it is possible to account for transactions in a commercially responsive way. Whilst the detailed policies are developed in the chapters that follow, the present chapter establishes the underlying concepts and provides an overview of the general approach.

An objective in developing the policies set out herein has been to maintain as close a relationship as possible between the underlying commercial activity and the related accounting treatment. This has been addressed within the context of SSAP 20 and the requirements of the Companies Acts, etc and the author is of the view that it is possible to establish a rational framework for foreign exchange accounting within these rules and guidelines. In those cases where current accounting standards or other constraints might be considered to prevent the adoption of a commercial approach, the difficulties are identified and discussed so that it is at least possible to adopt the most appropriate treatment for internal management accounting purposes.

Whilst it is recognised that the approach recommended in the following chapters is already standard practice for many UK companies, this is often not the case in so far as the treatment of certain hedging arrangements are concerned.

This chapter also considers the general concepts of base currency and the monetary/non-monetary classification of balance sheet items, and then reviews in overall terms the contents of chapters 7, 8 and 9 relating to transaction accounting, balance sheet translation and consolidations. It concludes with some recommendations concerning the treatment of economic exposure and some suggestions for a more comprehensive disclosure of currency positions.

GENERAL CONCEPTS

This section establishes the overall approach of this book to foreign exchange accounting and discusses the structure of the remainder of this chapter and the chapters which follow. It explores the concept of 'base currency' and then discusses the importance of the differentiation between monetary and non-monetary items.

Base currency

The starting point in accounting for foreign currency transactions is to determine precisely what constitutes a 'foreign currency'. This is actually somewhat more complex than it may at first appear, in that it means that one has to define the 'base currency' for the business entity concerned.

SSAP 20 employs the concept of a 'local currency' which it defines as being 'the currency of the primary economic environment in which (the entity) operates and generates net cashflows'. SFAS 52 employs the concept of 'functional currency' which it defines as: 'the currency of the primary economic environment in which the entity operates'.

It is important to recognise that the base currency of a business entity may bear no relationship to its local statutory reporting currency or the currency of the country in which it is either operating or incorporated. It rather has more to do with the whole way in which that entity operates, and which currency has the greatest influence over those operations. It must also be appreciated that individual operating divisions within a single legal entity may well have different base currencies as a result of their differing operations. It is, in most cases, desirable for a business unit to use its base currency as the one in which all transactions should ultimately be recorded. Any need to translate those accounts into another currency (perhaps for head office or local statutory reporting purposes) can then be treated in exactly the same way as the translation of the financial statements of an overseas operation. It is recognised that it may be necessary, of course, also to maintain fairly detailed records in the local statutory currency where this is required by local regulations, etc.

When considering the question of an entity's base currency, it is important to recognise that one can really only separate base currencies within a single business unit where there is a distinct operation which is clearly conducted under a different economic environment to the rest of the organisation. If we consider a UK incorporated company, with an integrated UK based trading operation, it is generally not possible to argue that it has two separate base currencies for different types of transactions unless those transactions can be clearly related to separate operating areas. A good example of where it might be possible to identify two base currencies within a single operation might be a UK subsidiary which has one division which re-exports products imported and manufactured by its foreign parent, and another division which manufactures and sells its own products locally.

Although SSAP 20 provides little guidance as to how one determines the 'local currency', SFAS 52 does contain, in an appendix, a number of suggestions as to the kinds of factors which should be taken into account in determining functional currency. The following guidelines have been developed from a number of sources, but are consistent with the suggestions in SFAS 52.

1   Management and appraisal

The single most important factor is probably the way in which the entity is managed, and the process by which its performance is evaluated by its parent company or shareholders. Certain companies quoted on The UK Stock Exchange, for example, have share prices which are primarily responsive to movements in foreign exchange rates rather than, perhaps, the success of the underlying company's operations. This is perhaps as good an indication as any that the base currency of the company concerned is at least partly in a currency other than sterling. Aspects such as remuneration packages (and in particular the determination of bonuses), a parent company's currency hedging approach, longer-term plans and budgets and similar managerial concerns, are all factors which might indicate a particular base currency. It should be recognised, however, that the exercise of significant management control, and the resultant use of the parent company's currency for decision-making purposes, does not in itself necessarily indicate that the currency of the parent company's country is the base currency for its foreign operations.

2 *Cashflow considerations*

The nature of an entity's cashflows, and the way in which they are managed within the corporate group, frequently provide a good indication as to the entity's base currency. Where the majority of cashflows are in the entity's local currency it is unlikely that the base currency will be anything other than that local currency. Where, on the other hand, the cashflows are an integral part of those of the parent, there is a high volume of inter-company transactions, and it is possible to observe extensive interrelationships between the cash operations of the entity and those of the parent, it is likely that the base currency will be that of the parent.

The question of financing is also one that needs to be considered in some detail when considering the entity's base currency; the raising of local equity or debt finance often indicating a reliance to some extent on the local currency. It becomes important in such situations for the entity to generate sufficient funds to service that debt or equity in the local currency.

3 *Currency management*

The way in which foreign currency exposures are managed within the group may, of itself, indicate the parent company's view as to the base currency of its subsidiaries. It has already been seen in chapter 4 that there are a number of options open to large international groups as regards the centralisation or decentralisation of the group's currency management activities. Some companies choose to view, as a matter of policy, certain of their overseas operations as a long-term structural exposure, without making any attempt to hedge them. Although a hedged foreign operation rarely gives any indication as to the base currency of the foreign affiliate, a policy of *not* hedging such operations is sometimes evidence that the overseas affiliate is viewed as having its own local base currency.

4 *Costs and revenues*

The extent to which an entity is dependent upon manufacturing or overhead costs denominated in a particular currency, and hence the proportion of the total 'value added' of a product which is in effect denominated in that currency, may well be indicative of the entity's base currency. Where, however, the value added, although denominated in a local currency, is perhaps 'priced' in relation to overseas costs, this factor may well be less significant.

The way in which an entity sets its sales prices and the nature of its sales markets both provide evidence as to the entity's base currency. Care must be taken, however, to ensure that locally-based prices are not simply the result of overseas costs and current exchange rates, rather than, for example, a function of locally-incurred costs and/or local competition.

It must be recognised that although the above factors should in general all be considered together, aspects such as the way the business is managed and the foreign currency management techniques of either the parent or the entity itself are likely to be the primary influences over the choice of base currency. It is certainly arguable that the other factors should be taken into account by management in determining the way in which currency exposures should be managed, but this is a separate issue. Where there appears to be little evidence as to any obvious currency in which an entity is managed, and where there is an absence of sophisticated currency management techniques, these other factors may assume far greater significance.

Although it is probably dangerous to suggest that the base currency should be the local currency in the absence of evidence to the contrary, it is probably true that this is actually the attitude taken by the majority of companies. To the extent that this is reflected in the way in which those groups subsequently manage their currency exposure, there should be no adverse impact, but a more sophisticated consideration as to the most appropriate base currency for an operation would in many cases be highly desirable.

The importance of establishing the base currency for a business entity is that it is normally appropriate to maintain the primary accounting records of that entity in that particular currency. Where the base currency is also the local (or statutory) currency, such an approach may well be required by law. The recommended approach to transaction accounting and balance sheet translation set out in the following sections is within the context of a business entity having established its local base currency. Although the examples set out in this book assume, for convenience, that the base currency established is sterling, the approach set out herein is, of course, equally applicable to any other base currency.

Chapter 9 deals with the question of consolidations and the discussion there should be considered in the context of consolidating a series of separate business entities, each having their own individual base currency. The approach in the case of the consolidation of a series of business entities with the same base currency is essentially the same as that which is applied in the case of a consolidation involving a number of separate domestic entities.

Monetary and non-monetary items

A foreign currency transaction is one which involves the creation or disposal of a foreign currency denominated asset, liability, commitment or contingency. The only real difficulty in accounting for such transactions originates from having to record the foreign currency asset, liability, commitment or contingency in the base currency rather than in the underlying foreign currency. It is, in other words, necessary to attribute at some point a base currency equivalent to the foreign currency amount. The need to do so may arise at the point where the transaction is entered into, at the time of settlement, or at some future date, depending on the nature of the transaction concerned.

A foreign currency transaction, in accounting terms, can comprise one or more items denominated in a foreign currency. It might, for example, simply involve the exchange of foreign currency cash for inventory priced in that foreign currency, or it may involve the purchase of the foreign currency itself in exchange for sterling. It is, of course, also common for there to be transactions between two different foreign currencies, not directly involving sterling.

To the extent that a foreign currency transaction involves a foreign currency amount, it is necessary to determine whether or not that amount can, in the future, be treated as a sterling denominated balance, or whether it is necessary to continue treating it as a foreign currency denominated item.

The decision as to whether or not to translate the amount into sterling on a permanent basis should be governed by a view as to whether or not the underlying item in question continues to retain characteristics which involve the foreign currency concerned. An asset, acquired in foreign currency for use in a UK business, can generally be treated as a sterling denominated item subsequent to acquisition, because the fact that it was originally acquired for foreign currency (as opposed to sterling) becomes largely academic. It should be provided with a sterling value which allows for the proper accounting for that item in the future. This would, for example, apply in the case of the purchase of overseas inventory or, perhaps, the acquisition of a fixed asset located in an overseas location.

The contrary position is true in the case of, for example, a foreign currency cash balance which is being maintained to allow the company to effect settlement of future purchases of foreign currency denominated inventory. It is quite clear in this case that it is necessary to treat the currency cash balance as a foreign currency denominated item, as to do otherwise would be misleading in terms of its value at any future point in time. It would, in other words, not be appropriate to allocate a permanent sterling equivalent value to foreign currency cash.

The above thinking has led to the development of the monetary/non-monetary concept, whereby monetary items are generally considered to retain their foreign currency characteristics, whilst non-monetary items are given a permanent sterling equivalent at the point where they arise, thereafter being treated as sterling denominated items.

This book examines accounting for foreign exchange under the two broad headings of 'transaction accounting' and 'translation accounting'. The former considers the way in which individual transactions should be recorded in the sterling books of account, whereas the latter considers the treatment of those balances which continue to retain their foreign currency characteristics after the original recording of the transaction.

The segregation of assets and liabilities between monetary and non-monetary becomes confusing in the case of items such as marketable securities which, whilst having a monetary 'value', are not necessarily treated as a monetary 'item' when they are carried in the accounts at historic cost. This is conceptually correct, of course, as using the historic exchange rate is totally consistent with the concept of historic cost accounting. Where there are marketable securities carried in the balance sheet at valuation, it becomes clear that they should be treated as being a monetary item and subjected to periodic revaluation. Exactly the same rationale can be applied to trade inventory.

The only time that a currency revaluation is required is therefore where there are monetary items denominated in a foreign currency. It is necessary to take account of all foreign currency monetary assets, liabilities, commitments and contingencies in the periodic revaluation process carried out in connection with the preparation of an entity's accounts in its base currency. As with the original recording of a transaction, the revaluation process must also take account of the prevailing commercial circumstances at the balance sheet date, using the foreign exchange rates most appropriate to the currency positions under consideration.

In some cases it is necessary for a business entity to utilise a currency for its main accounting records which is other than its base currency. This might be necessary, for example, where it is necessary to use the local currency for statutory purposes, but where the base currency has been determined to be that of an overseas parent. In such cases, it is necessary to remeasure the balance sheet and income statement into the base currency prior to considering such questions as consolidation, etc. The objective of that remeasurement process is essentially to translate the statements into a form which would be identical with that which they would have had, had the accounts actually been kept in the base currency itself. The process to be employed is, accordingly, exactly the same as that utilised for the recording of foreign currency transactions in an entity's base currency.

TRANSACTION ACCOUNTING

The underlying concept of transaction accounting is that, having determined the base currency, one wishes to record all transactions in that currency, whether or not they are local or foreign currency transactions. The base currency equivalent of any foreign currency amount is then determined on the basis of the economic facts prevailing at the transaction date, whether that means using the actual rate ruling at that time or some other rate determined by the commercial circumstances then existing. Once recorded in the base currency, the fact that the transaction originally involved a foreign currency ceases to be relevant unless some remaining monetary asset, liability, commitment or contingency denominated in that foreign currency continues to exist.

The standard approach

The normal approach to transaction accounting is that one records the transaction in the base currency accounts at the rate ruling on the transaction date. Chapter 7 shows that this should, in general, be the spot rate of exchange ruling on the transaction date. The only exceptions to this general rule are mentioned below.

The rationale for using the spot rate of exchange revolves around the concept of 'opportunity cost' applied to any foreign currency funds which are available to settle the related currency obligations and/or which will subsequently be acquired for the purposes of such settlement. The discussion in chapter 7 takes the reader through a series of fairly simplistic examples to demonstrate the basic rationale involved. It is important to recognise that the use of the spot rate of exchange at the transaction date remains valid whatever the nature of the transaction and irrespective of when any related monetary amounts payable or receivable are eventually settled. There should be no confusion between the translation exposure originating from a foreign currency transaction and the accounting approach to be adopted in relation to that transaction. The two issues are fundamentally different.

The problem of currency transaction accounting therefore becomes one of determining the effective translation date, and chapter 7 recognises that there are diverse practices in this area. It is recommended that in general the transaction date should be the date on which the currency commitment first arises, irrespective of when it might be recorded as such in the company's accounting records.

Use of the spot rate of exchange prevailing on the transaction date is generally appropriate for both monetary and non-monetary items. Whereas non-monetary items retain their sterling values indefinitely, however, monetary items essentially comprise foreign currency assets or liabilities which are subject to fluctuation in sterling terms as exchange rates move. They are accordingly taken into account in the balance sheet translation process.

Exceptions to the rule

The use of the spot rate of exchange ruling on the transaction date is a concept which can generally be applied to the majority of foreign currency transactions, whether or not they result in 'on balance sheet' or 'off balance sheet' items. Complications may arise in certain cases in determining the transaction date, but in general this should be taken as the date on which any exposures relating to the transaction first arose. There are, however, a number of instances where use of the spot rate of exchange might be inappropriate and these generally concern transactions where some other rate has been agreed in advance of the transaction date.

The most obvious example of where it would be inappropriate to use the transaction date spot rate of exchange is where the transaction itself is carried out under the terms of a contract which specifies that some other rate will apply. In such a situation, it is more appropriate to consider the transaction as having been redenominated in sterling as at the date on which the underlying contract was entered into. Although this is a fairly straightforward concept, certain complications can sometimes arise where the contract relates to contingent arrangements between the two parties concerned.

The other common exception to the rule is where a transaction hedge is entered into to 'fix' the applicable exchange rate in advance of the transaction date. This should be differentiated from an exposure hedge which seeks to eliminate any currency exposure arising from unsettled monetary transactions existing subsequent to the transaction date. The effect of a transaction hedge is essentially the same as the effect of having a contracted rate applying to the transaction. It achieves the objective, in other words, of redefining the foreign currency transaction in sterling terms.

In the case of both contracted rates and transaction hedges, it is the rate specified in the appropriate contract which should be used for the purposes of recording the subsequent transaction. Chapter 7 explores the reasons why it is appropriate to use the implicit forward rate of exchange in a forward contract or any other form of hedging arrangement, rather than, for example, the spot rate ruling at the date when the hedge is entered into. The chapter also argues that where a transaction hedge is entered into through the use of a balance sheet currency position – for example through the acquisition of foreign currency funds in advance of the transaction date, it should, in theory, still be the forward rate of exchange ruling at the hedge date which should be used for the purposes of recording the transaction. This is because the 'financing element' represented by the forward premium or discount at that time is, in effect, no more than an adjustment to the underlying sterling value of the transaction. It is fundamentally different, in economic terms, to the premium or discount arising on the hedge of a balance sheet exposure.

Some companies seek to use their balance sheet for the purposes of hedging known structural currency positions. They might, in other words, try and maintain a permanent currency imbalance in an attempt to hedge known future currency transactions over a predetermined period of time. Chapter 7 argues that there is no real difference between using the balance sheet to effect global hedging of known structural exposures and arranging a specific hedge to cover a known future transaction. It is accordingly recommended that in both cases, an attempt be made to bring any financing gain or loss arising from having entered into that hedge into the calculation of the exchange rate to be used for recording any subsequent transactions.

Where a hedging arrangement attempts to combine both a transaction hedge and an exposure hedge, ie where the hedge covers both the transaction itself and any exposure originating from that transaction, it is argued that, although the theoretical approach would require that the two elements of the hedge be broken down and treated in different ways, a more pragmatic approach might be to treat the entire hedge as relating to the subsequent balance sheet exposure. The effect of such an approach is essentially to redesignate the transaction date as being the hedge date, and thus it could be argued that the spot rate ruling on that earlier date is more appropriate than the spot rate ruling on the subsequent transaction date.

Chapter 7 also explores the approach to be adopted where there is more than one rate of exchange, the question of asset revaluations and the particular circumstances which need to be taken into account in the case of trading activities. Where the company is carrying out a mark to market based trading activity (for example in a commodity or a security), it is generally inappropriate to fix the sterling equivalent of any foreign currency transactions as of the transaction date. It is normally more appropriate to treat any underlying non-monetary items as being, in effect, monetary items subject to periodic revaluation.

Translation into base currency

The above approach to transaction accounting is also appropriate where it is necessary to translate financial statements from a local currency into an entity's base currency. In such circumstances, the only additional problem is likely to be the fact that actual or historic exchange rates may be 'lost' in the accounting system, thereby requiring the use of average rates of exchange. Whilst average rates might be appropriate for the translation of period income and expense, they are unlikely to be suitable for the translation of non-monetary items which arose over the course of the period.

This problem will often be able to be addressed by considering the materiality of exchange rate movements over the period in question and concluding that they were insignificant, or by considering the materiality of the activity concerned to the group in question as a whole. Generally, however, it is difficult to devise a suitable approach to translation from a local currency into an entity's base currency, unless comprehensive historic data exists concerning the exchange rates ruling on the relevant transaction dates. In such circumstances, it is therefore sometimes necessary for accounting systems to be developed with reporting facilities in both the base and the local currency. The multicurrency accounting systems described in chapter 10 are generally able to address this particular requirement.

BALANCE SHEET TRANSLATION

The question of translation arises in foreign currency accounting because of the need to continue to view certain monetary items as being denominated in their underlying currency. It will be recalled from the discussion above that it is generally inappropriate to record such items at a fixed sterling amount, it being preferable to treat them as foreign currency items, subject to consolidation into the base currency at the appropriate rates ruling at the balance sheet date.

The translation of foreign currency items into the base currency on a periodic basis is potentially the most complex area of foreign exchange accounting. This is due to the fairly complex hedging arrangements which can now be entered into and the desirability of taking account of economic exposures when evaluating the base currency equivalent of a particular foreign currency position.

The standard approach

Chapter 8 explores translation exposure as a concept and concludes that, in general, it is appropriate to utilise the balance sheet closing rate for the purposes of valuing unhedged currency positions. This approach, which is consistent with SSAP 20, is justified on the basis that it is theoretically possible for the company to 'close out' such positions at the balance sheet date – thereby fixing the base currency equivalent of the foreign currency amounts in question. The fact that management chooses not to do so, and that further exposure accordingly exists in the subsequent accounting period, is attributable to that subsequent accounting period rather than the current period. The most appropriate measure of the value of the position as at the balance sheet date is accordingly the spot rate ruling at that time.

Translation gains and losses originate from the fact that one is using a rate to translate monetary items into the base currency which is different to that ruling at either the original transaction date or the last revaluation date. Such currency gains or losses should in most cases be taken to income during the period in which they arise.

Much has been written of the 'misleading impression' sometimes given by taking account of translation exposure. Such comments usually refer to translation exposure as 'accounting exposure' on the basis that it is not 'real' and is simply a figment of the accountant's imagination. Chapter 8 explains why this is clearly not the case and, using some simple examples, demonstrates that an exposed monetary position is, from the standpoint of the company concerned, a very real exposure which should be taken into account when preparing periodic sets of accounts. The fact that the loss might not eventually be realised because exchange rates move in the opposite direction is just as irrelevant as any other event occurring subsequent to the balance sheet date and included in the results of the subsequent period. It is not generally appropriate to 'restate' base currency equivalents of foreign currency exposures simply because the 'realised' gain or loss is different to that anticipated at the time when the financial statements are prepared.

Hedging

Much of the Reference Section of this book is concerned with the more complex hedging arrangements now available to the majority of major companies. The detailed accounting implications of those hedging arrangements vary from product to product. There are, however, a number of general principles which can be applied to all cases.

In the first place it is important to differentiate exposure hedges from transaction hedges. An exposure hedge is entered into with the intention of reducing or eliminating the foreign currency exposure created, generally as a result of an earlier currency transaction. It has nothing to do with the recording of the transaction itself and the rate applied in determining the base currency equivalent of any non-monetary item arising from that transaction should not be affected by having entered into an exposure hedge – whether the hedge was entered into prior to the transaction, on the transaction date itself, or subsequently. This is demonstrated by way of example in chapter 8.

It is essential to take account of any exposure hedges when effecting a revaluation of a company's foreign currency monetary items. Failure to do so will result in the presentation of a misleading picture.

A confusion often arising when dealing with exposure hedges is that the rate implicit in the hedge often embodies a forward premium or discount (or the equivalent thereof) and the question accordingly arises as to how that 'interest element' of the exchange rate should be handled. An underlying theme running through this book is that it is essential to differentiate between the underlying foreign exchange rate and the interest differential implicit in any forward foreign exchange contract or the equivalent. This is particularly true in the case of exposure hedging where the rate being fixed by the hedge is generally the spot rate ruling at the point where the hedge is entered into, rather than the forward rate employed by the hedge itself. The appropriate accounting treatment is, accordingly, to apply the spot rate ruling on the date on which the hedge was entered into when revaluing the underlying hedged foreign currency position, with any forward premium or discount (or the equivalent thereof) being taken to income over the life of the hedge as part of the company's overall net financing activities.

This approach should be contrasted with the use of the forward rate (including any premium or discount) when dealing with the recording of a transaction subject to a transaction hedge.

Non-monetary items

We have already established that, in general, non-monetary items should be converted into a base currency equivalent on the date on which the underlying transaction was entered into. It is not then, in general, appropriate to effect a revaluation of what has become, to all intents and purposes, a base currency denominated item. Chapter 8 explores certain situations where this may not actually be the case due to the nature of the underlying non-monetary item. A particular example of this is where the non-monetary item comprises an equity investment, perhaps in a subsidiary or an affiliate, which is perceived by the company as being an exposure in the underlying foreign currency, perhaps due to the expected flow of future foreign currency revenue.

Although SSAP 20 generally requires that non-monetary items be held at their historic sterling amount, there is little guidance on the approach to the hedging of such items where a company chooses to treat them as being a monetary type exposure. There is, in the case of a hedge of an equity investment, specific provision in SSAP 20 allowing the company to match the hedge against the underlying investment. Chapter 8 argues that such an approach can also be employed in other cases where there is a hedge of what might appear to be a non-monetary position. In the case of an equity investment and its related hedge, SSAP 20 argues that one should reserve account for any gains or losses on both the underlying investment and the related hedge. Chapter 8 explores this concept and compares it with the approach advocated by that Statement in the case of consolidations. It is concluded that although there is little basis for reserve accounting in such a situation, the approach can, with one or two small amendments, be made to 'give the right answer'.

Reserve accounting is not available in the case of other non-monetary hedges and, indeed, SSAP 20 generally requires that any non-monetary items be retained at their historic exchange rates. Chapter 8 argues that where the commercial substance of a non-monetary item is such that it is more in the nature of a monetary item, and where the resultant exposure has been hedged by the company, it is appropriate to have regard to this in accounting for the hedging transaction. In other words, although it might be necessary to continue accounting for the 'non-monetary' item at the historic exchange rate, when carrying out the periodic revaluation of the company's currency exposures, it is appropriate to take account of the underlying monetary nature of the 'non-monetary' item at the same time as one takes account of the related hedge. The effect of such an approach will be that, although the balance sheet carrying value of the non-monetary item might still be at its historic rate, the amount taken to income in relation to it will reflect its underlying monetary nature and the related hedging of same.

The latter approach is essentially the same as that advocated below in relation to 'economic exposures', whereby it is suggested that it is necessary, in certain circumstances, to take economic exposures into account in effecting any periodic revaluation.

Off-balance-sheet exposures

The recommended approach in relation to off-balance-sheet exposures is that they be treated, in currency terms, in the same way as balance sheet assets or liabilities. They are, accordingly, taken into account in the periodic revaluation of the company's currency positions. It is important to remember, however, that many off-balance-sheet items comprise future commitments which would not normally be accounted for in a true sense until some point in the future. An example of this would be a long-term operating lease. Chapter 8 argues that, in such cases, it is generally inappropriate to book any currency gains or losses arising on the forward exposure. Similarly, any hedges of that exposure should be treated as transaction hedges until the date on which the transaction itself falls to be accounted for. The only exception to this is, as one would expect, where the transaction date has already effectively passed and the fact that the item is off-balance-sheet is merely due to the accounting convention being employed. In such situations, it is appropriate to take account of both the exposure and any hedges of that exposure as at the balance sheet date.

Chapter 8 also examines the question of contingencies and argues that any foreign currency exposure included therein should be taken into account in evaluating the overall amount of the contingency. To the extent that the contingency is hedged (perhaps using, for example, a currency option) it is necessary to match the hedge and the exposure. To the extent that a contingent profit or loss is recognised in the financial statements, it is clearly appropriate also to take account of any foreign exchange implications attaching thereto. Although it may be possible to ignore any option type currency hedges relating to an off-balance-sheet contingency, there is a problem where the contingency is hedged using either cash or a commitment type hedge.

CONSOLIDATIONS

As long as one has properly determined the underlying base currency for each operating entity within the group, many of the problems traditionally associated with carrying out a multicurrency consolidation are eliminated. Although there has been a considerable amount of discussion concerning the relative merits of the 'temporal method' as opposed to the 'closing rate/ net investment method', it is argued in chapter 9 that there is, in effect, only one method of multicurrency accounting: the closing rate/net investment method.

The temporal method should be used, according to SSAP 20, when consolidating the results of a foreign enterprise which is more dependent on the economic environment of the investing company's currency than that of its own local reporting currency. The implications of such a scenario, however, are that the base currency of the foreign enterprise must be, by definition, the same as that of the investing company – so that the consolidation process becomes one involving two companies using the same base currency, rather than a consolidation using two different currencies. If, as noted earlier, the foreign enterprise uses a different currency for the maintenance of its local accounting records, it is necessary to use the approach employed for transaction accounting to translate those records into the base currency prior to effecting the consolidation.

Chapter 9 reviews these arguments in a little more detail, but most of the discussion of consolidations is devoted to an examination of the closing rate/net investment method now advocated by both SSAP 20 and SFAS 52.

Background

There has been, as noted previously, a significant amount of discussion as to the appropriateness or otherwise of the closing rate/net investment method, with those arguing against the approach pointing to the following disadvantages:

(a)Inconsistency. It is sometimes considered that employing the temporal method for some companies and the closing rate/net investment method for others will lead to confusion and the manipulation of accounts.

(b)Shareholders' perception. It is argued that the parent company's shareholders are primarily interested in the results of the group's operations as measured in their own currency, irrespective of whether or not there are currency gains or losses on net overseas investments. Such authorities argue that it is necessary to include all the results of operations in the income statement of the parent company, and that this must include the gains or losses arising on any net currency exposures.

(c)Objectives of consolidated accounts. There is a view that consolidated financial statements should represent the results of a group's activities 'as if those activities had all been carried out by the parent company'. This is viewed as being inconsistent with the closing rate/net investment method under which items normally carried at historic cost are shown in the consolidated financial statements at historical cost (in foreign currency terms) translated at closing balance sheet rates. It is argued that the resulting numbers are meaningless in that they represent an amalgamation of historical cost and current rates.

SSAP 14, *Group Accounts*, in fact defines consolidated financial statements as being 'one form of group accounts which presents the information contained in the separate financial statements of a holding company and its subsidiaries as if they were the financial statements of a single entity'. This is sometimes sighted as being an inconsistency with SSAP 20 which implicitly provides for an accounting approach which does *not* assume that the underlying objective is to produce the accounts as if the financial statements were those of a single entity. The latter approach would, of course, require the use of the temporal method. The extent to which SSAP 14 and SSAP 20 are inconsistent is, however, surely less important than the overriding objective of the accounts giving a true and fair view.

(d)Inflation. It is sometimes argued that the use of the closing rate/net investment method is consistent with a current cost basis of accounting but that the historical cost approach is more consistent with the temporal method, particularly where inflation is fairly low. The combination of the historical cost basis of accounting and the use of the closing rate/net investment method for consolidations is said to be illogical, and to result in amounts in the balance sheet which are neither historic cost, current cost nor market value and which serve no useful purpose to the users of the accounts. The introduction to SSAP 20 in fact refers to the question of countries experiencing hyper-inflation and says that:

'Where a foreign enterprise operates in a country in which a very high rate of inflation exists it may not be possible to present fairly in historical cost accounts the financial position of a foreign enterprise simply through the translation process. In such circumstances, the local currency financial statements should be adjusted where possible to reflect current price levels before the translation process is undertaken'.

The Accounting Standards Steering Committee issued a Technical Release (TR504) addressing some of the above criticisms and this argued that the closing rate/net investment method was appropriate for the following reasons:

1. The holding company's investment is normally in the net worth of a business operation rather than in its individual assets and liabilities.
2. The method of translation ensures that the translated results and relationships do not differ significantly from those reported prior to translation.
3. The method acknowledges the fact that operations which are conducted in currencies and in economic environments other than those of the parent are essentially different from the parent's own operations. And
4. Translation of the historical cost accounts at closing rates is merely a restatement of assets and liabilities for the purposes of consolidation and does not constitute a revaluation.

The key issues

As both the temporal and the closing rate/net investment methods result in monetary items in the subsidiary entity being translated into the parent's base currency at the closing balance sheet rate of exchange, the only real issues which need to be addressed in considering the two approaches are the way in which non-monetary items are carried in the consolidated balance sheet and the way in which currency gains or losses are then handled in the income statement. Under the temporal method, all currency gains and losses are taken to income, whereas under the closing rate/net investment method the gains or losses attributable to the parent's net investment in the subsidiary are taken to a special reserve account. This book suggests that the closing rate/net investment method required by SSAP 20 is supportable from a commercial standpoint to the extent that the net investment can be viewed as a structural currency position of the parent. The arguments are briefly reviewed in the following paragraphs and are explored in greater depth in chapter 9.

A particular difficulty which needs to be addressed is the concept of a 'foreign currency asset'. It will be recalled from the earlier discussion of base currency that a non-monetary foreign currency item ceases to be a foreign currency item as soon as it has been translated into the base currency. It is, of course, consistent with that approach that from that point in time it becomes a 'base currency item'. An implication of the closing rate/net investment approach is that when such non-monetary items are recorded in the accounts of the subsidiary, they are in fact treated in the same way as any monetary items recorded in the subsidiary when they are consolidated into the parent. There is, however, no inconsistency in these approaches as it has already been established that the foreign currency non-monetary item has become an item denominated in the base currency of the foreign entity – which is entirely consistent with the idea of that foreign entity being a self-contained currency unit with its own base currency.

The reasonableness of this approach can be demonstrated when one considers the example of a fixed asset located overseas and denominated in the base currency of the overseas operation. The asset cost will be translated into the local currency of the parent at the closing balance sheet rate. It is appropriate to view the fixed asset as a 'foreign currency asset' because it is producing revenues in that foreign currency, will be replaceable at a cost denominated in that foreign currency and is likely to be operated in such a way that uses overheads and other costs also denominated in that foreign currency. It is surely natural to view such an asset in exactly the same way as any monetary item denominated in that currency. The asset has been, and is likely to remain, commercially part of a foreign currency unit which is separately identifiable and is operating in an environment using its own base currency.

It is also of relevance to note that the only viable alternative to using the closing balance sheet rate would seem to be the historic rate (ie adopting the temporal method), and that using the latter moves completely away from the concept of the subsidiary operation having its own base currency. Its base currency would in effect become the same as that used by the parent, something which would clearly not be the case in a great many cases.

The main issue as regards the consolidation of a subsidiary operation's income statement relates to the treatment of any gain or loss arising on the parent company's net investment in the subsidiary. The gain or loss arising when the subsidiary has its own base currency is, under the closing rate/net investment method, taken to reserves rather than being shown in the income statement. To the extent that the parent company has fully hedged its currency exposure to the subsidiary by way of a foreign currency borrowing, the gain or loss on the related hedge is also taken to reserves. The effect should be substantially the same as if both the gain or loss on the net investment and the gain or loss on the hedge were taken to the income statement. The only point at which the issue becomes relevant is, accordingly, when the parent company has chosen not to hedge its net investment in the overseas subsidiary or where it has only arranged a partial hedge.

Where a company has chosen not to hedge or to only partially hedge its net investment in an operation involving a different base currency to its own, it is in commercial terms, essentially adopting a structural foreign exchange position vis-à-vis that exposure. It is the impact of any movement in foreign exchange rates applied to that structural currency position which is shown in reserves and which is a measure of the group's gain or loss as a result of that structural position. Although it is true to say that the shareholders of the parent company are, accordingly, unable to see the entire results of the group's investment in that operation in the income statement, they do have a better understanding of the underlying profitability of that operation as measured in its own base currency. The treatment of the gain or loss arising on the structural position should perhaps be viewed in the same light as the treatment of periodic revaluations of fixed assets which are, of course, also generally taken to reserves. They represent, in other words, the results of long-term strategic decisions by the group's management, rather than necessarily relating to the underlying ongoing profitability of the operations concerned.

Although the above may be viewed by some as a somewhat tenuous argument in support of the current generally accepted accounting approach, it is, in the author's view, a good starting point from which to move in developing a more comprehensive approach to multicurrency consolidations, embodying the more realistic treatment of hedging and taking into account, where appropriate, economic exposures. The movement on reserves reflecting the results of a structural currency exposure should be considered to be part of the positional data disclosed by a company for the benefit of its shareholders. This aspect is further considered below.

DISCLOSURES

Mention has already been made of the way in which many companies now choose to cite movements in foreign exchange rates as the reason for a lack lustre performance in a particular area. Chapter 3 explored in some detail the nature of foreign exchange exposure and the way in which gains and losses can arise both in a 'one-off' trading sense and over a period of time as a result of positional mismatches. That chapter also explored the idea of 'economic exposure' and suggested that such exposures might be far more significant to many companies than might initially appear.

Although the accounting methodology explored in this book should result in a realistic approach to accounting for historical activities, it is not possible for an accounting approach on its own to convey to the users of a set of financial statements information concerning the current prospects of the company or group as regards currency exposure. In the same way that an increasing number of companies are now providing information concerning their business activities and, for example, the geographical split of revenues, etc, it is surely important for at least the larger international corporates, to begin to disclose information concerning their current and ongoing currency positions. It would also seem to be desirable that, in doing so, they take account, where appropriate, of known economic exposures.

The remainder of this chapter,therefore, reviews the additional disclosures which would seem to be desirable in order for the user of a set of financial statements to be able to appreciate properly the true financial position of the company.

Economic exposure

The concept of economic exposure was discussed in chapter 3 where it was demonstrated that there could be significant differences between the perceived and actual foreign currency exposure of a company. Economic exposure is, of course, fundamentally different to either transaction or translation exposure, in that it can only be computed as a result of a complex analysis of the company's underlying business activities, often in a very detailed way. To be performed effectively, it requires detailed information concerning the pricing and, in many cases, the cost structure of the company's competitors; information which may well not be readily available.

The difficulty in accounting terms emerges when a company has identified certain economic exposures which it decides to hedge or which, as a result of certain other transactions, it perceives as having already been hedged. The hedge may, in accounting terms, produce an exposed currency position which would under normal circumstances be revalued, and the question accordingly arises as to whether or not one should attempt to match the hedge against the economic exposure, thereby eliminating it from any revaluation process. Whilst such an approach is totally supportable within the context of trying to obtain a realistic accounting result, it necessarily creates problems where there is no guarantee that a company has identified all of its economic exposures. Should one allow the company to ignore hedges against recognised economic exposures, but not take account of other exposures inherent in the company's organisation which, for one reason or another, have *not* yet been recognised?

Although it might in theory be highly desirable for all companies to account properly for economic exposure in the preparation of their periodic financial statements, it is recognised that this will not be possible in the vast majority of cases. It is also accepted that many economic exposures are, by their nature, both obscure and potentially rather small. The identification of such exposures is both time-consuming and, in some cases, of little practical value to the company's management. Where, however, there exists a fairly obvious economic exposure, or where the company has decided to identify *all* significant exposures of this type, then an attempt should surely be made to take account of those exposures when evaluating the company's overall hedging activities. It is likely, after all, that the company might wish to hedge those exposures (at least on a selective basis) and it would be totally misleading to then treat such hedging transactions as outright positions.

This book accordingly recommends that where a hedge can be shown to constitute an effective hedge of an economic exposure, it be ignored in the periodic revaluation process and treated, in accounting terms, in the same way as a transaction hedge. Where such an approach is adopted it is suggested that the company attempt to identify any further economic exposures with a view to describing these exposures and its hedging of them in a note to the accounts. This approach to the hedging of identified economic exposures is, of course, consistent with that recommended in relation to the global hedging of identified structural exposures.

Positional disclosure

There are few, if any, large companies which currently disclose details of their foreign currency positions, although it is fair to say that many investors make assumptions regarding the long-term structural position of certain companies when buying or selling their shares.

If the financial statements of a company are supposed to show a true and fair view of that company's financial position at any point in time, surely it is necessary for there to be some kind of disclosure as to the company's current and prospective currency exposures. Although it would seem inappropriate, at this time, to set out a blueprint for such disclosure, it would seem desirable at least to indicate the nature and approximate size of any inherent structural currency positions, the extent to which any such positions may have been hedged, whether or not the group envisages any fundamental shifts in those structural positions and, perhaps, the methodology employed for monitoring and controlling short-term trading positions. It would, for example, be useful if a company were to disclose the period over which it traditionally attempted to hedge future currency exposures.

Although it is recognised that suggestions of additional corporate disclosures generally tend to be drowned in a chorus of objections, it is suggested that the importance of some of these matters is such as to warrant very careful attention by those responsible for the preparation of periodic financial statements.

CHAPTER 7

Foreign currency transactions

BALANCE SHEET RELATED TRANSACTIONS

A simple cash transaction
Foreign currency payables and receivables
Foreign currency commitments
The general case

SOME EXCEPTIONS TO THE GENERAL CASE

Contracted rates
Transaction hedging
Other rates of exchange

DEALING ACTIVITIES

Nature of a dealing activity
The normal approach
The impact of interest
Controlled arbitrage

OTHER TRANSACTIONS

Commitments and contingencies
Revaluations

This chapter considers the way in which foreign currency transactions should be recorded in the local currency or base currency books of account. It is accordingly directly applicable to foreign currency transactions entered into by either a UK entity or any overseas operation having sterling as its base currency, but can also be applied in general terms to transactions being recorded in any non-sterling base currency by either a UK or an overseas company. The policies set out in this chapter are also applicable to the retranslation into base currency of transactions recorded, for example, in a local currency.

In general terms it is possible to define a foreign currency transaction as any transaction which either creates or disposes of a foreign currency denominated asset, liability, commitment or contingency. Such transactions range from those involving the purchase or sale of an asset with a price denominated in a foreign currency, to the actual purchase or sale of the currency itself.

It should be recognised that the only real difficulty in accounting for currency transactions originates from having to record the asset, liability, commitment or contingency in the local base currency when the underlying economic value or obligation is actually denominated in a foreign currency.

The majority of currency transactions involve either initially, or in due course, the acquisition or disposal of foreign currency. The transaction giving rise to these currency cashflows, however, is frequently entered into either earlier or later than any related exchange of currency. The timing of the transaction itself is often critical to the exchange rate used in accounting for it, whereas it is the timing difference between the transaction date and any related cashflows which generally gives rise to currency exposures and, consequently, to currency gains or losses. The transaction itself, and the way in which it is accounted for, should not on its own usually give rise to any foreign exchange gain or loss.

The present chapter is concerned solely with transaction accounting and does not deal with the treatment of any foreign currency balances held for the purposes of settling foreign currency transactions. The existence of unhedged foreign currency cash or other foreign currency denominated monetary items can give rise to translation exposure, which is the subject of chapter 8.

BALANCE SHEET RELATED TRANSACTIONS

The majority of foreign currency transactions originate from the acquisition or disposal of either an asset or a liability in exchange for foreign currency. Such transactions include an asset being purchased in a foreign currency; inventory being sold into an overseas market; or the drawing down of a foreign currency loan.

These transactions are distinguishable from the fact that they involve the creation or elimination of either a balance sheet asset or liability (including on-balance-sheet commitments) and therefore exclude off-balance-sheet commitments or contingencies, which are examined in a later section. The initial discussion is also limited to transactions involving assets and liabilities held in the balance sheet at historic cost. The treatment of foreign currency transactions relating to dealing activities where assets are held at market values is also considered in a later section of this chapter.

A simple cash transaction

Let us consider the scenario in which a UK company purchases inventory from a foreign location and is required to pay for that inventory on the same day in a foreign currency. One can view this as essentially two separate transactions: the purchase of the foreign currency in exchange for sterling (which may well have taken place at an earlier date); and the purchase of the inventory with the foreign currency. If the company intends to use the inventory in its UK manufacturing activity it will wish to register it in its accounts as a sterling asset which can then be utilised in the production process. In simplistic accounting terms the transaction can be documented as follows:

1.   *Debit* foreign currency cash   FC 'A'
        Credit sterling cash   £'B'

2.   *Debit* inventory   £'C'
        Credit foreign currency cash   FC'D'

The foreign currency amount 'A' in the above example is determined by a combination of the spot rate of exchange at the time and the amount of sterling exchanged 'B'. The only difficulty arises in determining the carrying value of the inventory – £'C'. Where the currency is acquired and the inventory is purchased on the same day, it would, in economic terms, naturally be realistic to record the inventory at the same rate of exchange ie at £'B'. This is, of course, generally not the case, so that it becomes necessary to determine *which* rate of exchange is most appropriate for computing the sterling value of the inventory.

Let us assume that the company maintains a foreign currency bank account out of which it purchases its foreign currency inventory, and that there are ongoing decisions being made by management as to the amount of cash being held in that foreign currency account. Those decisions will be driven by a combination of management's views as to the company's future foreign currency requirements, their assessment of the relationship between future movements in exchange rates and current interest rate differentials, and perhaps other considerations. On the assumption that there is free convertibility between the foreign currency and sterling, the 'opportunity cost' of maintaining the foreign currency cash balance at a particular level on any day is the sterling equivalent of the currency amount at that day's spot rate of exchange.

In other words, the company could choose to exchange the currency cash balance for sterling at that day's current rate of exchange. Management's decision to hold some of the company's surplus funds in a foreign currency rather than sterling is really no different to a decision to place certain of its funds on long-term deposit rather than, say, on overnight call. It can be thought of as an integral part of the overall use of the company's financial resources.

If one accepts the foregoing argument it follows that using the foreign currency cash for the purchase of inventory on any particular day is, in commercial terms, the same as using sterling which has been sold into the foreign currency on that same day at the then prevailing rate of exchange. In other words, the appropriate rate of exchange to be used for the purposes of valuing the inventory in sterling terms is that ruling on the transaction date, irrespective of when the foreign currency cash is actually acquired.

Foreign currency payables and receivables

If we now consider the same example of a company importing foreign currency denominated inventory but with a delay in ultimate cash settlement, it becomes necessary to account for a foreign currency obligation between the time of acquiring the inventory and the ultimate settlement of the currency payable. The accounting entries in this situation would be as follows:

1. *Debit* foreign currency cash   FC'A'
       Credit sterling cash   £'B'

2. *Debit* inventory   £'C'
       Credit foreign currency payable   FC'D'

3. *Debit* foreign currency payable   FC'D'
       Credit foreign currency cash   FC'D'

It will be seen that the foreign currency accounting entries are essentially similar to the earlier scenario with the only additional step arising from the delay in cash settlement. The actual settlement of the payable for currency cash does not, in itself, comprise a foreign currency transaction – it is merely the satisfaction of a foreign currency obligation through the payment of foreign currency cash.

It is possible to apply the same arguments to this example as to the previous one. Whether the foreign currency is purchased prior to the transaction date, on that day itself, or at some subsequent date, should not determine the rate of exchange to be applied in valuing the inventory in sterling terms. The rate ruling on the date on which the foreign currency payable is settled is just as irrelevant as that existing when the foreign currency is acquired, probably having far more to do with the credit periods being offered by the supplier and the company's own ability to manage its overall cashflows.

The sterling carrying value 'C' in this latest example should accordingly once again be determined by the exchange rate ruling on the day on which the obligation to pay the foreign currency price of the inventory is incurred (ie the transaction date).

The difference here, of course, is that settlement of the currency obligation is not taking place at the same time as the inventory is acquired, so that a question arises as to whether or not one uses the spot rate of exchange, or a forward rate determined, perhaps, by the expected date of settlement of the related payable. As the forward premium, or discount, is (as discussed in chapter 2) no more than a reflection of the interest rate differentials between the foreign and local currencies, it is no more in economic terms than an adjustment to the implicit interest gain to the company in not having to settle its payables until some time after they have arisen. In the same way in which one would not, under traditional accounting concepts, discount the cost of sterling priced inventory to reflect delays in ultimate cash settlement, one should clearly not do so for foreign currency denominated inventory. The appropriate rate of exchange to be used in determining the inventory cost accordingly remains the spot rate ruling on the day on which the related currency obligation is incurred.

The reader may notice at this point that no account has been taken of the currency exposure arising should the company decide not to purchase foreign currency on the transaction date. It could be argued that the proper way to account for the foreign currency inventory is also to take account of the 'cost' to the company of closing out the resulting exposure, perhaps via a forward currency purchase. Would it not therefore be more correct to use a forward rate of exchange, irrespective of whether or not this includes the interest adjustment implied by the forward premium or discount?

Such an approach would clearly be incorrect. Not only does it result in inconsistent treatment as between sterling and foreign currency purchases of inventory, it also relies on the false assumption that the underlying accounting principle to be applied must be based on the company having no residual currency exposure.

Foreign exchange exposure is now a fact of life to the vast majority of UK businesses and an objective of accounting for currency transactions should be to ensure that any gains or losses arising from that exposure are properly reported. If the company in our example chooses not to hedge the foreign currency payable, then the gains or losses arising between the transaction date and the settlement date will be determined by the net movement in the spot rate of exchange over that period. If the company *does* decide to effect a hedge of that exposure, either through the purchase of the foreign currency on the transaction date, or through the use of a forward foreign exchange contract or the equivalent, then there should be no currency gains or losses arising from the transaction.

The interest implications of arranging the exposure hedge, either originating from the interest differential between the sterling and foreign currency funds, or from the forward premium or discount (the effect of which should be virtually identical), should quite properly be treated as an adjustment to interest income or expense. It must after all be remembered that the net interest income or expense of any company is determined by a number of factors – one of which is the way in which that company manages its working capital. There is no accounting principle which states that all of a company's working capital should be assumed to be denominated in sterling, and the process of entering into an exposure hedge can be thought of as simply an integral part of managing the company's foreign currency cashflows.

This issue is explored further in chapter 8 in the context of balance sheet translation.

Foreign currency commitments

We can now extend our analysis one stage further to consider the situation existing when the company enters into a commitment to acquire overseas inventory at an agreed foreign currency price, but does not actually take delivery until sometime later. Let us also assume, for the purposes of illustration, that the acquisition of the related foreign currency does not take place until *after* the commitment has been incurred. In such a situation, we can show the accounting entries which would be required as follows:

1.	*Debit* inventory receivable	£'C'	
	Credit foreign currency payable		FC'A'
2.	*Debit* inventory	£'C'	
	Credit inventory receivable		£'C'
3.	*Debit* foreign currency cash	FC'A'	
	Credit sterling cash		£'B'
4.	*Debit* foreign currency payable	FC'A'	
	Credit foreign currency cash		FC'A'

It will be seen that, once again, there are actually still only two foreign exchange transactions, and the first of these is when the inventory receivable is recorded as a sterling asset on the date on which the foreign currency obligation is incurred. In a situation such as this, some companies still choose to record the inventory receivable as a foreign currency asset until such time as it is, for example, received in the UK. It can be demonstrated that this is an unrealistic approach if one compares this example to the previous one. The nature of the foreign currency commitment is essentially just the same, irrespective of whether or not the inventory has actually been delivered. The fact that the inventory has not yet arrived should not influence the sterling cost applied to it, and the proper approach is clearly to use the rate of exchange prevailing at the point where the currency commitment arises. The same arguments exist against using the forward rate as were reviewed in the previous example – leading to the conclusion that it is the spot rate ruling on the date on which the commitment arises that should be used to value the inventory in sterling terms.

We shall see below how this generalised approach to balance sheet related transactions does not necessarily hold when considering a commitment that does not relate to an asset or liability carried on the balance sheet, or where the related asset or liability is regularly revalued or 'marked to market'.

The general case

So far the discussion in this chapter has been limited to an examination of the way in which one accounts for the purchase of foreign currency inventory. The analysis can easily be extended to cover the acquisition of any other asset denominated in a foreign currency. Whether the asset is of a short-term or long-term nature should not influence the exchange rate to be used when recording its value in sterling.

It is also very straightforward to extend the approach to cover the sale of an asset. Where, for example, there are sales denominated in a foreign currency, the sterling equivalent of the proceeds should be determined by the spot rate of exchange ruling at the time of sale. This should be the case whatever the expected timing for settlement of any related foreign currency receivables.

SSAP 20 requires that 'each asset, liability, revenue or cost arising from a transaction denominated in a foreign currency be translated into the local currency at the exchange rate in operation *on the date on which the transaction occurred*'. It is quite clear that, in all of the examples examined so far, the transaction actually occurred on the date on which the foreign currency obligation arose, and the correct approach is to use the spot rate of exchange ruling at that time.

The same concept applies in the case of foreign currency costs or revenues which arise from non-asset-based transactions, for example the acquisition of services (such as overseas consultancy services) or the imposition of overseas taxation. The approach to be adopted in translating these items into the base currency is essentially the same as in the case of an asset-based transaction. The appropriate rate of exchange will generally be the spot rate prevailing on the transaction date.

In the earlier examples we have chosen to define the transaction date as being that on which the foreign currency obligation arose. It is reasonable to extend this approach to most other situations, so that the problem then becomes one of defining the effective date on which the obligation arises. In the case of the provision of services, for example, it might be considered that the obligation arose over the period of time in which the services were provided. In the case of a taxation charge relating to a particular item of foreign currency income, it would be reasonable to argue that the obligation arose at the same time as the related income. If, therefore, a particular rate is being used for a certain source of foreign currency income, it would be reasonable to utilise that same rate for any related taxation.

Many companies choose to adopt a less sophisticated approach in the case of translating foreign currency items originating from non-asset based transactions, essentially utilising the rate ruling at the point where the obligation is first recognised in the books of account. The extent to which such a practice is acceptable will, of course, largely depend upon the materiality of the amounts concerned to the overall business.

Some industries currently use a very diverse range of different approaches in this area, many of which are inconsistent with the general concepts discussed above. The insurance market, for example, traditionally books premium income using rates of exchange prevailing at the point where the premium is recognised, whereas claims arising under the policies relating to that premium income are generally booked at the rates of exchange existing when the claim is first recorded. There are a large number of variations on this approach: involving average rates of exchange; cash settlement rates; etc. Whatever the approach adopted, it is often not entirely consistent with the underlying objective of trying to ensure that the exchange rate utilised is that prevailing on the 'transaction date'.

SOME EXCEPTIONS TO THE GENERAL CASE

Having established that the normal approach to transaction accounting involves the application of the spot rate of exchange existing on the transaction date, it is now necessary to examine briefly the exceptions to that rule.

The following paragraphs explore the idea of the exchange rate relating to a particular transaction having been determined in advance of the transaction date, either by way of a contracted rate or through the use of transaction hedging. The final section examines the use of average exchange rates and addresses the question of currencies having two or more separate exchange rates.

Contracted rates

In some instances involving foreign currency transactions it is possible for a company to arrange for a contracted rate of exchange to be applied to the transaction prior to the actual transaction date.

Contracted rates are particularly common in certain long-term contractual business relationships, where one party to the transaction wishes to protect themselves from future currency movements. It is one of the more straightforward forms of currency hedging that is available without having to enter into specific hedging transactions, and is frequently encountered in the construction industry and in certain overseas government contracts.

It is important to recognise that the underlying economic objective of using a contracted rate in an international transaction is to shift the currency exposure arising on that transaction from one party to the other. It can, accordingly, have the same effect as an arrangement involving the issuing of invoices in a foreign currency or an agreement to acquire an overseas asset in one's own base currency.

From the standpoint of a UK purchaser, the existence of a contracted rate for an overseas asset purchase in essence does no more than fix the pricing under the contract in sterling terms. The fact that the rate employed might be a combination of the spot rate, the forward premium or discount, and an element of service fee, should not detract from the underlying point that if the contract had been drawn-up entirely in sterling terms, it would not necessarily have been thought of as a foreign currency transaction.

Turning to the case of a UK supplier who agrees to effect future sales on the basis of a predetermined exchange rate, it can be seen that the effect is the same as if that supplier had chosen to issue price lists denominated in the foreign currency concerned. The foreign exchange exposure in such a situation has, in effect, been shifted from the overseas purchaser onto the UK supplier. It is quite clear in such a situation that the supplier has taken on a very real currency exposure in terms of his future sales. How should any sale subsequently made under that contract therefore be accounted for?

In addressing this last question, it is useful to compare the idea of a long-term fixed rate contract with a series of transactions undertaken on the basis of a foreign currency price list. The only difference between these is that in the case of a long-term contract, the supplier has committed himself to sell at those prices well in advance of the sale actually taking place. This is, however, not really any different to any other kind of long-term sales contract whereby the overall profitability of the arrangement can be affected by future events. An unexpected movement in the foreign exchange rate is not really any different to an unexpected increase in manufacturing costs. The supplier has simply chosen to fix his future revenue on the basis of his current perception of future costs (and exchange rates) at the time that the contract is entered into.

Any 'prefixing' of a foreign currency transaction into sterling should be treated in exactly the same way as any other sterling-based transaction. In other words, the sterling equivalent of the foreign currency amount should be considered to have been determined at the point where the contract was entered into rather than on any subsequent 'transaction date'. The fact that there is a foreign currency amount underlying the sterling equivalent becomes largely irrelevant from the date of the contract.

Any contract which has the effect of defining what would otherwise be a sterling item in foreign currency terms should be treated in exactly the same way as any other foreign currency denominated transaction. The fact that the underlying item is denominated in sterling becomes largely irrelevant and the amount in question can be treated in exactly the same way as any other foreign currency item. The exchange rate to be applied to that foreign currency amount would accordingly be the spot rate ruling on the eventual transaction date, rather than any rate inherent or implied by the contract to which the transaction relates.

The whole area of contracted rates can become more complicated where the contract is drawn up in the form of an option arrangement allowing, for example, a purchaser to acquire inventory up to a certain predetermined level at a predetermined effective exchange rate over, say, six months. In such a situation, the supplier may well have in effect taken over the foreign currency exposure relating to the transactions but does not, of course, actually know at the commencement of the contract how much inventory is eventually likely to be delivered. The supplier has accordingly taken on a form of contingent exposure in terms of future sales. Although this has major repercussions for the supplier in terms of his ability to manage his resultant currency exposures, it has no direct impact on the way in which the transactions themselves should be accounted for. In the absence of any transaction hedging (see below) the appropriate rate to be used in translating the sales into the supplier's base currency will be the spot rate ruling on the transaction date, irrespective of the rate implicit in the underlying contract. The sale is still, in economic terms, a foreign currency denominated transaction rather than one carried out in the base currency of the supplier.

In summary then, when dealing with contracted rates it is important to recognise the economic effect of the underlying contract. If the effect is to transfer the foreign exchange exposure from one party to the other, one needs to ask what the effective underlying currency is for any transactions carried out under that contract? Having then determined the effective currency for those transactions one can account for them in the normal way. In other words, any transactions under a contract which has the effect of restating them into sterling should be accounted for as sterling transactions, whereas any transactions which have been, in effect, restated into a foreign currency should be treated as foreign currency transactions, and should utilise the prevailing spot rate of exchange on the transaction date in the normal way.

It is interesting to note that the effect of some long-term contracts can be to create a form of 'structural position', the economic effect of which can be similar to any 'natural' structural positions of that kind. Although it might be necessary to take such exposures into account when evaluating the overall hedging activities of the company (see chapter 8) it does not in general impact the way in which any transactions originating from the contract are accounted for.

Transaction hedging

It is important to differentiate between the hedging of a foreign currency transaction and the hedging of any exposure arising from that transaction. If we again consider the scenario of a company purchasing inventory from overseas, but delaying payment of the resultant creditor until some time in the future, a transaction hedge might comprise a forward foreign exchange contract entered into some time prior to the transaction date, with the objective of 'fixing' the sterling cost of the inventory at that time. Such a hedge is not the same in economic terms as the forward transaction which might have been entered into on the transaction date to hedge the settlement of the related creditor. The latter form of hedge is simply an alternative to acquiring the foreign currency on the transaction date and holding it (on deposit for example) until the settlement date. It should, in itself, have no impact on the exchange rate used to record the underlying transaction.

The nature of a transaction hedging arrangement is such that there will generally be no related balance sheet asset or liability. Such a hedge can be effected either through a cash based transaction (ie advance acquisition of currency funds etc) or by way of a forward transaction or the equivalent.

As we are concerned with hedging a future transaction (ie an off-balance-sheet commitment of some sort), it is not possible to relate the premium or discount on the transaction hedge to any form of funding arrangement. It is rather the cost (or benefit) to the company of deciding to fix the exchange rate on the transaction prior to the transaction date. The premium or discount can accordingly be thought of as simply being one aspect of the overall pricing of the subsequent transaction in sterling terms. Had, for example, the currency exposure been borne by the other party to the transaction, the predetermined transaction value would have been in sterling.

It can accordingly be seen that the economic impact of a transaction hedge is essentially no different to the effect of the parties to the transaction having entered into a contracted rate arrangement. It has the effect, in other words, of converting a foreign currency transaction into a sterling transaction. As the transaction hedge is an integral part of the overall value of the transaction, it should be taken into account when subsequently recording the transaction itself. If, for example, a company decides to enter into a transaction hedge in relation to the future acquisition of foreign currency denominated inventory, and does so through the use of a forward foreign exchange contract, then it will be the rate specified in that contract which should subsequently be used to determine the sterling equivalent of the inventory cost on the transaction date. Whether a company uses a contracted rate of exchange included in the underlying transaction documentation or whether it achieves the same result through an external forward contract should not have any effect upon the way in which the transaction is subsequently accounted for.

SSAP 20 in fact refers to the question of transaction hedging in para 46 where it states that 'where a trading transaction is covered by a related or matching forward contract, the rate of exchange specified in that contract *may* be used'. Although the use of the forward contracted rate is not *required* under the Standard it is necessary to use that rate if one wishes to maintain consistency in the accounting approach adopted. It is also reasonable to extend the concept to other forms of hedging arrangement rather than simply limiting it to forward foreign exchange contracts. There would appear to be nothing in SSAP 20 to prevent the extension of the idea to other forms of transaction hedging.

It is important then to recognise the difference between using a forward foreign exchange contract to hedge a transaction and using the same kind of contract to hedge a balance sheet exposure. Whereas in the former case, any forward premium or discount is included in the valuation (in sterling terms) of the subsequent transaction, in the latter case (as will be explored further in chapter 8) the premium or discount is treated as being an integral part of the company's overall financing activities, ultimately being taken to interest income or expense..There is a fundamental economic difference between attempting to eliminate the currency exposure relating to a future transaction and attempting to eliminate any exposure arising as a result of that transaction. In the first case one is simply attempting to fix the foreign currency transaction in sterling terms whereas in the second case, the foreign currency exposure has already been (or is about to be) incurred, and the hedge is entered into with the objective of reducing or eliminating that exposure in the future.

It has been mentioned that an alternative form of transaction hedging might be for the company to use its balance sheet, perhaps by acquiring any foreign currency funds required well in advance of the transaction date. This is similar to the scenario explored in one of the earlier simple examples where the company maintained a pool of foreign currency funds for the purposes of purchasing foreign currency inventory. It can now be seen that in order to be consistent with the use of a forward foreign exchange contract for the purposes of transaction hedging, it will be necessary to 'capitalise' any interest differential arising as a result of holding the foreign currency cash as opposed to the company's base currency into the subsequent valuation of the ultimate transaction. There should, in other words, be no difference in the effective exchange rate used for the foreign currency transaction simply because of the way in which that transaction is hedged.

In theory this would mean that where a company acquires foreign currency in advance of the transaction date with the objective of hedging the transaction itself (as opposed to any exposure flowing from that transaction) then the proper way to proceed would be either to utilise the forward exchange rate then prevailing for the purposes of recording the subsequent transaction (taking any implicit premium or discount between that forward rate and the spot rate relating to the actual acquisition of foreign currency to income as an adjustment to interest income or expense), or alternatively, to capitalise any interest differential over the period of the hedging arrangement and then take it into account in the recording of the subsequent transaction. This is clearly a fairly complex process which most companies would probably choose to avoid. It might, in addition, be argued that the foreign currency funds were simply part of the revolving fund of financial resources which were being managed in such a way as to minimise the company's overall short term exposures to its known structural currency positions. In a broader sense, it is not uncommon for companies to have balance sheet currency exposures which offset, at least in some degree, the structural exposures that they can foresee over the short term. Is it possible, or even desirable, to attempt to translate these balance sheet exposures into the equivalent of a transaction hedge in relation to as yet uncompleted transactions?

In economic terms there would seem to be no real difference between the specific hedging of a future transaction and the generalised hedging of a known series of future transactions. It would also seem to be irrelevant as to whether the hedging is carried out through the use of a forward foreign exchange contract or by using the company's balance sheet.

This book accordingly recommends that where a company is using either specific or generalised hedging (either on or off the balance sheet) of future known or expected transactions, that the effective 'cost' of those hedging arrangements be deferred and taken into account in the recording of the subsequent transactions. This would result in the exclusion of the hedging arrangements from any periodic revaluation (chapter 8). It is further recommended that the approach adopted in this area should form part of the additional disclosures that are suggested in chapter 6.

In practical terms, of course, effecting a pure transaction hedge in the knowledge that there will be delayed settlement of the transaction, will simply result in a currency 'gap' exposure arising between the transaction date and the settlement date. For that reason, most companies normally choose to enter into a hedge in the first instance which also covers the gap exposure – ie in effect covering both the transaction exposure and the positional risk. This creates a problem in that only a part of the hedge relates to the underlying transaction; the remainder relates to the financing of the transaction.

The correct treatment of a hedge which covers both the transaction itself and the subsequent gap exposure is to separate that element relating to the transaction hedge from the portion covering the gap, and then use only the former in valuing any related balance sheet asset or liability. (An example of this is included in Reference Section B.4.) A more pragmatic approach is to treat the entire hedge as relating to the gap exposure, and then account for it in the way described in chapter 8. Such an approach can be partially justified if one argues that the 'transaction date' should be treated as being the date on which the hedge was entered into. In other words, the foreign currency exposure can be thought of as having originated, not on the transaction date, but on the date on which the transaction was hedged. Unfortunately, if this were the case, it should, in theory, be the spot rate ruling on the earlier 'hedging date' which should be used for the purposes of recording the transaction, rather than the spot rate ruling on the subsequent 'transaction date'.

In general then, where a composite hedge is carried out to cover both the foreign currency transaction *and* the translation exposure deriving from that transaction, it is recommended that, if the transaction is particularly material, an attempt be made to separate the hedge into these constituent elements, accounting for each element as discussed in this chapter and chapter 8. If such a separation proves to be impractical, or if the transaction is less material, then the entire hedge should be treated as relating to the resultant translation exposure with the transaction itself being treated in the same way as if it had been unhedged. In the event of the latter approach being adopted on a regular basis, careful attention should be paid to the period elapsing between the hedge date and the transaction date. If that period becomes unusually long, the approach should be reconsidered.

It can be seem from the above that there are a number of questions which emerge in the area of transaction accounting, flowing both from the inconsistencies inherent in the way in which the 'transaction date' can be defined and the difficulty sometimes experienced in handling global transaction hedges. The most appropriate treatment in a practical sense is likely to consist of a compromise between what would be theoretically appropriate and what is desirable from a practical standpoint. It must also be recognised that, unless the non-monetary item resulting from a foreign currency transaction continues to exist at a financial reporting date, the effect of using an erroneous rate for the purposes of transaction accounting will generally only be a misallocation between operating income, currency gain or loss, and interest income and expense. Although the approach adopted might be of considerable significance in the case of certain capital or long-term financing transactions, it is generally far less so where one is considering the purchase of overseas inventory or the handling of foreign currency sales.

Other rates of exchange

Some countries have more than one exchange rate, eg a commercial rate and a financial rate. This raises the question as to which rate should be applied when translating a foreign currency transaction amount. SSAP 20 makes no reference to the matter although it is considered in SFAS 52. Transactions should in general be translated and recorded at the rate at which it would have been possible to settle the exposure at the transaction date. Where two rates of exchange are in use, this may mean that they are both used for different types of transaction.

The examples that we have considered so far in this chapter all examine the accounting treatment applicable to a single transaction. The accounting implications become far more complex where there are a large number of foreign currency transactions.

In view of the difficulties sometimes encountered in collating and recording currency data, SSAP 20 allows the preparer of financial statements to utilise average rates of exchange for the translation of currency amounts, rather than necessarily using the actual rates relating to the individual underlying transactions. Such an approach is often considered necessary when translating financial statements from an entity's local currency into its base currency. The option of using average rates is only permitted by SSAP 20 as an approximation to actual rates 'if the rates do not fluctuate significantly'.

It is quite clear that, in economic terms, the use of any kind of average rate of exchange will produce a less accurate answer than using actual rates. If the number of foreign currency transactions are sufficiently large to require a complex accounting system, it is likely that the exposures inherent in the company's operations would also be such as to warrant such a system. The added complexity in the accounting approach should, accordingly, be seen as an investment against the business risks of incurring unacceptable currency exposures, rather than simply as a result of having to account for those transactions in a particular way. If there are relatively few foreign currency transactions, it should not be particularly onerous to utilise a simple manual system to maintain details on an 'actual rates' basis.

Although the use of average rates of exchange may be appropriate in some circumstances, such an approach should only be seen as a compromise solution, not as an acceptable method in itself.

DEALING ACTIVITIES

This section briefly reviews the question of dealing activities whether they be those involving commodities or securities, or the actual trading of foreign currencies themselves. The particular issues which need to be addressed in considering a dealing operation include the definition of the most appropriate base currency, the preponderance of monetary items as opposed to non-monetary items, the need for a comprehensive mark-to-market approach, and the accounting problems that can emerge when a mark-to-market treatment interfaces with the more traditional historic cost approach. These issues are examined in turn.

Nature of a dealing activity

Dealing activities may encompass any number of specialised products, including physical commodities, futures transactions relating to those commodities, financial securities or physical amounts of currency, etc. Their common characteristic is generally that the primary business activity is one of buying and selling the products in question for the purposes of making profit, rather than necessarily being involved in either the production or use of the product itself. Many commodity trading companies, for example, may be involved in the growing, preparation and shipment of agricultural commodities, and may have downstream operations which then process that commodity into a finished product. Somewhere within the world-wide operation, however, there is likely to be a discreet 'trading operation' which absorbs a variety of functions for the group ranging from the transhipment activity through to the eventual disposal of the commodity. The extent of the 'trading activity' in such a situation can probably best be identified by the way in which it functions and is managed, rather than delineating it on the basis of the actual activities carried out.

The key managerial point about a dealing operation is that the only sensible way to evaluate its profitability is to monitor over time the movement in the market value of any positions held. To do otherwise will run the risk of recognising apparent profits whilst leaving losses hidden in future unprofitable positions. It accordingly follows that there is a need, at least internally, for a comprehensive market based revaluation (or 'mark-to-market') of all positions associated with the trading activity on a regular ongoing basis.

The mark-to-market approach can be carried out in a number of ways: on a consolidated basis for a number of products; on a product-by-product basis; or even at individual dealer level. Many companies attempt to evaluate performance by 'trading desk' and virtually all try to monitor results by product or commodity. With different products or commodities being denominated in different foreign currencies, and the underlying activities of the operation perhaps being monitored in another currency, the question of exchange accounting becomes extremely central to the ongoing monitoring of activity.

The accounting principles appropriate to a dealing activity involving either a commodity or a financial security will generally also be appropriate to a pure foreign exchange trading operation. This is because the nature of a commodity or financial security in a trading operation is essentially the same, in accounting terms, as an underlying amount of the foreign currency in which the particular product is denominated. They are all treated, in other words, as monetary items.

The normal approach

There are, in absolute terms, few differences between a dealing activity and any other situation where one has to account for foreign currency transactions.

The position is generally more complex because of the need to determine the most appropriate underlying base currency, and the systems solutions tend to be more complex due to the nature and volume of the transactions concerned. The underlying principles of accounting, however, are, in the final instance, essentially the same.

Because the dealing activity consists of the buying and selling of monetary items, it is not really necessary to calculate base currency amounts for any foreign currency items. Such items continue to be foreign currency denominated items subject to periodic revaluation throughout the time in which they are held. To the extent that one also needs to account for non-monetary transactions such as, for example, the acquisition of fixed assets, the same rules apply as in any other situation.

The kinds of multicurrency accounting systems referred to in chapter 10 are generally able to account for trading transactions in 'source currency', thereby obviating the need to assign a base currency equivalent to any foreign currency amounts. All balance sheet and off-balance-sheet assets, liabilities, commitments and contingencies are then revalued to market rates on a periodic basis which, in many cases, will probably be daily. Many trading based systems now carry out such a revaluation on a real time basis.

The way in which forward foreign currency commitments are revalued should reflect the way in which the underlying transactions relating to those commitments are treated. If, for example, one is attempting to evaluate in sterling terms the market value of a commodity future denominated in US dollars, and the futures position has been partly hedged through a forward foreign exchange contract, it will be necessary to revalue both the commodity future and the forward foreign exchange contract using then market rates. In the same way that the commodity future will be revalued at the current forward rate for that position, it is clearly appropriate also to revalue the foreign exchange hedge using the forward rate. If the two futures transactions are hedging a cash position in the commodity concerned, there is likely to also be some financing element relating to the cash position. If that financing is in a foreign currency, then both the cash commodity position and the financing will need to be converted into the appropriate base currency at current spot rates of exchange. Such a sequence of transactions will naturally result in a continued exposure relating to the remaining period of the fully hedged transaction in which the foreign currency funding needs to be continued. In other words, there is a future interest cost inherent in revaluing the entire hedged position to market. It thus becomes necessary to take account of that future interest cost in evaluating the overall value of the hedged position.

The present book does not attempt to address the detailed considerations which need to be borne in mind when accounting for a dealing activity, but it is important, in the context of foreign exchange accounting, to explore briefly the particular complication arising where the company does not utilise a comprehensive mark-to-market approach across all of its activities.

The impact of interest

Problems typically emerge whenever an operation involves 'cross-trading' between two particular product areas where the accounting approach adopted is inconsistent. This happens whenever a mark-to-market based trading operation interfaces with a more traditional 'accruals' based historic cost type accounting approach. This may arise, for example, where a secondary market bond trader acquires stock from the inventory of the primary bond issuing operation of the same company. If the latter adopts an 'accruals basis' of accounting, and the secondary market maker utilises a mark-to-market concept, difficulties can arise whenever stock is transferred between them. The most common situation where this is encountered in the financial services area is the interaction between the foreign exchange markets and the money markets.

Due to the linkage between forward foreign exchange rates and interest rate differentials, there is frequently a considerable amount of arbitrage between the foreign exchange markets and the money markets. Such arbitrage is carried out in substantial volumes by the international banking community and, to a lesser extent, by the treasury departments of major corporates. This arbitrage activity is, of course, essential to the efficient operation of the markets and ensures that the relationship between interest rate differentials and forward premiums and discounts is maintained. Unfortunately, most corporates and the vast majority of banks, still account for their money market activity on an accruals basis, whereas the common approach to foreign exchange trading involves, for the reasons already discussed, a regular marking of all positions to market. Whenever there is an arbitrage transaction between the two markets, the question arises as to the most appropriate accounting treatment. If there is an accruals based approach for interest and yet a mark-to-market treatment for foreign exchange positions, it becomes extremely easy to manipulate profit figures and to switch profits or losses between the two activities.

A typical interest arbitrage transaction

Assume that the company is a dollar-based operation with access to both the money markets and the foreign exchange markets at inter-bank rates.

On 14 June it arranges the following four transactions:

1. It borrows DM10 million for three months from 16 June until 16 September at an annual rate of interest of 4%.
2. It sells these Deutschmarks into US dollars at the then spot rate of exchange (1.8600), yielding $5,376,344.
3. It places the US dollars on three month deposit from 16 June at an annual interest rate of 6.5%.
4. Finally it arranges a forward foreign exchange contract, value 16 September, to purchase DM10,100,000 using US dollars. The rate obtained is 1.8497, thus requiring $5,460,345.

The cashflows on 16 September will be as follows:

Repayment of US dollar deposit	$5,376,344
Interest on US dollar deposit	87,366
Purchase of Dm10.1 million	(5,460,345)
	$ 3,365

The DM10.1 million will be sufficient to repay the Deutschmark loan plus the accrued interest thereon.

The $3,365 represents the overall arbitrage profit on the series of transactions and is fixed at the outset, being independent of any subsequent movements in exchange rates. The arrangement is, in other words. a fully-hedged series of transactions. How will the $3,365 be shown in the accounts?

If the spot rate does not move over the three months of the transaction, the result of the arrangement would probably normally be shown in the company's accounts as follows:

Interest income	$87,366
Interest expense (DM 100,000 at 1.86)	(53,763)
Currency loss (impact of 1.86–1.8497 on DM 10.1million)	(30,238)
	$ 3,365

Alternatively, had the spot rate increased over the three months to, say, 1.92 the result may have appeared as follows:

Interest income	$87,366
Interest expense (DM 100,000 at 1.92)	(52,083)
Currency loss:	
Principal (DM 10 million at 1.86–1.8497)	(29,938)
Interest (DM 100,000 at 1.92–1.8497)	(1,980)
	$3,365

Although the net result does not change, the movement in the spot rate does amend the allocation of the result as between net interest and currency loss. From a broader standpoint, of course, the whole idea of there being any foreign exchange impact is irrational in that the series of transactions essentially relate to a fully hedged funding arrangement.

In a banking environment, a fully-hedged interest arbitrage transaction would be known as a 'deposit swap' and by identifying such transactions at their inception, a reclassification is generally made between currency profit/loss and net interest. The currency loss is then amortised over the life of the transaction and the various currency exposures created by the loan, the deposit and the forward transaction are all eliminated from the revaluation process. This avoids fluctuations in currency profit/loss arising as a result of the periodic revaluations over the life of the arrangement.

If, however, the transactions are not recognised as a linked series in this way, and if the company employs accrual accounting for its loans and deposits and yet a mark-to-market for its foreign exchange positions, there can be very significant differences between the profit actually reported for any period and the underlying commercial reality.

Revaluation of an arbitrage position

If the earlier interest arbitrage arrangement had not been recognised as a linked series of transactions at the point of inception, and if exchange rates had fluctuated over its three-month life, what would have been the impact on reported results?

The following calculations assume that the forward position is treated as having created a speculative gap position which, in accordance with common practice in many foreign exchange dealing environments, is accordingly being subject to periodic revaluations at forward market rates. The balance sheet spot position includes the underlying loan and deposit together with the accrued interest on same and is subject to a periodic spot revaluation. The interest itself is recognised on a straightforward accruals basis and is translated each month-end at spot rates of exchange.

For the purposes of the example we assume an initial strengthening of the Deutschmark, but then a fairly continuous depreciation over the remainder of the period. This depreciation is assumed to arise as a result of a gradual increase in US dollar interest rates in relation to Deutschmark rates, with a corresponding increase in comparable forward discounts. The spot and forward rates assumed in the example are as follows:

	Spot rate	Forward rate attributable to 16 September
16 June (inception)	1.8600	1.8497
30 June	1.8100	1.8000
31 July	1.8600	1.8532
31 August	1.9100	1.9075
16 September	1.9600	n.a.

Using these rates, net interest would be reported at each date as follows:

	Income	*Cumulative interest*			*Period interest*
		Expense		*Net*	
	$	DM	$	$	$
30 June	14,561	16,666	9,208	5,353	5,353
31 July	43,683	50,000	26,882	16,801	11,448
31 August	72,805	83,333	43,630	29,175	12,374
16 September	87,306	100,000	51,020	36,346	7,171
					36,346

By revaluing accrued interest at each month-end at the then spot rate of exchange, net interest is bearing the impact of revaluing the previous month-end accrued position. The other items which need to be revalued, and which would result in the booking of a translation gain or loss at each period end, are the deutschmark loan and the forward US dollar sale. The impact of revaluing the DM10 million loan at the spot rate of exchange and the DM 10.1 million forward contract at the forward rate of exchange may be summarised as follows:

Spot revaluation

		Cumulative revaluation		Period
				movement
	$	DM in $	Net	
30 June	5,376,344	5,524,862	(148,518)	(148,518)
31 July	5,376,344	5,376,344	—	148,518
31 August	5,376,344	5,235,602	140,742	140,742
16 September	5,376,344	5,102,041	274,303	133,561
				274,303

Forward revaluation

		Cumulative revaluation		Period
				movement
	$	DM in $	Net	
30 June	5,460,345	5,611,111	150,766	150,766
31 July	5,460,345	5,450,032	(10,313)	(161,079)
31 August	5,460,345	5,294,889	(165,456)	(155,143)
16 September	5,460,345	5,153,061	(307,284)	(141,828)
				(307,284)

The overall accounting relating to this series of transactions would accordingly be shown in the accounts as follows:

US$

	Foreign exchange gain (loss)			Net	Net
				interest	profit
	Spot	Forward	Net		
30 June	(148,518)	150,766	2,248	5,353	7,601
31 July	148,518	(161,079)	(12,561)	11,448	(1,113)
31 August	140,742	(155,143)	(14,401)	12,374	(2,027)
16 September	133,561	(141,828)	(8,267)	7,171	(1,096)
	274,303	(307,284)	(32,981)	36,346	3,365

It can be seen from the above that, although the overall profit on the transaction is still $3,365, the way in which it would have been recognised in the accounts would have resulted in the booking of a profit in the first half-month of well over twice this amount, and then a run of losses in the remaining two-and-a-half months to amortise that overstatement of profit.

Accounting for deposit swaps, or cross-currency fundings as they are sometimes known, has long been a contentious issue in international banking. Although some trading rooms have been content to operate within a fairly rigorous definition of what constitutes a deposit swap, others have sought a far more flexible approach embodying the concept of 'one-sided' or 'pool' swapping. When utilising a pool swapping approach, the dealer is in effect allowed to designate any individual forward transaction as being part of a theoretical swap against the 'pool' of loans and deposits on the books of the bank. The spot leg of the swap is derived from the forward leg and the overall profitability follows automatically from the forward rate, the current spot rate and the dealer's stated 'assumed' interest cost/benefit. A few banks have taken this process to its natural conclusion and have chosen to amortise all forward premiums and discounts over the life of the transactions, taking all forward positions into account in the spot revaluation.

Whatever approach is adopted and whatever the controls imposed over the dealer's designation of individual transactions, the only real answer to the problems of inconsistent accounting in this area can be a move towards greater consistency. In the banking market, this is already beginning to take place (at least for internal management accounting purposes) by ensuring that the money market book is periodically marked-to-market and compared with any gains or losses incurred on the foreign exchange side. For most international corporates, with less reason for moving towards a comprehensive mark-to-market and possibly without the sophisticated systems to allow them to do so, the most satisfactory solution will probably be to rely on a tighter control over arbitrage activity.

Controlled arbitrage

The most straightforward means of reducing the risk of manipulation and ensuring that the accounting approach adopted is reasonable is to try and ensure that there is a proper differentiation between the money market and foreign exchange trading activities. This can be achieved by ensuring that all external foreign exchange trades are entered into by a limited number of foreign exchange dealers; by limiting the extent of foreign exchange trading allowed by the money market dealers and by ensuring that all such activity represents trades between themselves and the foreign exchange traders; by carefully controlling and monitoring the gap positions allowed to be opened up, even temporarily, by the foreign exchange traders (whose role should be the trading of foreign exchange rather than interest rates) and by ensuring that there is a daily agreement of activity as between the back and front offices. If a sufficiently rigorous control environment can be imposed, it is possible to argue that all interest arbitrage transactions originated by the money market traders are money-market-based activities which should be accounted for on an accruals basis, whereas all external foreign exchange transactions (and any internal foreign exchange transactions which the foreign exchange traders carry on with the money market traders) should be treated, from the standpoint of the foreign exchange activity, as being foreign exchange originated activity which should be marked-to-market.

This is the approach (sometimes inadvertently) adopted by many of the international banks now operating in these two markets. The practical application of the concept usually involves the use of internal deals, and controls are introduced to try and identify all arbitrage or deposit swaps transactions. Unfortunately the control environment in some banks is still sufficiently weak for there to be considerable room for manipulation by a dealer keen to hide losses or advance profits, and it is a problem which many banks have suffered from over the course of the last two decades. With the increasing deregulation of the money markets and the growing ability of large corporate treasury operations to become as actively involved in interest arbitrage as the banks, it is inconceivable that a large number of corporates are not now suffering from the sorts of problems experienced by the international banking community in the 1970s. Recent cases of apparent 'currency fraud' in the European corporate market may simply be the tip of the iceberg in this context.

OTHER TRANSACTIONS

The remainder of this chapter considers those transactions which do not result in an immediate acquisition or disposal of an asset and, accordingly, do not necessarily have a direct impact on the balance sheet. It also reviews the question of periodic fixed asset revaluations.

Commitments and contingencies

There are many currency transactions which can result in the creation or elimination of foreign currency commitments or contingencies. These range from long-term obligations such as lease commitments or guarantees, down to much shorter-term transactions, such as forward foreign exchange contracts. Many of the currency hedging products available today are of an 'off-balance-sheet' nature.

The detailed way in which many of these transactions should be accounted for can be complicated by the nature of their construction. This is particularly true in the case of longer-term hedging transactions.

The majority of off balance sheet commitments and contingencies are monetary items which need to be considered in the context of translation exposure. The general principles to be adopted in this area are accordingly discussed in chapter 8 with many of the individual transactions being considered in more specific detail in the Reference Section.

A foreign currency denominated financial commitment such as the obligation to make future payments under a long-term lease is similar to any sterling-based obligation of the company. Proper disclosure of the transaction would require that reference be made to the fact that the payments were denominated in the currency concerned, and the committment to make future currency payments should be taken into account in any assessment of the company's overall structural exposure to the currency concerned.

Revaluations

A final form of transaction which needs to be considered is where a non-monetary item, such as a building, is subject to revaluation. Fixed assets, in particular, are sometimes subject to a company-wide periodic revaluation in accordance with the company's adopted accounting policies. When a property is located overseas it is important to determine whether or not the foreign exchange rate applied to the asset value should be the original historic rate or the rate ruling at the date of revaluation.

In the same way that any revaluation of a sterling asset is no more than an attempt to place a 'current value' on the asset in question, it is clearly irrational to revalue an asset denominated in a foreign currency other than by using the current rate of exchange. The historic exchange rate becomes as irrelevant as the historic cost once the revalued amount of the asset is included in the accounts. In terms of the discussion earlier in this chapter we are accordingly treating the revaluation date as a new transaction date.

A related issue is how the currency element of any gain or loss arising on the revaluation should be shown in the accounts. Companies such as general insurance companies might, for example, under their normal accounting policies, show any currency gains or losses in the income statement, but any unrealised appreciation in property investments as a movement on reserves. In such circumstances, should the currency gain on a revalued property be credited to reserves or to income?

It could be argued that within the context of a company's reported results, it is perhaps largely irrelevant whether an accretion in value on revaluation has occurred as a result of the movement in a foreign exchange rate or, for example, an increase in the underlying value of the asset concerned. There will, after all, be many cases where, because of fundamental economic readjustments in the economy in question, these effects would be expected, at least partly, to offset. Furthermore, as the asset has (in accounting terms), already been converted into a 'sterling item', is it rational to then record a subsequent gain or loss on exchange?

The contrary argument might be that the revaluation reserve should reflect the uplift in value of the asset in underlying currency terms, rather than in the local base currency, because this better reflects the underlying commercial circumstances. It might also be argued that the foreign exchange gain or loss is in the nature of a realised item, as opposed to the revaluation uplift which is clearly unrealised. This view might be particularly important, for example, if there were currency losses offsetting the valuation uplift; is it the gross uplift or the net which should be treated as undistributable?

The revaluation of the asset is, as already mentioned, in the nature of a new transaction, suggesting that it can be thought of in terms of a 'release' of the old asset and the 'reinstatement' of a new one at the current spot rate of exchange. It could also be compared to the pricing of trading stocks maintained in the balance sheet at their current market value. Both concepts would support the idea of taking any currency impact arising from the revaluation to income rather than to the revaluation reserve.

On balance, the approach favoured in this book is to credit the revaluation reserve with the local currency equivalent of the underlying currency valuation uplift, and to take any currency gain or loss arising from the retranslation of the historic pre-revaluation balance direct to income. This approach is consistent with that advocated in chapter 9 in relation to the treatment of a consolidated subsidiary's revaluation reserve.

It would in general seem appropriate to reconcile the increase in asset carrying value and the amount credited to revaluation reserve by way of a note to the accounts.

CHAPTER 8

Balance sheet translation

AN OVERVIEW

Simple translation exposure
The general case
Translation hedging
Periodic revaluation

HEDGING

Trading exposures
Foreign equity investments
Other balance sheet exposures

OFF BALANCE SHEET EXPOSURES

The question of set-off
Commitments
Contingencies
Economic exposure

Chapter 7 reviewed how foreign currency transactions were recorded in the local currency using, in most cases, the prevailing spot rate of exchange on the transaction date. That rate determined the local currency amount at which the related asset or liability (such as the inventory in the example used) was to be recorded. Balance sheet items such as inventory are non-monetary items which, once translated into the local currency, are not subject to subsequent revaluation. They become, in effect, items denominated in the local currency.

Transactions such as the acquisition of inventory create, in their turn, monetary items such as accounts payable or receivable. It will be recalled how, in the examples used, the existence of these balances reflected the timing difference between the transaction date and the date of ultimate currency settlement. It will also be recalled that, unless they were hedged in some way, they resulted in a currency exposure existing for the period between the transaction date and the settlement date. To the extent that there is an unhedged monetary exposure during a period in which exchange rates move, there is a currency gain or loss to the company concerned.

Chapter 3 referred to this form of currency exposure as 'translation exposure' although any gain or loss arising from that exposure only becomes apparent either when the currency position concerned is 'closed out' or when it becomes necessary to produce consolidated sterling accounts. The production of those sterling accounts involves the translation of currency balances into sterling, thereby comparing the current sterling equivalent of any foreign currency exposures to the corresponding sterling amount either as at the last revaluation date or at the point where the exposure was originally recorded.

AN OVERVIEW

The following sections develop an overview of the recommended approach to translation accounting, with the more complex issues of hedging and off-balance-sheet exposures then being explored in greater depth in later sections.

Simple translation exposure

Let us consider the second example reviewed in chapter 7, page 101 of a company importing foreign currency denominated inventory but experiencing a delay in ultimate cash settlement. The accounting entries in this situation were as follows:

1. *Debit* foreign currency cash   FC 'A'
       Credit sterling cash   £ 'B'

2. *Debit* inventory   £ 'C'
       Credit foreign currency payable   FC 'D'

3. *Debit* foreign currency payable   FC 'D'
       Credit foreign currency cash   FC 'D'

It will be recalled from chapter 7 that the foreign exchange rate applied in order to determine the value of 'C' was the rate ruling on the transaction date, rather than that applying as at the date of acquiring the cash or at the point where the currency payable was ultimately settled.

If one explores this example in a little more detail, it will be seen that there are essentially two particular points where a currency exposure can arise. The first of these is the period between the acquisition of the foreign currency and the transaction date. During this period the company is holding foreign currency cash of 'A' without any corresponding liability. There will, accordingly, be a currency gain or loss dependent upon the size of that position ('A') and the movement in exchange rates between the two dates. If precisely the correct amount of foreign currency cash had been acquired (i e 'A' = 'D'), the currency gain or loss on this exposure would have been £'B' − £'C'. If the foreign currency cash had been acquired with a view to hedging the subsequent transaction it would, as discussed in chapter 7 be theoretically more correct to treat it as a transaction hedge and account for the subsequent transaction accordingly.

The other point where a currency exposure arises in this example is where the amount of foreign currency acquired is greater than that necessary to settle the foreign currency payable. This would result in there being a residual amount of foreign currency left after the transaction date which was not matched by a corresponding currency liability. That exposure would continue to exist until such time as the amount of currency was either sold or appropriated for some other purpose. The gain or loss on that exposure would be a function of any movements in exchange rates over the period in question, and the amount of foreign currency held (FC'A' − FC'D').

It is important to recognise that there is no currency exposure on the amount of foreign currency 'D' between the transaction date and the settlement of the currency obligation. The cash and the amount payable are offsetting exposures and any interest impact flowing from holding the cash in currency rather than in sterling is simply part of the overall financing of the transaction. Chapter 7 explored the possibility of using the forward rate of exchange to account for a transaction where there was delayed settlement. The approach was rejected in favour of using the spot rate of exchange, largely in recognition of the fact that the forward rate of exchange included a premium or discount which had more to do with the financing of the delayed settlement than with the transaction itself.

In the above example, had the company not been in possession of any foreign currency as at the transaction date, it would have had an exposed currency position of FC 'D' from the date of the transaction until such time as the exposure was closed out, for example by way of the acquisition of currency cash at the time of settlement of the payable. In the case under discussion, however, the company has hedged this foreign currency exposure by ensuring that it has sufficient foreign currency available. It was not, accordingly, exposed to movements in exchange rates in relation to the amount of the foreign currency payable.

An alternative approach available to the company would have been to hedge the exposure created by the foreign currency payable in some other way. This would have been possible, for example, by using a forward foreign exchange contract, with a value date at or shortly before the expected date of settlement of the currency payable. Had the company entered into a forward contract as of the transaction date, the exchange rate applying to that forward contract would have consisted of the combination of the then spot rate of exchange and any applicable forward premium or discount.

An exposure hedge such as this is simply an alternative to acquiring foreign currency on the transaction date and holding it (on deposit for example) until the settlement date. The rate specified in that contract should, in itself, have no relevance to the exchange rate used in translating the underlying transaction. The purpose of the hedge is to protect the company from movements in exchange rates between the transaction date and the settlement date. It would, as discussed in chapter 7, still have been appropriate to use the spot rate of exchange for recording the inventory amount 'C'.

The above discussion has explored ways in which the company can hedge the foreign currency exposure created by a simple currency transaction and it has been seen how the existence, nature, and indeed, timing of any hedging arrangement has nothing whatever to do with the way in which the underlying transaction has been accounted for. The exposure hedge is, rather, taken into account when considering the value of any residual foreign currency monetary items subsequent to the transaction date. This process is further explored below.

The general case

A more general way of considering the exposures created by our simple transaction is to think in terms of the three key dates:

(a) Transaction date. The date on which the transaction is entered into.

(b) Hedging date. The date on which the currency exposure arising from the transaction is hedged.

(c) Settlement date. The date on which the cash settlement of any monetary items resulting from the transaction takes place.

There are clearly a number of possible combinations of these three dates depending upon the timing of the recognition of the currency exposure and whether or not it is hedged prior to settlement. The alternatives can briefly be summarised as follows:

(a) Unhedged scenario. In this case one would have only a transaction date and a settlement date, with the currency required for settlement, for example, being acquired only at the point of settlement. A currency exposure would exist between the transaction and settlement dates and could give rise to a translation gain or loss in the event of a balance sheet being prepared at any time after the transaction date.

(b) Simultaneous hedging. If the hedging and transaction date are the same, and the hedge is a 'perfect one', there is no translation exposure between the transaction and settlement dates.

(c) Pre-determined hedge. As in the simple example examined previously, the hedge may be put in place in advance of the transaction date. In such a situation there is no foreign currency exposure between the hedge date

and the transaction date and, assuming that the hedge is effective, no exposure between the transaction date and the settlement date. Chapter 7 explored the idea of pre-transaction date hedging and concluded that the cost or gain arising from that portion of the hedge covering the period up to the transaction date should be included in the determination of the sterling equivalent of the subsequent transaction. The portion of the hedge attributable to the period between the transaction and settlement dates was to be treated as an exposure hedge. It was suggested that in such a situation a pragmatic approach might require that the entire hedge be treated as relating to the period between the transaction date and the settlement date, and/or that the transaction date be redefined as that on which the hedge was entered into.

(d)Post-transaction–date hedge. If there is a delay between the transaction date and the hedge date, there is a currency exposure in the intervening period. No exposure will exist between the hedge date and the settlement date.

Currency exposures arise in the various scenarios explored above as a result of the timing difference between the transaction date and either the hedge date or, in the case of an unhedged transaction, the settlement date. Currency gains or losses occur where there are movements in exchange rates between the transaction date and the hedge date/settlement date. The gains or losses are often referred to as either transaction gains/losses or translation gains/losses, depending on whether or not the exposure has yet been eliminated. As soon as the exposure is 'closed out' the gain or loss on the transaction is generally considered to be 'realised' and is usually referred to as a transaction gain or loss. If it is necessary to prepare financial statements prior to the exposure being eliminated, the translation of exposed monetary positions at then current rates of exchange produces what are generally referred to as translation gains or losses. All translation gains and losses would, of course, become realised gains and losses if the company were to 'close out' all of its currency positions at the date on which the financial statements are prepared.

Translation hedging

The question of translation hedging is a subject covered later in this chapter but it is necessary to explore the broad principles at this point prior to addressing the question of periodic revaluations.

The simplest form of translation hedge is generally the purchase or sale, as appropriate, of the foreign currency subject to exposure. A perfect hedge of the exposure will generally require that the hedging transaction is put in place on the date on which the exposure arises, ie the transaction date in the case of an exposure originating from a foreign currency transaction. The idea of such a hedge is to prevent future currency gains or losses on the underlying exposure, and this is achieved, of course, by in effect fixing the sterling value of the foreign currency amount. A more correct way of viewing the hedge is to see it as eliminating the exposure itself, resulting in there being no net currency position which is subject to currency fluctuations.

If the translation exposure flowing from a foreign currency transaction

Translation exposure

Unhedged scenario

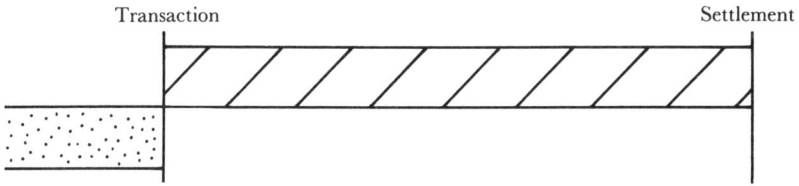

Transaction   Settlement

Simultaneous hedging

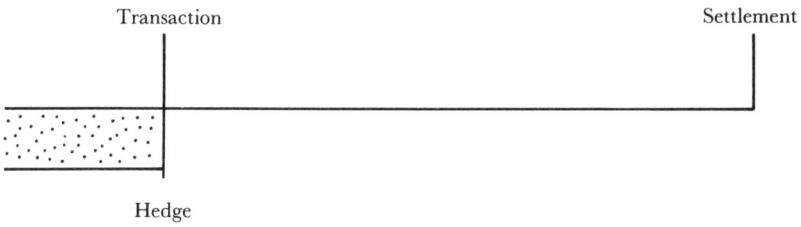

Transaction   Settlement

Hedge

Pre-determined hedge

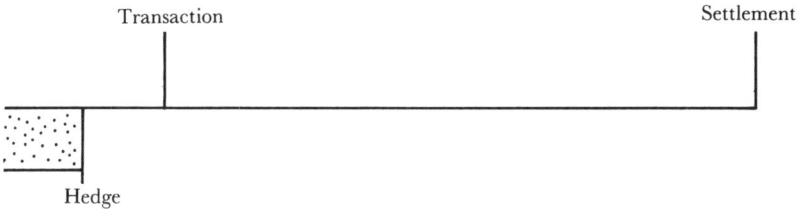

Transaction   Settlement

Hedge

Post-transaction-date hedge

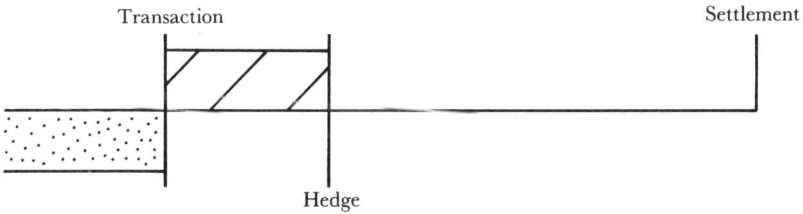

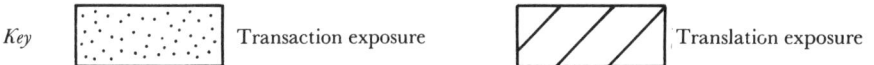

Transaction   Settlement

Hedge

Key   Transaction exposure   Translation exposure

is hedged on the transaction date via a cash transaction, it will be necessary to carry out the purchase or sale of the relevant foreign currency at the then spot rate of exchange ie the same exchange rate will apply to the translation hedge as has been used to record the underlying transaction. It is quite clear then that, as long as the appropriate amounts of foreign currency have been bought or sold, there will be no residual translation exposure and the entire transaction will have been carried out and completed at the spot rate of exchange ruling on the transaction date. The use of any other rate for the purposes of the translation exposure (for example the forward rate relating to the anticipated date of settlement of the exposure) would be inconsistent with the concepts discussed in chapter 7 relating to the underlying accounting approach to be adopted in respect of the transaction itself.

It flows from this analysis that, if one uses a different form of translation hedging – for example a forward foreign exchange contract, this should not, in itself, give rise to a different treatment to that which would have been the case had the hedge been entered into in the cash market. In other words, the fact that one is choosing to hedge the translation exposure other than through the cash market, should not change the underlying accounting in relation to the exposure.

If one were to hedge an exposure using a spot foreign exchange contract, any implicit financing gain or loss arising as a result of then holding cash balances in the foreign currency becomes a part of the company's overall financing operations. In the same way, if a forward transaction is used to hedge a currency exposure, it should be the spot rate of exchange ruling at the date on which the transaction is entered into that is taken into account in determining the nature of the hedge, with any financing element represented by the forward premium or discount on the transaction being treated as interest income or expense.

By extension, it can be seen that this approach applies equally well whenever the exposure hedge is actually entered into. If, for example, an exposure is allowed to 'run' for some time prior to being 'closed out', it should not matter whether or not the closing out takes place via a cash transaction or a forward market deal. The effect, in both cases, has been to eliminate any future exposure to movements in the spot rate of exchange. In economic terms, the sterling equivalent of the foreign currency amount of the exposure has, in effect, been fixed at the then spot rate of exchange, with any difference between that spot rate of exchange and the rate implicit in, say, the forward transaction being treated as an integral part of the company's subsequent financing activities. This is normally achieved in practice by capitalising the financing element and then amortising it over the life of the hedge as an adjustment to interest income or expense.

We return to this matter again later in this chapter under the overall subject heading of hedging.

Periodic revaluation

It can be seen that whenever there is a delay in the settlement of a foreign currency transaction, there is an exposure to movements in the applicable exchange rate between the transaction date and either the hedge date or settlement date. If one is preparing a set of accounts between these dates it is necessary to consider which exchange rate to use to convert those foreign currency monetary items into sterling.

It would, if desired, be theoretically possible to eliminate all future exposures arising from the currency positions being carried as of the date on which the accounts are being prepared. This would simply require suitable hedging transactions to be put in place, either by way of a purchase or sale of the appropriate currencies or through some other approach. Any decision to *not* hedge the exposures can accordingly be considered to be a positive management decision to continue maintaining them into the subsequent accounting period. A realistic assessment of the gain or loss accruing *up to the date of preparation of the accounts* is therefore determined by the gain or loss which *would* have been incurred at that time had management decided to close out the exposures.

There are a number of ways in which the exposures could have been eliminated, including the purchase or sale at the balance sheet date of the amounts of foreign currency ultimately required. Alternatively, it might have been possible to purchase forward foreign exchange contracts timed to match the expected settlement dates of the outstanding monetary assets and liabilities. It has already been argued that whenever a currency exposure is hedged, whether at the transaction date or subsequently, it is appropriate to consider the sterling value of the currency amount as having been fixed at the then spot rate of exchange. Any financing arrangements relating to the hedge, such as the forward premium or discount on a forward currency transaction, should be accounted for as part of the company's overall financing activities. The same rationale can be applied in the case of a theoretical closing out of exposures through the revaluation process. The currency gain or loss to date on those exposures can generally be calculated by converting any remaining foreign currency assets, liabilities or commitments into sterling at the spot rate of exchange ruling on the balance sheet date.

SSAP 20 rationalises the use of the closing balance sheet rate on the basis that 'short-term monetary items will soon be reflected in cashflows'. It argues that because of these cashflow effects, it is normally appropriate to recognise such gains and losses as part of the profit or loss for the year. This suggests that the year-end rate is being used because it is an 'approximation', in some sense, to the rate that will eventually be applied in settling those transactions. This would seem to be rather misleading in that there are clearly very sound commercial grounds for using the closing spot rate in any case.

The period-end rate is relevant to management's performance up to that date. The fact that the relevant exchange rates might have moved by substantial amounts shortly after the balance sheet date should surely be viewed in exactly the same way as, for example, the unexpected imposition shortly after the balance sheet date of a higher tax rate. It is in other words, an event relating to the subsequent accounting period.

The standard pursues its rationale for using the balance sheet rate when considering the question of long-term monetary items.

'Although it is not easy to predict what the exchange rate will be when a long-term liability or asset matures, it is necessary, when stating the liability or asset in terms of the reporting currency, *to make the best estimate possible in the light of the information available at the time*; generally speaking translation at the year end rate will provide the best estimate, particularly when the currency concerned is freely dealt in on the spot and forward exchange markets.'

The standard goes on to argue that because long-term monetary items are different to short-term items, it is also

'necessary to consider on the grounds of prudence whether the amount of the gain, or the amount by which exchange gains exceed past exchange losses on the same items, to be recognised in the profit and loss account should be restricted in the exceptional cases where there are doubts as to the convertibility or marketability of the currency in question.'

If one accepts that there is an economic rationale in attempting to evaluate the results for a period on the basis of the management decisions taken during that period, there should be no underlying difference in the treatment of short-term and long-term monetary items. The reference in the standard to convertibility and marketability of the currency in question is particularly misleading as such a consideration should, surely, also be taken into account in the case of *short-term* monetary items.

It is sometimes argued that SSAP 20 requires that where there are doubts as to convertibility or marketability of a currency, any unrealised profits should be reflected in reserves rather than in the income statement. There would seem to be no basis for this treatment and it is possible that the standard has in fact simply been misread by certain commentators in this respect. In the event of there being doubts concerning convertibility or marketability of a currency, a realistic attempt should be made to evaluate the most likely value of the underlying assets or liabilities and use that figure for the purposes of both the balance sheet presentation and the determination of the exchange gain or loss to be reflected in the accounts. There would seem to be no justification for reserve accounting in such a situation.

Questions can sometimes arise concerning the appropriate rate to be employed in the case of a multi-tiered exchange rate system. In the case of an exposure deriving from a trading transaction, the same approach should be employed as was recommended in chapter 7 in relation to the underlying transaction accounting. In other words, the most appropriate rate is that which would apply on the balance sheet date if the outstanding settlement was to be effected at that time. The decision is sometimes more difficult in the case of longer-term exposures, particularly those which originate from capital type transactions. In general, any outstanding currency exposure will ultimately result (even if only in the very long term) in a foreign currency cash settlement of some kind, and the rate to be employed for balance sheet translation purposes should be that most likely to be used for the purposes of eventual settlement. For some capital type exposures this is likely to be the rate in use for dividend or profit remittances, whereas for others it might be the rate applied to capital repayments, etc. The decision should be taken on the basis of current views as to the most likely future operations of the group and, whatever rate is eventually used, should still follow the basic approach of utilising the *current* rate of exchange.

HEDGING

Many of the complexities encountered in foreign exchange accounting are the result of having to account for complex hedging arrangements. SSAP 20 makes passing reference to hedging when referring to the fact that it is permissible to use the rate implied by a forward foreign exchange contract when that contract can be related to an underlying balance sheet exposure. There are a large number of possible hedging products now available to most companies in respect of their foreign currency exposures although the accounting implications of same generally follow the same broad principles. The current chapter sets out the general policies that are considered to be most appropriate in this area, irrespective of the actual hedging technique eventually used. Although the examples used tend to employ, for convenience, forward foreign exchange contracts as the hedging medium, the concepts involved can be applied to any of the other forms of hedging technique discussed in the Reference Section.

Trading exposures

Chapter 7 has already explored the concept of transaction hedging, by which it is possible to fix a foreign exchange rate in advance of the subsequent transaction date. It was pointed out in that discussion, however, that today companies are increasingly keen to hedge their overall exposure, including any gap exposure between the transaction date and the settlement date. Hedges are accordingly entered into with a view to matching the ultimate settlement, rather than as a simple transaction hedge.

Let us examine another example from chapter 7 involving the purchase of inventory from overseas with a delay in payment of the resultant creditor until sometime later. We shall further assume, however, that the company has chosen to hedge the overall transaction by taking out a forward foreign exchange contract at the point where the original obligation was incurred. In accounting terms, such a sequence of events could be depicted as follows:

1. *Debit* inventory receivable   £'C'
       Credit foreign currency payable   FC 'A'

2. *Debit* forward currency purchases   FC 'A'
       Credit forward sterling sales   £ 'B'

3. *Debit* inventory   £ 'C'
       Credit inventory receivable   £ 'C'

4. *Debit* foreign currency cash   FC 'A'
       Credit forward currency purchases   FC 'A'
       Debit forward sterling sales   £ 'B'
       Credit sterling cash   £ 'B'

5. *Debit* foreign currency payables   FC 'A'
       Credit foreign currency cash   FC 'A'

In the above situation, as long as transactions 1 and 2 take place at the same time, the foreign currency payable, FC 'A' has been hedged by the forward currency purchase. When that contract matures there is a receipt of foreign currency cash of the amount required to continue hedging the foreign currency payable. In the event of transactions 4 and 5 not taking place at the same time there is, of course, a residual gap exposure relating to the timing difference between cash receipt and cash payment.

The hedge in the above example does not actually change the way in which the inventory receivable or the foreign currency payable are initially booked. The then current exchange rate is still the one that is applied in calculating the sterling value of the inventory receivable. The purpose of the hedge is rather to protect the balance sheet position (a short position of FC 'A') from future movements in the exchange rate – ie it fixes the sterling value of that position. In order to obtain a proper overall view of the company's exposure to currency movements it is essential to take account of the forward hedge. For example, if one were to produce accounts for the company in the period between transactions 3 and 4, there would be an apparent exposed foreign currency payable position of FC 'A' unless one also took into account the foreign currency hedge (ie transaction 2). Failure to take the hedge into account in the preparation of the company's financial statements will accordingly result in the presentation of a misleading picture.

SSAP 20 says in relation to translation that 'where there are related or matching forward contracts in respect of trading transactions, the rates of exchange specified in those contracts may be used.' This would suggest that it is possible (or even desirable) to use the forward rate of exchange embodied in the hedge rather than the spot rate applicable at the time that the hedge was taken out. There are circumstances (such as in the trading operations discussed in chapter 7) where use of the forward hedged rate might be appropriate, but in general this is in fact unlikely to be the case.

As discussed earlier in this chapter, it should in general be the spot rate of exchange ruling at the time that the hedge is entered into which is used for the purposes of fixing the sterling equivalent of the hedged position. It is that spot rate which should, accordingly, be taken into account in the periodic revaluation process. Any difference between that spot rate of exchange and the rate implicit in the hedge is likely to relate to the interest differential between the two currencies concerned and should be treated as comprising an integral part of the company's financing activities.

In order to ensure that the use of a forward hedge achieves the same result as if a cash hedge been entered into, it is necessary to amortise the premium or discount, or any other financing element of the hedge, over the life of the hedging transaction. The way in which that amortisation takes place and the period over which it is amortised is likely to be a function of the hedging transaction itself rather than anything to do with the currency exposure being hedged. If, for example, the hedging transaction is entered into for a period extending beyond the expected settlement date of the exposure, it is the longer period that should be used for the purposes of amortising any premium or discount, rather than the period of the exposure.

In general then, a translation hedge should have no impact on the exchange rate used to record the non-monetary item giving rise to the exposure, and the rate implied by the hedge should not, necessarily, be that applied in revaluing any monetary exposure being hedged. The rate to be applied to the monetary exposure for revaluation purposes will be the spot rate ruling on the date on which the hedge was entered into. The forward premium or discount or any other form of 'hedging cost' should be taken to income over the life of the hedge as part of the company's overall net financing activities.

Hedges may, of course, be taken out at any time during the life of a foreign currency exposure and need not, in a business sense, be related to any one particular transaction. Although SSAP 20 refers to only forward contracts and to particular 'trading transactions', it would not seem to have been its intention to limit the provision to this extent, and it is now generally assumed to apply to other hedging products and to exposures arising from groups of transactions whether or not separately identifiable.

Foreign equity investments

Apart from the passing reference to the use of forward contracts for the hedging of trading transactions, the only other explicit reference to hedging in SSAP 20 is in connection with foreign equity investments.

Where a company has chosen to use foreign currency borrowings to finance, or provide a hedge against, a foreign equity investment, then, subject to certain conditions being met, SSAP 20 allows the equity investments to be denominated in their underlying currency and to perform a periodic revaluation into the local currency. Any gains or losses arising on that periodic revaluation can then be 'offset' against gains or losses arising on the related borrowing. The statement requires a company adopting this approach to offset the respective effects of these revaluations in reserves, rather than flowing them through the profit and loss account.

The objective of SSAP 20 in this area is to address the anomaly that would otherwise be created by accounting in different ways for the two sides of what would appear to be a fully-matched transaction. In the normal course of events, the foreign equity investment would be treated as a non-monetary item which would be fixed in sterling terms as from the original date of investment. If the company wishes, however, to view the investment as being essentially denominated in the underlying currency, and then to hedge that exposure by borrowing funds to match the investment, it is quite clear that it would be inappropriate to revalue the foreign currency amount of the debt whilst maintaining the equity investment at its original historic exchange rate. The solution offered by SSAP 20 is, accordingly, to treat the foreign equity investment as being a foreign currency item subject to periodic revaluation, and to take the effects of that revaluation, together with the impact of any revaluation on the hedge, direct to reserves.

It will be seen in the following section that the case of hedging a foreign equity investment by way of a foreign currency borrowing is in fact simply one example of a much wider group of potentially anomalous situations. It should also be appreciated that there is no longer any need for the company to effect a 'cash' hedge, there being a number of alternative approaches now open to it. SSAP 20, in its current form, would appear to restrict the 'offsetting in reserves' approach to foreign equity investments which have been hedged through a foreign currency borrowing and even seems to suggest that there should be reserve accounting for any mismatch between the revaluation impact on the investment and on the debt. The latter situation arises where the foreign currency borrowing is in a different currency to that of the investment or where there is something of a mismatch between the amounts involved. The latter can frequently arise where there has been an accretion in value of the equity investment as a result of earnings subsequent to the date of the original investment.

The fact that management has chosen to hedge the overseas equity investment presumably reflects their desire to create in economic terms a sterling investment. In such a situation, it would seem reasonable to treat any unhedged portion of the overseas investment as an exposed currency position, with any currency gains or losses arising from it being reflected in income for the period in question. Reserve accounting for any mismatch between the foreign investment and the related borrowing would seem to be illogical.

The position can become extremely complex where the company views its overseas equity investment as simply a constituent part of its exposure to that currency and, at the same time, decides to follow a fully-hedged strategy. In such circumstances, it is possible that there will be a variety of hedging techniques employed to eliminate the exposures created by the equity investment and other positions in that currency, and any attempt to identify separately the various component parts of the equity hedging strategy may be doomed to failure. The proper accounting treatment in such a situation must surely be to revalue the overseas equity investment at current rates, in the same way as any monetary asset would be revalued. Any hedging transactions can then also be revalued as appropriate, with the offset taking place in the income statement rather than in reserves. An alternative approach might be to ensure that a sufficient portion of hedging transactions is matched with the equity investment and revalued in such a way as to result in no net gain or loss on the position in question. Although this is, of course, very much a case of forcing the accounting to match the underlying commercial logic, it should at least achieve the desired result.

The way in which a company actually perceives its exposure towards a foreign equity investment is, of course, generally more complex than has probably been suggested so far. The investment is likely to comprise a variety of different exposures and the underlying question to be asked is precisely what the investing company is seeking to protect. To the extent that it perceives the investment as being a long-term (permanent) equity holding which it does not intend to realise, it is likely that any hedges entered into are in fact an attempt to protect the company against fluctuations in the future earnings flow from the foreign company, rather than as a hedge of the underlying investment itself. It is far from clear that the most appropriate way to protect a future flow of earnings is through a foreign currency borrowing.

Where, for whatever reason, the company wishes to hedge an overseas equity investment, it should initially decide whether it intends to hedge the 'balance sheet position' or whether the intention is in fact to hedge some future proposed transaction such as, for example, the ultimate disposal of the investment or a future flow of earnings. If the intention is to hedge the balance sheet value at any point in time then a borrowing in the foreign currency concerned may well achieve the desired result. If the intention is to hedge a future transaction relating to the investment, then the decision might be taken to utilise forward transactions or options rather than a cash borrowing. Whatever the approach adopted, it is important to relate the

intention of the hedge to the precise financial implications flowing from
it.

Where a foreign currency borrowing is used to hedge a foreign equity
investment, it is likely that there will be an interest differential between
the local currency and that of the overseas borrowing. That interest differential
will be taken into account as a part of the company's overall financing
activities rather than as a form of hedging cost.

If one were contemplating the ultimate sale of the investment and this
event had been hedged through a forward foreign exchange transaction,
the most appropriate course of action would be to revalue the investment
using the spot rate of exchange ruling at the time that the hedge was entered
into. One would, in other words, compare the spot rate of exchange when
the hedge was entered into with the spot rate ruling at the balance sheet
date and take the movement in those rates as being the 'offset' against any
currency gain or loss on the underlying equity investment. The amortisation
of the original premium or discount on the forward rate (and for that matter
any movement, in absolute terms, in the forward premium or discount) is
attributable to the 'financing element' of the hedge which would, had a
borrowing approach been adopted, have shown up in the overall cost of
funding. It is clearly appropriate to treat any interest differential arising
on a hedge created through a forward contract in exactly the same way.

SSAP 20 allows reserve accounting for a foreign equity investment and
the 'matching' borrowing where the following conditions are met:

'(a) in any accounting period, exchange gains or losses arising on the
       borrowings may be offset only to the extent of exchange differences
       arising on the equity investments;
 (b) the foreign currency borrowings, whose exchange gains or losses are
       used in the offset process, should not exceed, in the aggregate, the
       total amount of cash that the investments are expected to be able
       to generate, whether from profits or otherwise; and
 (c) the accounting treatment adopted should be applied consistently from
       period to period.'

Although the necessity for reserve accounting in this area is questioned,
it is accepted that the approach advocated by SSAP 20 will, in general,
provide an acceptable answer. That is not to say that the underlying concept
should not be extended to other areas (something which is examined in
the next section) but it does at least mean that the underlying result obtained
in the accounts should make sense. There would seem to be no prohibition
in taking any 'mismatch' arising as between the equity investment and the
hedge to income and this is the approach accordingly advocated in this
book. The net effect of adopting this strategy will, however, be to always
result in a nil impact on reserves: any gain or loss originating from the
investment being exactly offset by the gain or loss on the hedge. Although
the disclosure provisions of SSAP 20 would ensure that the figures are not
'lost' to the reader of the accounts, the approach does result in the whole
question of reserve accounting becoming somewhat superfluous.

An alternative way of looking at any mismatch in exposures arising on
an equity investment is to adopt the same approach as is employed in chapter
9 in the case of the revaluation of the net investment of a company in an

overseas subsidiary. In that case, it is argued that the rationale for the reserve accounting required by SSAP 20 could be seen as being a reflection of the parent's 'structural position' in the subsidiary's base currency. It is suggested in that chapter that the idea of reserve accounting can, accordingly, be viewed in the same context as the periodic credits to reserves arising as a result of, for example, a fixed asset revaluation. Depending upon the company's individual circumstances, this argument could be used to justify reserve accounting for any mismatch between the equity investment and its hedge.

Other balance sheet exposures

It has already been noted that the status of hedged foreign equity investments is essentially the same as certain other hedged non-monetary items. A similar logic can, for example, be applied to inventory held for resale in a foreign currency or currency prepayments, etc. In such cases, the fact that these items are generally treated as being non-monetary, would normally require a 'historic' exchange rate policy whereas, in economic terms, the items are more in the nature of a 'monetary' exposure. It is the definition of 'monetary items' and the fact that certain non-monetary items may in effect constitute currency denominated exposures which give rise to the problem in this area.

The special treatment of foreign equity investments envisaged above applies in those situations where management has decided to hedge those investments, thereby explicitly accepting that they are foreign currency denominated items. It has been seen that this might be appropriate where the company is either looking at a future transaction in the equity of that company (for example a sale of the investment) or where the hedge is, in effect, simply an attempt to protect future flows of foreign currency revenue flowing from the investment. It is quite clear that similar considerations can relate to certain other non-monetary items such as, for example, a fixed asset located in an overseas country which is scheduled for sale in the near future, inventory held for resale overseas, deferred taxation (where the ultimate taxation liability will be denominated in the foreign currency), or certain prepaid expenses where it might be more appropriate to treat the balances as being denominated in a foreign currency.

In all of the above cases, the traditional approach envisaged by SSAP 20 is to treat these items as being, in effect, sterling denominated, their foreign currency nature having been lost at the point where they were originally translated into sterling. Although the approach suggested in this book is consistent with that embodied in SSAP 20, it argues that it is important to ensure that in the overall evaluation of the company's foreign currency exposures, appropriate account is taken of the fact that certain 'sterling denominated' items might in the future yield foreign currency flows. This is a form of 'off balance sheet' exposure which needs to be taken into account in the periodic revaluation of the company's currency positions. A more convenient way of viewing these 'hidden monetary items' is to consider the underlying transactions which will create the monetary exposure as being *future* transactions. Any hedging of such exposure can then be considered to be in the nature of a transaction hedge, which should be accounted for as discussed in chapter 7.

In practical terms, the above means that any hedges of non-monetary items which are likely to give rise to future monetary exposures should be treated as transaction hedges and taken into account in recording the eventual transaction. They should accordingly be excluded from the periodic revaluation process, with any gain or loss being deferred and then brought into account when the monetary exposure arises.

Before concluding our discussion of translation hedging, it is important to remember that foreign currency exposures can arise from a variety of activities, many of which might not relate to trading activities. Exposures can arise, for example, as a result of the speculative investment of surplus funds in a foreign currency or the issuance of foreign currency denominated debt or equity. There is no particular reason why such exposures should not be treated in precisely the same way as those arising from trading transactions, with the currency amount essentially being converted into sterling at the spot rate of exchange ruling at the balance sheet date. The underlying concept of it being management's decision to maintain the exposure in question is just as valid (and probably more so) in the case of non-trading situations as with exposures arising out of trading transactions.

Any hedges entered into in relation to such exposures should, accordingly, be treated in the same way as hedges of trading transactions. The handling of any 'financing element' of the hedging product is no different and the overall criteria to be applied are essentially the same.

The detailed accounting approach to be adopted in respect of any particular hedging arrangement must take into account the underlying position being hedged and the commercial structuring of the hedge itself. The underlying concept in virtually all cases is that the sterling value of the foreign currency item being hedged is determined by the spot rate of exchange ruling at the time that the hedge is entered into, with any financing element forming part of the hedging arrangement either being recognised in an appropriate way over the period of the hedge or taken into account in the overall value of the transaction being hedged. More complex hedging scenarios are explored in the Reference Section.

OFF BALANCE SHEET EXPOSURES

Most large companies have numerous off balance sheet exposures, some of which will embody a foreign exchange risk. Such exposures range from straightforward commitments entered into during the normal course of business through to complex contingent exposures relating to, for example, the possible success or failure of a tender bid. The question as to whether or not an exposure is 'on the balance sheet' or 'off the balance sheet' is a combination of the underlying nature of the exposure and the extent to which it might relate to an asset or a liability which is itself 'off balance sheet'. The increasing use of off balance sheet finance by the corporate sector has given rise to a corresponding increase in off balance sheet exposures – many of which contain a foreign exchange element.

The other major area where off balance sheet currency exposure arises is where a company enters into a 'non-cash' hedging arrangement in relation to either a balance sheet or an off balance sheet exposure. Such off balance sheet hedges can range from simple forward foreign exchange contracts to complex option arrangements or currency exchange agreements. Any off balance sheet hedges should be accounted for in accordance with the broad concepts set out in the previous section, with the detailed treatment adopted taking account of the nature of the underlying exposure and the way in which the actual hedge is structured. Detailed examples in this regard are set out in the Reference Section. The remainder of the present chapter is concerned with those off balance sheet exposures which arise in the ordinary course of business rather than those created specifically for the purpose of hedging currency positions.

The question of set-off

Assets and liabilities can sometimes become 'off balance sheet' simply due to the way in which they have been netted on the face of the balance sheet. Although there might be good grounds for netting the underlying assets and liabilities, if this takes place where a residual foreign exchange exposure exists, then that exposure naturally ends up 'off balance sheet'. The question of set-off often arises in the case of financing transactions where a company is attempting to structure its balance sheet in a particular way, perhaps by adjusting the mix of floating and fixed rate funding. Traditionally, for example, if a company wished to reduce the ratio of its fixed rate to floating rate borrowings, but had no way of arranging for early redemption of the fixed rate debt, it was possible to enter into a 'back to back' facility with a financial institution, thereby effectively converting the fixed rate funding to floating rate. Such a transaction is now usually unnecessary as the same effect can be achieved by arranging an off balance sheet capital market swap.

Other areas where set-off is frequently encountered are when there is a cross-lending between unconnected companies and their respective local subsidiaries (an arrangement almost always involving foreign exchange exposures in the first instance) and situations involving guarantees relating to certain transactions entered into by related companies. Financial institutions have long applied slightly broader rules in determining whether or not particular assets and liabilities could be netted against each other; an issue which has taken on much more importance as a result of the recent increased focus on the question of capital adequacy ratios within the banking sector.

In the UK there is a general prohibition of set-off contained in the Companies Act 1981 (Sch 1, para 14), and for the non-banking sector, the netting of 'related' balance sheet items is usually unacceptable unless there is a very clearly established and enforceable legal right of set-off contained in the agreements between the parties. The situation in the US is less definitive than in the UK although the SEC has indicated that set-off is only appropriate in those cases where a clean legal right to offset exists.

In most cases, in order to be able to justify a set-off on the balance sheet, it is necessary to eliminate any residual foreign exchange exposure which might exist. This may, such as in the case of certain multicurrency swaps, be embodied in the underlying transaction documentation or might, alternatively, be handled through a separate hedging arrangement specifically entered into for the purpose of eliminating any residual exposure.

The extent to which an asset or a liability is removed from the balance sheet should have no direct impact on the way in which any related foreign currency exposure is accounted for. It will, accordingly, generally be necessary to effect a spot revaluation at the balance sheet date of all off balance sheet exposures in the same way as if they had been recorded on the balance sheet. The considerations to be addressed in determining how to effect that revaluation are the same as those explored in connection with balance sheet items.

Commitments

Certain commitments are traditionally not included on the face of the balance sheet. Examples include payments due under long-term property leases, contracted purchase orders (whether for inventory or fixed assets), sales commitments, and, of course, many of the off balance sheet financing transactions available in the market. To the extent that a commitment is denominated in a foreign currency, there is an exposure to future movements in the exchange rate between that currency and the local currency. Although the underlying obligation is not itself on the face of the balance sheet (for either traditional accounting, presentational, legal or other reasons), the foreign exchange exposure is still exactly the same. Such exposures should, accordingly, be viewed in exactly the same way as if they related to balance sheet assets or liabilities.

A feature of most commitments of the type referred to above is that they relate to future transactions of the company (in an accounting sense) and accordingly any income or costs deriving from those transactions are usually taken into account in future periods. For example the costs attributable to a long-term property lease and the revenue flowing from existing sales commitments, will generally fall into future periods of account. It is accordingly illogical to recognise a currency gain or loss which arises as a result of such commitments being denominated in the foreign currency, other than in the period in which the underlying transactions are themselves recognised.

It can be seen that this approach is consistent with the concept of transaction accounting already discussed in chapter 7. We are simply saying that the foreign currency exposure relating to a transaction is not taken into account until the 'transaction date'. It follows that any hedges of the exposures relating to those transactions should also not be taken into account until that date: an approach which is consistent with that applied to transaction hedges in chapter 7.

In some industries it is common for contracted losses to be recognised in advance of the date on which the revenues relating to a transaction might otherwise be booked. This is the case with certain long-term contracting industries or construction projects for example. Such an approach is, in effect, 'bringing forward' the transaction date into an earlier accounting period, and it is accordingly appropriate in such circumstances also to take account of any currency exposure implications. It is, in particular, necessary to take the effect of such currency exposures into account when determining the extent to which there is an overall loss on the contract.

Contingencies

The extent to which a contingency is recognised in the financial statements of a UK company is governed largely by SSAP 18, *Accounting for Contingencies*.

That statement defines a contingency as a condition which exists at the balance sheet date, where the outcome will be confirmed only on the occurrence or non-occurrence of one or more uncertain future events. The statement essentially requires material contingent losses to be accrued in the financial statements of a company where it is 'probable' that a future event will confirm a loss which can be estimated with reasonable accuracy at the time. It does not provide for the accrual of contingent gains.

To the extent that a contingency is denominated in a foreign currency, there is clearly a contingent foreign currency exposure attaching to it. In commercial terms, it is generally appropriate to view the entire exposure as a single contingency, but in terms of exposure protection it is frequently necessary to break it into its constituent parts. A contingent foreign currency exposure can, for example, be hedged using a foreign currency option. Where such an exposure is hedged using cash or a commitment type hedge, there would, of course, be a residual foreign currency exposure in the event of the contingency being eliminated. By eliminating the currency element of the underlying contingency, one is accordingly creating a separate currency contingency.

To the extent that a contingent profit or loss is recognised in the financial statements, it is clearly appropriate also to take account of any related foreign exchange implications. The approach and criteria would essentially become the same as when dealing with a commitment. Where a contingency is not taken into account on the balance sheet of a company it would generally be appropriate also to exclude the impact of any foreign currency exposure attaching thereto. It would, however, be necessary to take account of the implications of that exposure in determining the extent to which it might be necessary to recognise any loss arising from the contingency as a whole. Any 'option type' currency hedge arranged in relation to the contingency should, of course, also be ignored to the extent that the underlying contingency is not taken into account.

A complication arises where a contingent exposure is not accounted for on a company's balance sheet, but where the foreign currency element of that exposure is in fact hedged through either a cash or a commitment type transaction. Most authorities would argue that in such circumstances it would be necessary to treat the hedge as being unconnected with the contingency and to revalue it as an outright position as at the balance sheet date. Although this might be appropriate in the majority of such cases, it may well be technically incorrect in others. If the company is simply choosing to hedge the contingent currency exposure in the same way that a currency options trader would – ie using the cash or forward market on an incremental basis to limit exposure on the underlying option position (see Reference Section A.11), then the effect is essentially the same as if it had simply entered into an option contract. How should one take account of the hedge position in such circumstances?

In reality, of course, it is unlikely that a corporate contingency will be particularly comparable to the position of a currency options trader who will have a very well defined methodology for monitoring the underlying option exposure and then matching his cash or forward hedge to that position in a sophisticated mathematical way. This is generally not the case where one is dealing with corporate contingencies, as the extent to which the contingency is likely to come about is determined by a combination of both foreign exchange rates *and* the underlying probability of the contingency itself. It would, therefore, seem appropriate to treat any cash or commitment type hedges of a contingent position as outright exposures *unless* there were very definite reasons for doing otherwise.

A particular example of a foreign currency denominated contingency being, in effect, hedged by way of a cash transaction arises where the company has been *required* to purchase the foreign currency in advance of the contingency being determined. This might occur, for example, where a foreign court has asked for a fiduciary deposit to be paid into court pending settlement of an action against the company. The company has in effect been forced to hedge the foreign currency contingency. If the contingency is not recognised on the balance sheet the deposit is an exposed currency item subject to periodic revaluation and should be treated in currency terms just like any other foreign currency deposit.

Economic exposure

Chapter 3 briefly explored the nature of economic exposure and showed how its existence can completely change the underlying exposure arising from what might otherwise appear to be an outright currency position. Such economic exposures can exist either in isolation or in such a way as to be connected with either a balance sheet currency position or another off balance sheet exposure. A comprehensive review of a large international company's economic exposures will typically identify a large number of interacting risks – some of which will implicitly offset each other.

Economic exposure is, by its very nature, an exposure which impacts upon future transactions of the company. It is, accordingly, similar to the structural form of transaction exposure explored in chapter 7. Such exposures are, in general terms, ignored for the purposes of carrying out a balance sheet translation. The only difficulty in accounting terms accordingly arises when a company has identified certain economic exposures which it decides to hedge. The hedging might take place through the use of any one of a number of off balance sheet commitment type or contingent type hedging products, or might simply be achieved through the creation of a currency mis-match on the company's balance sheet. The result, in either case, is that there is an apparent exposed monetary position which, in economic terms, is perceived by the company as being a hedge of an identified economic exposure.

The approach to transaction accounting advocated in chapter 7 requires that any hedge of a future transaction should be excluded from the periodic revaluation process. The chapter recommends that this approach should be employed whatever the form of the hedging arrangement and whether it is in the nature of a specific or a generalised transaction hedge. It is argued that the 'cost' of the hedge (either the inherent forward premium/discount on a forward transaction or the funding implications of any balance sheet hedging) should be deferred and taken into account in recording the subsequent transaction.

Although economic exposure can be thought of as being similar to a structural form of transaction exposure, it is often much more difficult to measure the precise amount of the actual exposure. Furthermore, it is generally difficult to ensure that *all* such exposures have been identified. Do these additional complications mean that we are unable to treat a hedge of an economic structure in the same way as a generalised hedge of a structural transaction exposure?

In the same way that a company might choose to hedge certain structural positions but not others, it is perfectly acceptable to consider it as having only hedged certain of its economic exposures. The fact that there might be other, perhaps unidentified, economic exposures should not affect the way in which a hedge of an *identified* exposure is treated. Doubts concerning the amount of a particular economic exposure are a more difficult issue. Any hedge of an economic position should only be treated as such to the extent that it can be shown that the economic exposure is at least sufficient to allow the hedge to be fully compensating. If it appears that the hedge is excessive, or likely to 'over compensate' in relation to the exposure, then an appropriate portion of it should be treated as an outright position.

In summary then, where a hedge can be shown to constitute an effective hedge of an economic position, it should be ignored in any periodic revaluation and treated in the same way as a generalised transaction hedge. If only a portion of the hedge is required to protect the identified exposure, the remainder should be treated as an outright position in the normal way. Chapter 6 recommends that identified economic exposures and any hedging of same should be disclosed by way of a note to the accounts.

CHAPTER 9

Consolidations

As noted in chapter 5, many of the arguments surrounding foreign exchange accounting have concerned the most appropriate way of accounting for 'overseas operations'. The background to these discussions has already been covered in chapters 5 and 6 and the purpose of the present chapter is to set out an approach to consolidation accounting which is consistent with SSAP 20 and yet responsive to the underlying ideas embodied in this book.

This chapter is concerned with the consolidation of business 'entities' or 'operations' – which is not necessarily the same thing as a consolidation of the separate legal companies. The concepts explored can certainly be applied to the case of two individual companies, but it is important to recognise that they are also of relevance when consolidating the financial statements of *any* two operations which are separately accounted for – whether they are separate divisions of the same company, or individual divisions of different companies, and whether or not either one or both are located overseas. The terms 'subsidiary' and 'parent' used in this chapter should accordingly be interpreted in this light.

There are many complexities in consolidation accounting, particularly when one is dealing with large complex international groups. This chapter does not set out to be a comprehensive guide to consolidations, but is rather a summary of those particular problems which tend to be encountered in relation to foreign exchange.

A proper understanding of how to consolidate an overseas operation can really only be obtained by working through a detailed example. Such an example, which covers most of the matters discussed in this chapter is accordingly included in Reference Section D.

OVERALL CONCEPTS

The so-called 'temporal method' for consolidations is closely related to the concept of a business entity's 'base currency' (see chapter 6). In other words, it essentially applies where the base currency or the subsidiary being consolidated is the same as that of the parent company. It is important to recognise that this concept is valid, irrespective of the nature of either the parent or the subsidiary's reporting or local currency. It is, for example, perfectly possible for a UK operating division with a US dollar base currency to have an overseas branch operation, perhaps located in France, which might also have US dollars as its base currency. There would need to be a consolidation between the Paris branch and the UK operating division prior to any consolidation of the US dollar based operations with, perhaps, the sterling-based operations of the rest of the company.

As long as the two entities being consolidated have the same base currency, the resulting consolidated accounts will, subject to the normal complexities of consolidation accounting, simply reflect the arithmetical sum of the currency balances for the two companies concerned.

The typical complication which emerges, however, is that the subsidiary does not use its base currency for the purposes of its primary accounting records. For example, in the case of the above example, the French branch might (perhaps for regulatory purposes) use French francs as its local reporting currency. The need then arises to convert the French franc accounting data of the branch into the US dollar base currency prior to effecting the consolidation with the UK head office. It is this process which is generally referred to as the 'temporal method'.

It will be recalled from the discussion in chapter 7 that the approach to transaction accounting set out therein is also the underlying approach which should be adopted when translating financial statements from a local currency into its base currency. This is essentially because one is attempting to record the related transactions in the base currency in such a way that the result will be the same as if they had been recorded in that base currency from the very beginning. This is recognised in SSAP 20 where it refers to the fact that 'the mechanics of this (the temporal) method are identical with those used in preparing the accounts of an individual company'.

The 'temporal method', then, can be seen to be not so much a method of consolidating within a multicurrency environment as a means of translating the underlying accounting records of a subsidiary which have, for some particular reason, not been recorded in the appropriate base currency. It should not be seen as an 'alternative' to the more normal 'closing rate/ net investment method' of effecting a multicurrency consolidation.

The only additional complexity which tends to arise when one is trying to re-translate accounting records into the base currency is the possible loss of historic exchange rate data. Where there is a fairly high volume of foreign currency transactions and where the business entity concerned does not employ a full multicurrency accounting system such as that envisaged in chapter 10, it is quite likely that there will be insufficient information available to restate accurately the accounting records into the base currency concerned. It accordingly becomes necessary to consider using average rates of exchange for those transactions occurring over a particular period.

The use of average rates of exchange was explored in chapter 7 where it was concluded that whilst the use of average rates might be appropriate for the translation of income and expense, it is unlikely to be suitable for the translation of non-monetary items which arose over the course of the previous accounting period. Although in some cases the exchange rate movements over the period in question might be deemed to be immaterial, the size of foreign exchange fluctuations in today's market are such that it is generally difficult to conclude that this is the case. SSAP 20 allows the use of average rates of exchange 'as an approximation' to actual rates 'if the rates do not fluctuate significantly'.

THE CLOSING RATE/NET INVESTMENT METHOD

The remainder of this chapter deals with what is now the only generally accepted way of accounting for the consolidation of a number of separate business entities having different base currencies. It reviews the general approach adopted and then examines some of the complications which can emerge.

It must be remembered that the purpose of preparing a set of consolidated financial statements is to present a single picture of what is, in economic terms, probably two or more separate operations. The consolidation process is hampered by a number of difficulties in areas well outside of the foreign exchange field (accounting for goodwill, etc), all of which originate from the difficulty of trying to present a composite picture of those separate entities.

General approach

The concept underlying the closing rate/net investment method is that the parent sees its investment in a subsidiary entity as being one which is 'denominated' in the subsidiary's base currency. The company can accordingly be seen to have a 'net investment' in the subsidiary itself rather than an investment in the underlying assets and liabilities of that entity. The objective of the closing rate/net investment method is to consolidate the two entities within this framework.

The general approach to consolidation accounting in this context may be briefly summarised as follows:

(a) individual items in the subsidiary's balance sheet are translated at the closing spot rate of exchange ruling at the balance sheet date;
(b) any gains or losses arising on the parent's net investment in the subsidiary, as a result of movements in exchange rates over the financial period in question, are taken to reserves;
(c) the results for the period in the subsidiary are translated either at the closing spot rate of exchange or at the average rate of exchange for the accounting period;
(d) where an average rate of exchange is used for the translation of results, the difference between using that average rate and the result which would have been obtained had the closing rate been used, is also taken to reserves; and
(e) subject to certain conditions, the gain or loss on any hedge of the parent's net investment in its subsidiary is offset in reserves against any gain or loss arising on the net investment itself.

The following sections explore the above concepts in a little more detail and then examine a number of particular problems which emerge from this approach.

Relevant exchange rates

The translation of the subsidiary's balance sheet at closing spot rates of exchange generally presents few problems. The use of the spot rate of exchange should be seen very much as a convenient measure of the parent's base currency equivalent of its net investment in the subsidiary entity, rather than as a rate which has any particular kind of economic relevance to the future operations of the subsidiary. If the parent has an unhedged net investment in the base currency of the subsidiary, the theoretical 'value' of that net investment (within the context of historic cost accounting) is taken to be the parent's base currency equivalent of that investment at the prevailing spot rate of exchange. In reality, of course, the 'value' of the subsidiary to the parent is likely to be substantially different, probably better determined, for example, by the base currency equivalent of future expected flows of revenue, but this particular aspect of the entity's value should not be taken into account in the consolidation process any more than one would, for example, in the case of a local subsidiary.

A more difficult issue concerns the exchange rate to be used in translating the income statement of the subsidiary. SSAP 20 permits the use of either the average or the closing rate but provides no real guidance as to how the average rate should be calculated. Where an average rate is used, the difference between using that rate and the closing rate used for translating the balance of retained earnings, is taken to reserves. SFAS 52 requires that revenues, expenses, gains and losses are translated into the parent's base currency at the rates of exchange ruling on the date on which those individual items are recognised. In the absence of such sophistication, it allows an appropriate weighted average rate of exchange for the period in question.

The quandary as to whether or not to use the closing balance sheet rate or some kind of average/actual rate derives from the underlying dual objectives of consolidation accounting. As discussed in chapter 6, the use of the closing rate is more likely to better reflect the underlying financial activity of the subsidiary entity in its 'pre-translation' state, whereas an average rate more accurately reflects the profits or losses and cashflows as they accrue to the group over the accounting period in question. It was this difficulty which resulted in SSAP 20 allowing the use of either method. The practical difference between the two approaches is that it impacts the allocation of currency translation gains or losses as between the income statement and reserves.

Whatever the rationale for reserve accounting for any currency gain or loss arising on the re-translation of a parent's opening net investment in a subsidiary entity, it would seem to be desirable to treat profits or losses accruing over the accounting period in the same way. In other words, profits or losses accruing during the accounting period ought to be translated at the rates prevailing at the time when they arose, with any subsequent currency gain or loss arising as a result of the movement in rates between that time and the balance sheet date, being taken to reserves in the same way as for any retained earnings arising prior to the commencement of the accounting period itself. This is the approach that is preferred by SFAS 52.

It is accordingly recommended that, within the context of the reserve accounting environment advocated by SSAP 20, the most appropriate means of translating a subsidiary's income statement is to employ the actual rates of exchange prevailing at the time that the various items in the income statement arose. This is, of course, consistent with using as sophisticated a weighted average exchange rate as is available. Use of the closing balance sheet rate should be seen as a poor alternative to the use of average rates and should be used as an appropriate 'fall back' method where measurement of the average rate is impossible.

The example in Reference Section D utilises closing rates of exchange for the purposes of translating the income statement, as this provides a clearer guide to most other aspects of the consolidation process. Had actual or average rates been used, it would have resulted in a reallocation of income as between net profit and the foreign currency investment translation reserve.

Reserve accounting

The rationale for reserve accounting was explored in chapter 6 where it was suggested that an argument in support of the SSAP 20 approach was that the gain or loss could be viewed as the currency impact of the parent holding a structural position in the subsidiary's base currency. It was suggested that the idea of reserve accounting for the periodic revaluation of that net structural currency position could, accordingly, be compared to the reserve accounting employed for periodic revaluations of fixed assets. The gains or losses taken to reserves represent, in other words, the results of 'long-term strategic decisions' by the group – rather than measuring the underlying profitability of the operations concerned.

If one accepts this concept, it is of course entirely consistent to try and eliminate any currency gain or loss in those situations where the structural position embodied in the net investment has been hedged. If one is going to reserve account for the gain or loss arising on the structural position itself, it is appropriate to treat any hedge of that position in the same way.

SSAP 20 allows a parent to reserve account for the hedge of a net investment subject to certain specified conditions, and in the context of the hedge being taken out by way of foreign currency borrowings. The statement makes no mention of any other forms of hedging and could be interpreted as therefore implying that the gains or losses arising on a non-debt hedge of a net investment should be taken to income. Such an approach would clearly be misleading to the extent that the gain or loss on the underlying position is still being taken to reserves.

SSAP 20 allows for reserve accounting 'where foreign currency borrowings have been used to finance, or provide a hedge against, group equity investments in foreign enterprises'. The statement provides that reserve accounting for the hedge only be allowed where the closing rate method has been employed for consolidation purposes, and so long as:

(a) the exchange gains and losses arising on the foreign currency borrowings are only offset to the extent of the exchange differences arising on the underlying net investments in foreign enterprises;
(b) the amount of the foreign currency borrowings used to generate the offsetting gain or loss do not exceed, in total, the amount of cash that the net investments are expected to be able to generate, either through future profitable operations, sale, or some other means; and
(c) there is a consistent approach from period to period.

It should be noted that the statement 'allows' the use of reserve accounting for debt-hedges, but does not require that this approach be followed.

It is quite clear that there should be consistent treatment as between an exposed net investment and any debt-hedge and it is unfortunate that SSAP 20 does not appear to contemplate the case of a hedge being effected by means of something other than foreign currency debt. SSAP 20 in fact refers to 'foreign currency borrowings' being 'used to finance, or provide a hedge against' net equity investments, and it could be argued that many of the newer hedging products now available are, in effect, 'using foreign currency borrowings' as a basis for creating the product itself. In other words, although the foreign currency borrowings concerned are not on the face of the parent's balance sheet, they exist in some location and have been 'used' to create the hedge entered into by the parent.

Support for this more liberal interpretation of SSAP 20 can be found in Technical Release 603 which was issued by the Institute of Chartered Accountants in December 1985. This release deals with off balance sheet finance and window dressing, and argues in the case of the former that it would be appropriate for a company which had 'entered into an arrangement which was a substitute for, or equivalent to, borrowing' to take account in its balance sheet of 'its obligations under that arrangement'.

This overriding idea of 'substance over form' is particularly important in the area of exposure hedging. There are very distinct advantages in adopting a consistent approach in this area – whatever the nature of the hedging arrangement entered into, and this book accordingly advocates the use of reserve accounting for hedges of net equity investments – even if those hedges do not comprise borrowings by the company in the traditional sense.

If it is considered inappropriate to reserve account for such non-debt hedges, then the gain or loss arising on the hedge over the accounting period should be separately identified in the accounts and cross-referred to the movement in reserves arising from the net investment itself. This is an example of where additional disclosures are likely to be required in order to properly present the underlying financial position of the company within the context of having to comply with SSAP 20.

The absence of any definitive accounting guidelines in relation to off balance sheet hedging could quite easily be taken advantage of in this area by omitting to take account of any off balance sheet hedge of a net investment. It might be argued, for example, that SSAP 20 does not allow for reserve accounting of the hedge, but that to take any gain or loss to income would misstate income for the period in question. It might be argued that the footnote disclosure of the gain or loss arising on the hedge, and a statement to the effect that this offsets the gain or loss on the net investment shown in reserves, might be adequate. This would seem to be totally misleading in that it is quite clear that it would have the effect of misstating the net assets of the group. If the hedge is not accounted for in reserves, it would be essential for it to be taken into account in the period-end revaluation; taking any gain or loss to income and then effecting a footnote disclosure to explain that part of the currency gain or loss in income effectively offsets certain amounts taken to reserves.

SSAP 20 does not restrict, as does SFAS 52, the application of reserve accounting for debt-hedges to currencies which are either in the same currency as the underlying net investment or currencies which move in tandem with that of the investment. The UK accounting profession considered that SFAS 52 was a little too rigid in this regard and that it was, in any event, extremely difficult to identify which currencies could be said to move in tandem with each other. Whilst such a degree of flexibility is to be welcomed in a general sense, it is difficult to see in what circumstances it would be appropriate to apply a hedge in a currency which did not maintain a fairly close relationship to the currency of the underlying net investment.

The example in Reference Section D covers reserve accounting and, in particular, the partial hedging of a parent's net investment through foreign currency borrowings. Although it does not examine a non-debt hedging scenario, the concepts employed are essentially similar – with the basic rules of translation accounting (chapter 8) being followed in the normal way.

SPECIAL PROBLEMS

The remainder of this chapter looks at some of the less obvious questions which emerge in the area of multicurrency consolidations. Most of these are matters which are not addressed specifically by SSAP 20, and there is some evidence to suggest that there is still a degree of inconsistency in the treatment being employed by UK companies.

Associated companies

The approach to be adopted when dealing with associated companies is essentially the same as that employed for subsidiary business entities. To the extent that the associate is deemed to have a base currency which is different to that of the investing company, it is necessary to effect a multicurrency consolidation. That consolidation should employ the closing rate/net investment method and will result in any gain or loss arising on the investee's share of the associate's net assets as at the beginning of the accounting period being shown as a movement on reserves.

Particular problems which tend to arise when dealing with associates can include the determination of the associate's base currency, and what rate(s) to use for the purpose of translating results for the period. The criteria to be used in determining the base currency should essentially be the same as in any other situation, although it may be more difficult for the investing company to gain access to the necessary facts. This is also likely to be the case in determining the most appropriate rate to employ for the translation of results.

There are no particularly easy solutions to the above problems although, at the end of the day, the base currency of the associate can probably best be determined by the attitude of the investing company's management to the potential currency exposure implicit in the net investment. Any attempt to hedge that exposure in a particular way would, for example, probably provide very clear evidence as to the investing company's view as to the underlying base currency of the associate.

The difficulty in translating the results of operations for an associate is frequently that the actual underlying currency data has either been lost in the accounting process, or is not available to the investee company in its role as a non-majority shareholder. Resort is accordingly made in many cases to the use of an average rate of exchange, which is frequently an unweighted average for the period in question – simply because more accurate information is not obtainable.

Business combinations

The most recent formal guidance on accounting for business combinations in the UK is SSAP 23, issued in April 1985. This accounting standard sets out those conditions which must be met before a merger accounting approach is allowed and requires, in the absence of one or more of those conditions, that any business combination should be accounted for through the acquisition method.

Where a business combination is accounted for as an acquisition, the fair value of the purchase consideration is, for the purposes of the consolidation, allocated amongst the underlying net tangible and intangible assets of the acquired entity. That allocation is based on the fair value of those assets to the acquiring company, with any difference between the amount of the consideration and the aggregate of the fair values of the 'separable net assets' comprising goodwill. SSAP 22 recommends that such purchased goodwill be written off against reserves at the date of acquisition, but also allows for its amortisation over 'its estimated useful life' should the company so wish. Neither SSAP 23 nor SSAP 22 address the question as to how to account for a business combination in a multicurrency environment, and SSAP 20 is also silent on the issue.

There are three principal issues which emerge in this area. The first concerns the extent to which any goodwill not written off on acquisition should be included in the calculation of a company's 'net investment' in its subsidiary for multicurrency consolidation purposes. The second issue relates to whether or not, in restating acquired assets in the consolidated accounts to their fair values on acquisition, the restatement process should be carried out in the underlying currency of the assets concerned or in the base currency of the investing company. The final area of discussion concerns the treatment of goodwill held in the balance sheet of a consolidated subsidiary. These particular issues are examined in turn.

1   Definition of net investment

For the purposes of carrying out a multicurrency consolidation, a company's net investment in its subsidiary is normally defined as the net assets of that subsidiary, excluding any purchased goodwill. This is broadly consistent with the historic cost concept of accounting and avoids taking account of what is, in any event, only an intangible asset, in the determination of any net currency gain or loss taken to reserves. In that the author supports the immediate write-off of purchased goodwill at the time of its creation, he also believes that it is inappropriate to include such goodwill in the definition of a company's net investment in its subsidiary.

An argument in favour of *including* goodwill in the calculation of the net investment is that it represents future anticipated flows of revenue from the subsidiary entity and can be thought of as a structural exposure to the currency of that entity, in the same way as any other income earning asset. This would suggest that the goodwill should be treated as a foreign currency item, subject to periodic revaluation just like any other asset of the subsidiary. Taking account of purchased goodwill in this way, however, begs the question as to whether one should also take account of similar structural currency positions in the case of a subsidiary where goodwill, perhaps for historical reasons, has not been created in the group accounts.

Future anticipated flows of foreign currency revenue are simply a constituent part of the overall economic exposure of the group, and it is clearly unrealistic to try and account for some of this exposure by way of the consolidation approach, whilst probably totally omitting other exposures of a similar nature. The preferred approach is surely to treat all future anticipated flows of currency revenue in a consistent way across all subsidiary entities; taking them into account in calculating the overall structural exposure of the group rather than on a case-by-case basis in the consolidation process. It is accordingly recommended that for the purposes of carrying out a multicurrency consolidation, any purchase goodwill, to the extent that it is not written off at the date of acquisition, be stated in the base currency of the acquiring company and be excluded from the definition of that company's net investment in its subsidiary entity.

2 *Asset revaluations*

A somewhat more difficult issue concerns the extent to which any write-up in the fair value of acquired underlying assets should be treated as an adjustment to the underlying foreign currency accounts of the subsidiary entity – rather than as a consolidation adjustment booked in the parent's base currency. One way of achieving the former approach is, of course, to restate the actual assets in the subsidiary's underlying books of account, although the same effect can be achieved if desired through the consolidation process itself. The important factor is whether or not the value adjustments are treated as being foreign currency items or adjustments fixed at the time of the acquisition in the base currency of the parent.

Although one could argue that the value adjustments are simply part of the consolidation process and a result of the parent's decision to invest (and therefore nothing to do with the subsidiary), the effect of treating them in this way is to ignore totally the link that they have with the underlying assets. Such an approach results in the assets being translated at a composite of current and historic rates.

The preferred approach would on balance seem to be that any value adjustments to underlying assets should be effected in the underlying currency of the subsidiary entity, thereby resulting in the revalued assets being translated at each accounting date at current rates. This is consistent with the concepts underlying the 'net investment' approach, as the value adjustments *clearly* represent a part of the parent's original investment.

3 *Goodwill in the subsidiary*

The final issue which needs to be addressed relates to the treatment of any goodwill which exists in the accounts of the subsidiary entity itself. The issue here concerns the extent to which that goodwill figure should be treated in the same way as any other foreign currency asset of the subsidiary, or whether it is preferable to eliminate it from the parent's net investment in the subsidiary. In other words, to what extent should one restate the parent's net investment in order to eliminate purchased goodwill carried in the accounts of the acquired subsidiary entity?

It is quite clear that defining the purchase goodwill of a subsidiary entity as a foreign currency item will result in the value of that goodwill fluctuating, from one accounting period to the next, as exchange rates move. In the same way that it seems inappropriate to treat any purchased goodwill in the parent as being a foreign currency item, it seems equally inappropriate to treat any purchased goodwill in the subsidiary entity as being subject to currency fluctuations. It would also seem inappropriate to treat purchased goodwill in the subsidiary any differently to that held in the accounts of the parent, as the imposition of the subsidiary in relation to the acquisition of the underlying assets might simply have been arranged for local legal or taxation purposes. It is undesirable that such a decision should significantly impact the way in which the purchased goodwill should be accounted for at consolidated group level.

It is accordingly recommended that any purchased goodwill in the subsidiary's balance sheet be treated in the same way as if it had been recorded in the parent's accounts, being deducted from the parent's net investment in the subsidiary for the purposes of carrying out the multicurrency consolidation.

The example in Reference Section D employs the aforementioned recommended approaches in relation to the definition of the parent's net investment, the treatment of value uplifts to underlying assets and the handling of goodwill recorded in the subsidiary. The example shows the value adjustments being booked via the consolidation process rather than as an underlying restatement of the subsidiary's accounting records.

Intercompany transactions

The need to eliminate unrealised profits on intercompany transactions exists just as much in the case of a multicurrency consolidation as when one is consolidating two entities using the same base currency. The additional complication which arises is that there may have been exchange rate movements between the transaction date and the balance sheet date. As one is using the closing balance sheet rate to translate the balance sheet of the subsidiary entity, but may have accounted for the transaction in the parent company at the actual historic rate, any uncompleted transactions can result in the booking of unrealised gains or losses in the consolidation. The situation is best explored by way of a couple of examples involving the purchase of an asset by the parent from the subsidiary and by the subsidiary from the parent.

Inter company transactions

The following examples demonstrate the consolidation accounting entries which would generally be booked in order to eliminate the unrealised profit arising on the sale of inventory between a parent (A Co) and its subsidiary (B Co).

Example 1
Assume that the parent has acquired inventory at a cost of £100 which it then sells to its subsidiary (B Co) for £150. The base currency of B Co is Deutschmarks and the rate of exchange ruling at the transaction date is 3.00. If we assume that, at a subsequent balance sheet date, the inventory remains on hand with B Co. but the pound has depreciated to, say, DM 2.5, the following will be the entries processed on consolidation:

	B Co (DM)	B Co (£)	A Co (£)	Adjustments	Consolidated totals
Sales	—	—	(150)	(a) 150	—
Cost of sales					
Purchases	450	180	100	(a)(150)	130
Closing inventory	(450)	(180)	—	(b) 50	(130)
Cost of sales	—	—	100	(100)	—
Profit	—	—	(50)	(b) 50	—

The adjustments made above are as follows:

(a) elimination of inter company sale; and
(b) elimination of unrealised £ profit (£150–£100).

Although the inventory's original cost to the group was only £100, it is now shown in the consolidated accounts as having a cost of £130. This represents, in arithmetical terms, the original £ cost of the inventory plus its increase in value as a result of it having been denominated in DM during a period in which the pound has depreciated. The £30 represents, of course, the difference between £180 (DM 450 at 2.5) and £150 (DM 450 at 3.0)

Example 2
We now consider the opposite case of the subsidiary selling inventory to the parent. If we assume the same exchange rates as in the previous example, an original inventory cost of DM300 and an inter-company sale to the parent at DM450, then the consolidation entries would be as follows:

	B Co (DM)	B Co (£)	A Co (£)	Adjustments	Consolidated totals
Sales	(450)	(150)	—	(a) 150	—
Cost of sales					
Purchases	300	100	150	(a)(150)	100
Closing inventory	—	—	(150)	(b) 50	(100)
Cost of sales	300	100	—	(100)	—
Profit	(150)	(50)	—	(50)	—

The adjustments made are once again as follows:

(a) elimination of intercompany sale; and
(b) elimination of unrealised £ profit (£150–£100).

The profits of B Co have been translated into sterling at a rate of 3.0 on the basis that this is the most appropriate average rate for the results shown. Had the closing rate of 2.5 been used, the unrealised profit recorded in the subsidiary would have been £60, and the reversal of this would have resulted in a consolidated inventory cost of £110 rather than £100.

The objective of the consolidation should be to eliminate any unrealised profit arising as a result of the intercompany transaction, but not necessarily to eliminate any unrealised currency gain or loss. This is a logical approach so long as the transfer of any related asset or liability (inventory in the above examples) from one currency environment to another has the effect of changing the overall currency exposure of the group. This *will* be the case if the asset (inventory) is being held by the receiving entity for the purposes of either use in that entity's business, or onward sale within that particular currency environment. The same argument applies in relation to the transfer of a fixed asset between different currency environments as the future generation of revenues by that asset will take place in the new currency environment in which it is now located. The treatment is totally consistent with the overall concept of the two business entities concerned having separate base currencies.

Achieving the aforementioned objective in a practical sense is somewhat more complex than might at first appear. In the examples shown above it can be seen that where a parent entity sells inventory to its subsidiary, the effect of reversing the unrealised profits recorded by the parent will not necessarily 'restate' the inventory to its original cost to the group. Although we have agreed that any currency gain or loss as a result of the relocation of the inventory should have properly been taken into account in determining the cost base, a closer examination of Example 1 above will show that the currency 'uplift' of £30 is actually the uplift arising from the appreciation of the Deutschmark as applied to the *subsidiary's* inventory cost – rather than the *group's* original cost. It contains, in other words, an element of appreciation on the unrealised profit element. A more accurate calculation of the inventory appreciation would be to base it on the original cost to the group – thereby giving the same result as if the inventory had been transferred between the parent and the subsidiary at original cost. This would have resulted, in the example shown above, in a closing inventory cost figure of £120, representing the original sterling cost of £100 plus the £20 impact of the Deutschmark appreciation on the DM300 (£100) cost base. The £10 difference between the two approaches ends up either in income or in the foreign currency investment translation reserve.

The difficulty with this more accurate approach is that it is usually impractical to eliminate individual profit uplifts on a transaction-by-transaction basis at the point of sale, other than through a wholesale adoption of a policy involving transfers at cost. The latter, however, would be likely to provide the individual business entities with a number of unrelated problems connected with their evaluation of profitability, etc. As there is generally not a major income statement impact arising from the way in which the uplift is treated, and as the amounts involved are, in the majority of cases, probably not that significant, it is suggested that a pragmatic approach be adopted such as that set out in Example 1 above. In the event of the amounts of 'intercompany inventory' on hand being significant at the end of a period in which there have been major fluctuations in exchange rates, it is suggested that the alternative approach be considered as a far more accurate assessment of the group's consolidated position.

The other problem area which emerges in relation to inter company transactions concerns the translation of unrealised profits arising in a subsidiary. In the second example above, it can be seen that the carrying cost of the group inventory is determined by the way in which the subsidiary's profit and loss is translated. In the example shown, the inventory is carried at a value which implies an exchange rate which was valid at the point where the inventory was transferred to the parent. As noted in the Example, had the consolidation been effected using the closing rate rather than the average rate, the effect would have been to increase the carrying value of the inventory by £10 – representing the impact of translating the subsidiary's net income. It is suggested that a more realistic result is obtained by using as close a rate as possible to that prevailing on the transaction date – suggesting that as realistic an average rate as is achievable should be used wherever possible. If the closing rate has to be used, and if the amount of unrealised profits becomes significant in relation to the group's operations, it is suggested that consideration be given to reversing out of the asset cost in the parent the effect of any currency impact on the unrealised profit.

Intercompany accounts

Many intercompany transactions give rise, at least initially, to an intercompany current account balance. The treatment of such accounts when producing a consolidated balance sheet is to translate them into the parent's base currency at the closing spot rate of exchange. Problems can arise where a transaction is not recorded by the parent and the subsidiary at the same time, or where one party to the transaction uses a different exchange rate for the purposes of recording the transaction. Such problems can generally best be resolved by addressing the nature of any timing mismatch and correcting for any resulting misstatement as appropriate.

Whatever the source of an intercompany current account, any movement in exchange rates will be likely to generate a currency gain or loss in either the accounts of the parent or the accounts of the subsidiary – depending on the currency of the intercompany account. If the account is denominated in the currency of the subsidiary, any exchange rate movement will be reflected as a currency gain or loss in the accounts of the parent. Conversely, if the account is in the parent's base currency, there will be a currency gain or loss arising in the subsidiary which would normally be accounted for in the subsidiary's base currency income statement prior to effecting the consolidation. If the account is denominated in a third currency, it may give rise to gains or losses in the accounts of both the subsidiary and the parent.

The only real complication in this area is where the intercompany account, though originating from a series of intercompany transactions, is in effect used by the parent as a means of either financing the subsidiary or, perhaps, for hedging its net investment in that subsidiary. Whether or not the account is denominated in the currency of the subsidiary, if it represents an amount due to the parent which perhaps rarely results in cash settlement, it is quite possible that the parent views it as being an integral part of its funding of its investment in the subsidiary concerned.

In general terms, any long-term, intercompany balances in favour of the parent should be examined to ascertain whether, from the standpoint of the parent, they represent part of its funding of that subsidiary. Conversely, any long-term amounts due to the subsidiary should be reviewed to ensure that they are not, in economic terms, partial repayments of other long-term funding arrangements, or a method of hedging the parent's investment in the subsidiary's share capital.

Non-equity investments

SSAP 20 recognises that it is possible to finance a subsidiary entity by way of long term loans or 'intercompany deferred trading balances'. It argues that 'where financing by such means is intended to be, for all practical purposes, as permanent as equity, such loans and intercompany balances should be treated as part of the investing company's net investment in the foreign enterprise'. Such balances are accordingly taken into account in determining the gain or loss to be taken to reserves in the consolidated accounts as a result of the impact of exchange rate movements on the parent's net investment.

It is naturally extremely difficult sometimes to determine whether or not an intercompany current account is in reality simply a means by which the parent is financing its subsidiary. It is an example of a situation where there is little by way of accounting guidelines available, and it becomes important to look at the underlying commercial reality in order to determine the proper treatment. One can review intentions, the ability to settle the balance in the foreseeable future, the origin of the intercompany account itself, the extent to which it 'rolls over' through the settlement of older parts of the balance, and the longer term intentions of the parent. To the extent that the account is considered to be part of the long-term financing of the subsidiary – it should be deemed to comprise part of the parent's net investment in that subsidiary.

Long-term debt financing whether by way of a rolling current account balance or specific long-term debt, can either be in the currency of the parent, the currency of the subsidiary or in some third currency. Where it is denominated in the currency of the subsidiary it can be treated in the same way as any equity investment in that subsidiary – in effect representing a structural position of the parent in the currency of the subsidiary; the currency position itself being represented by the individual assets of that subsidiary. If it is in the currency of the parent, it comprises a liability of the subsidiary to the parent in the parent's currency. It would not be subject to periodic revaluation in the consolidated accounts of the parent but would, of course, result in a currency gain or loss to the subsidiary which would, under normal circumstances, be taken to income in the subsidiary's accounts. This is consistent with treating the subsidiary as having a separate base currency to that of the parent, and addresses the underlying commercial situation as viewed from the subsidiary's standpoint of being financed in a 'foreign currency'.

Confusion can arise in this area as it is sometimes considered that the parent can reduce its currency exposures by lending funds in its own currency rather than using the currency of its subsidiary. This is, of course, something of a mis-perception in that the exposure of the parent is essentially evidenced by the net assets of the subsidiary rather than in the way in which it chooses to finance those net assets. It can reduce that exposure by borrowing in the currency of the underlying subsidiary but not, in reality, by simply lending it funds denominated in its own base currency. The presumption underlying the subsidiary having a separate base currency is that it will need to convert the parent's financing into its own base currency for the purposes of employing it in its business. It is, accordingly, perfectly correct to record a currency gain or loss in the accounts of the subsidiary in relation to any funding by the parent which is denominated in the parent's base currency.

There are a number of ways in which a parent *can* use the funding of its subsidiary in order to reduce any exposure which might be created as a result of its investment in the subsidiary. Let us consider the case, for example, of a company which wishes to establish a trading operation (with a dollar denominated base currency) in Tokyo but is required by local statute to capitalise the local operation in yen. In order to eliminate what might otherwise be a yen exposure, the parent could arrange for any yen cash invested in the subsidiary to be lent back to the parent – thereby squaring the transaction. The underlying base currency of the subsidiary could then be designated as being US dollars with no yen exposure arising on the investment itself. The same effect could be achieved by purchasing the yen in the UK and selling it again in Tokyo, or by entering into one of the newer forms of currency swap with a financial intermediary. Whatever the route taken, the effect of the arrangement is to eliminate the exposure of the parent to any movement in the exchange rate between sterling and yen. The parent is then able to fund its subsidiary in dollars in whichever way it chooses. The borrowing from the subsidiary (or the arrangement that achieves the same result) should accordingly be treated in exactly the same way as any other borrowing against an equity investment – offsetting the gain or loss arising on both sides of the transaction against each other in reserves. The same effect could be achieved by including the borrowing in the computation of the parent's net investment in its subsidiary.

It is interesting at this point to explore the status of 'third currency borrowings', whereby either the parent or the subsidiary raises funds in a third currency to be used by the other company. If, for example, the subsidiary requires finance in a third currency, it might be able either to raise those funds directly itself or, as an alternative, do so through the parent. Assuming that the decision to fund one company via the other has nothing to do with the intercompany funding arrangements themselves, the way in which the debt is raised should not affect the accounting treatment in the consolidated group accounts. This *will* be the case unless it is erroneously treated as being part of the parent's net investment in its subsidiary – in which case the treatment could be substantially different.

Reserve accounting in the subsidiary

Whenever the subsidiary employs reserve accounting, it is necessary to monitor separately the currency revaluation impact on those reserves. The most common example of this is where properties are held at valuation in the subsidiary entity's accounts and any revaluation gains and losses are taken to a revaluation reserve.

The problem here is that one is consolidating a revaluation reserve account which is, itself, based upon a revaluation of certain of the subsidiary's assets in the appropriate base currency. The asset itself has been restated at its current revaluation in that same local base currency. The parent's net investment in its subsidiary will be a combination of the original asset cost plus the subsequent revaluation. Any gain or loss arising on that net investment in currency terms can also be analysed as between the gain or loss attributable to the original cost and that arising on the subsequent revaluation. How should the currency gain or loss on the parent's net investment in the revaluation reserve be treated?

The two alternative approaches are to take any currency gain or loss on the revaluation reserve either to the foreign currency investment translation reserve or to the revaluation reserve itself. The advantage of the former approach is that it results in the translation reserve bearing the full impact of any movements in exchange rates as applied to the parent's net investment in its subsidiary. The disadvantage is that it results in the revaluation reserve being translated at a composite rate (depending upon the rates prevailing at previous balance sheet dates) as well as leading in some cases to a mismatch between the original cost of the asset in current sterling terms and the amount of the revaluation reserve. Some argue that it is in any case, preferable to allocate the total currency adjustment arising on the underlying revaluation of the net investment between the translation reserve and the revaluation reserve, thereby ensuring that the revaluation uplift on the fixed asset is equal to the revaluation reserve in the consolidated accounts. This approach also results in the revaluation reserve being translated at the closing balance sheet rate of exchange.

Although there might be something conceptually appealing about the idea of the revaluation reserve being equal to the overall revaluation uplift, there would seem to be no real justification for treating an asset subject to revaluation any differently to any other asset. The foreign currency translation reserve should reflect the impact of the currency movements on all of the parents' net investment, irrespective as to whether or not a portion of this relates to a revalued asset. Where that net investment is hedged, for example, it would make little sense to have to allocate a portion of the hedge gain or loss to the fixed asset revaluation account. On balance it would accordingly seem preferable to allocate all of the currency gain or loss on the parent's net investment to the translation reserve, and then explain by way of the fixed asset note that a portion of the overall base currency uplift is attributable to foreign exchange and the remainder to an underlying uplift in value. The latter would, of course, then be equal to the amount shown as a movement on the revaluation reserve. This approach, which is consistent with that advocated in chapter 7 in relation to company only revaluation reserves, is the one adopted in the Example in the Reference Section.

When a revalued asset is sold, the profit on the transaction is, of course, the difference between the sales proceeds and the most recent valuation. In the same way that it will be necessary to reclassify the revaluation reserve as distributable earnings, it will also be necessary to reallocate any currency gain or loss taken to that reserve.

Statement of source and application of funds

Once the consolidated balance sheet and income statement has been prepared, there are essentially two separate ways of constructing a statement of source and application of funds.

A direct comparison of the consolidated balance sheets at the commencement and end of the reporting period will generate 'gross' movements in balance sheet items which will include, in essence, the impact of any foreign exchange movements on the subsidiary's assets and liabilities. Although this approach accordingly results in a funds flow statement which can be reconciled directly back to the profit and loss account and the balance sheet, it is somewhat misleading in that the movements identified include the exchange impacts which are, by any definition, non-cash items.

A preferred approach is, accordingly, to derive the 'net' movements by extracting from the gross movements the exchange impact on the foreign subsidiary's opening balance sheet. This is a far more complex process which entails calculating the foreign exchange impact of the rate movements over the year as applied to the subsidiary's opening balance sheet, and then adjusting the results to take account of any items already separately extracted by way of the adjustment to the foreign currency investment translation reserve.

The Example in Reference Section D includes the preparation of a statement of source and application of funds on the preferred net basis.

CHAPTER 10

Systems and controls

This present chapter explores the fundamental aspects of a multicurrency accounting system and comments upon many of the reporting formats which it might be expected to be able to produce. It discusses the alternative systems solutions to the basic problem of multicurrency accounting and suggests a number of criteria which should be taken into account in determining the preferred approach. In view of the very large number of alternative systems solutions now readily available on the market and the extremely large number of in-house 'purpose-built' systems, an attempt has been made to keep the overall discussion as general as possible. It should be recognised that some accounting systems use terminologies which may well be inconsistent with those used in this chapter.

MULTICURRENCY ACCOUNTING

Any accounting system, whether it be a sophisticated multinational mainframe-based computer system or the limited manual accounting records of the corner grocer, is perfectly capable of recording transactions in foreign ·currencies. This can be achieved simply by recording those transactions in sterling at the appropriate rate of exchange and then maintaining separate (manual) accounting records to retain the original currency information to the extent that this might be required. Such an approach, however, tends to become very quickly unworkable and prone to error so that as soon as the number of non-sterling transactions increases, a decision must be taken to establish some form of multicurrency system.

The nature of a multicurrency accounting system can range from extra cash columns in a manual ledger (to account for non-sterling bank accounts) through to comprehensive international banking packages, capable of processing numerous transactions in all of the world's currencies. The precise needs of any particular operation will be driven by the volume and nature of its foreign currency activities and the extent to which it wishes to manage its currency exposures. Some companies may choose to enhance their sterling accounting system in such a way as to be able to handle non-sterling transactions in a limited way, whereas others may opt for the alternative of a new purpose made system. In the latter case, a new system could be designed to replace all or just a portion of the present accounting system.

This section identifies some of the criteria that should be taken into account in deciding upon the optimum systems strategy for any particular company.

Corporate structure

The corporate structure and, in particular, the role of any group treasury function, will be critical in determining the system needs of the organisation. If, for example, there is a centralised treasury function responsible for managing and controlling all foreign currency exposures, and if all operating divisions are then told that they may not run any foreign currency positions themselves, it is quite likely that it will be possible to restrict the multicurrency system to the central treasury operation. The converse would be true if the treasury function operated more in the role of a corporate adviser and if local operating units were allowed to retain a certain amount of discretion in managing their own currency exposures.

It is also likely that whilst some operating units may have relatively few foreign currency transactions, others might have a large number. A centralised purchasing division, for example, might acquire goods from a large number of overseas suppliers, although group management might decide to 'bill on' those goods to individual operating divisions in sterling.

The underlying nature of any overseas operations also needs to be examined, as there is a need to determine the base currency in each case. If this is other than sterling, there needs to be a mechanism whereby the local currency financial information can be translated into sterling for reporting purposes, either in the overseas location or in the UK. If the UK operation is a subsidiary of an overseas company it may well need to maintain records in both sterling and the currency of its parent in order to address both statutory and parent company reporting requirements. Some operating units in the UK might have a base currency in, say, US dollars, and any arrangements made will have to address the need to be able to subsequently translate the dollar results into sterling for reporting purposes.

All of the above factors are likely to influence, to some degree, the extent to which the group's accounting systems need to be established on a multicurrency basis. There are no particular 'golden rules' in this area – the optimum solution essentially being a function of the way in which management wishes to control the activities of the group. The author's overall observations as to the most appropriate structure in this regard were discussed in chapter 4.

Information needs

Chapter 5 reviewed the reasons for information having to be available in both a 'consolidated' and a 'currency only' format. Consolidated information is required for periodic financial reporting, regulatory reporting and the monitoring of certain exposures. Currency information is required in order to be able to monitor currency risk – both in terms of the overall open position and any gap positions which might exist. Those requirements generally mean that any multicurrency accounting system needs to have the facility for viewing individual transactions, either on a currency or on a sterling equivalent basis. This central requirement has been a key factor in the design of multicurrency accounting systems over the course of the last decade or so.

In view of the need to monitor gap positions as well as overall open positions, there is an additional demand placed on the accounting system: that of value date recording. This is particularly true when the company has entered into forward foreign exchange contracts or other off balance sheet hedging transactions, all of which require a careful monitoring of the date on which ultimate cash settlement is to take place. The information that needs to be captured by the accounting system in the case of a simple forward foreign exchange contract, for example, is likely to include: the two currencies concerned; the amounts of each of those currencies; the implicit exchange rate; the counterparty with whom the transaction was entered into; the deal date; the value date; the broker (and sometimes the amount of brokerage); settlement instructions (generally for both sides of the transaction); and an indication as to the reason for having entered into the transaction (e g is it a hedge?). That information then needs to be able to be accessed in order to produce currency ladders, average rates, settlement details, etc. The information needs in relation to more complex hedging products can be even more onerous.

Reporting requirements

It is important to recognise that, unless a company is prepared to trade in only one currency, it is virtually impossible to eliminate all foreign exchange risks. The provision of regular and sophisticated management information on a company's exchange exposures is accordingly a fundamental contribution to management's ability to be able to control the operations of the company. The following is a brief summary of the reporting requirements which are likely to exist in a fairly large corporate environment.

1   Strategic reports

Strategic reports should be prepared on a periodic basis to assist management in determining the longer-term approach to be adopted in its management of the company's currency exposures. These are the reports which should identify any economic exposures and, in particular, any structural flows of foreign currency. Such reports should set out clearly the implications of these economic/structural exposures within the context of the company's day-to-day activities.

Strategic reports are likely to focus upon the long-term cash projections of the group in each currency, and to suggest options which may be available to cope with imbalances and/or temporary cash shortages. The majority of trading companies have some form of long-term structural cashflow and it is important for any short-term foreign exchange trading decisions to be taken in the full knowledge of the longer-term situation.

Finally, the strategic reports need to look to the future and try to identify potential changes, either in the structural relationships themselves or in external factors which might impact upon the currency exposures inherent within them.

2   Tactical reports

In most large companies it is necessary for management to receive daily reports on the company's foreign exchange positions so that rapid decisions can be taken in relation to hedging, etc. In many cases the taking of day-to-day decisions will be delegated to the corporate treasury function, but even then it is generally preferable for a periodic (perhaps weekly) report on currency positions to be circulated to senior management. The precise form of any daily tactical reporting will be a function of the nature of the company's operations and the number of foreign currency transactions. The simplest scenario might be the receipt by the chief accountant of the previous night's closing position on each overseas currency bank account, together with a summary extraction of known future currency transactions. The more sophisticated treasury functions of many larger international corporations now have real time screen dealing systems which rival many of London's international banks.

The actual content of daily tactical reports should include both overall open positions and any forward gap positions in each currency. It would be normal for such reports to compare 'end-of- day positions' with any limits established by management in relation to such positions. These reports can accordingly be seen as fulfilling something of a 'control' function – reviewing the previous day's, or previous week's, activity on an 'after-the- event' basis.

3   Operating reports

The treasury function will require certain operating reports in order to be able to control the group's exposures on an ongoing basis, and be able to control and settle those transactions which it has entered into itself. Operating reports will include summaries of all foreign currency transactions throughout the group (perhaps over a de minimis amount) including full details as to value dates etc. This information will need to be merged with the foreign exchange trading activities of the treasury area in order to obtain an overall view as to the company's positions. Such reports typically include short-term cash projections for the various currency bank accounts and foreign exchange 'ladders' setting out the value dates for all forward foreign exchange exposures. Separate reporting arrangements may be employed in relation to options trading and for any other 'non-standard' exposures.

Reports will be required each day setting out the settlement of any foreign exchange transactions previously entered into. In addition to assisting in the control of currency bank accounts such reports can also be of considerable value in the subsequent reconciliation process.

4   Other

There may be other reporting requirements, such as those dictated by the head office or outside regulatory organisations. Head office reporting in particular is now frequently a sophisticated and integral part of the world-wide management of foreign currency resources. It is important in such circumstances to ensure that there is a proper understanding of each reporting location's responsibilities, and that all those involved appreciate precisely what is being included in the definition of various currency positions.

CONTROL CONSIDERATIONS

Chapter 4 discussed the importance of a company's accounting system in terms of management's ability to control foreign exchange risk. Such risks, which we might refer to as business risks, arise whenever a company is transacting business in foreign currencies. A central objective of the accounting system is to be able to provide such information as is necessary for management to be able to control those risks in the most appropriate way.

When a company chooses actively to manage its foreign exchange exposures by entering into spot, forward and other currency hedging transactions, there are a large number of additional risks which originate from the operational side of that business activity. In the following discussion these are referred to as operational risks. Before examining business and operational risk in a little more detail, however, this section examines the crucial question as to how the corporate can be sure that all currency exposure information is being properly collated.

Data capture

Chapter 4 reviewed alternative approaches to the management of foreign currency exposure. Whatever approach is eventually adopted, a critical requirement of the unit responsible for controlling exposure is that it has as much information as is possible concerning the company's current, and prospective, currency exposures. This problem of data capture is often overlooked by those responsible for establishing centralised treasury accounting systems until too late in the implementation process. A proper understanding of the current and prospective information flows concerning currency exposure is critical to designing an effective exposure management system.

One of the most obvious areas where treasurers find difficulty in 'establishing the facts' is in terms of a group's economic exposure. Whilst it might be fairly easy, probably through empirical observation or a review of historical trends, to determine what structural currency flows exist within the group, it is far more complicated to ascertain the nature of potential interactions between the group's operational units and third parties such as competitors or suppliers.

Many treasurers even have difficulty in ensuring that they are aware of routine currency activities in some operating divisions, and there is frequently a problem in identifying potential changes in future currency flows. The only real solution to this problem tends to be an educational programme aimed at divisional management, with the objective of increasing their awareness of actual and potential currency exposure. It is then necessary for the treasurer to rely heavily on the view of his colleagues in the various operational units in building up a global view as to the group's true currency risks. Earlier mention has already been made of the tendency for general management to be fairly ill-educated on the subject of foreign exchange exposure, and this generally makes the treasurer's task even more complex than might otherwise be the case.

Data capture is also a problem in terms of the day-to-day management of the group's currency positions. There is little point implementing a sophisticated centralised treasury operation, built around the concept of managing, say, a 12-month forward cashflow profile if information on those future currency flows is not readily available from the underlying operating areas. The treasurer is likely to require timely information concerning all expected or contracted currency exposures over the future planning period on a regular basis, and this requires both an understanding in the operating units as to the nature of this requirement as well as the ability to then identify the exposures as and when they arise. The practical difficulties in this area sometimes lead large international corporates to restrict their planning horizon to, say, three months, or even a shorter period, and then to rely more heavily on the treasurer's understanding of the group's structural flows and economic exposures than might otherwise have been necessary.

The final and most immediate challenge for the designer of a group-wide currency information system is the need for day-to-day management of the group's currency positions. The treasurer needs to be provided with real time information concerning expected currency cashflows, particularly in relation to the non-receipt of expected foreign currency amounts. The systems established to accommodate these requirements may range from daily telephone calls to real time screen link-ups between unit financial controllers and the central treasury. The maintenance of centralised group-wide currency bank accounts can, of course, have a major beneficial impact in this area.

Where the centralised group treasury is charged with managing exposures on an international basis, all of the aforementioned problems of data capture are magnified a hundred fold. It becomes necessary to cope with the problems of an international trading operation in parallel with those particular difficulties associated with managing the group's currency positions. With currency markets now open 24 hours a day, the group treasurer needs to decide whether or not to continue managing positions himself or whether there should be some kind of delegated authority to other geographical areas in relation to, say, closing out large exposures arising during the course of their local trading day.

Business risks

The business risks arising from foreign currency activities have already been explored in some detail in earlier chapters. They can, however, broadly be summarised as follows:

1   Overall net position

The overall net position is defined as that position in any currency which is exposed to changes in the spot rate of exchange between that currency and sterling. The position generally comprises the net of all assets, liabilities and off balance sheet commitments (excluding any fully-hedged positions) in that currency. It excludes the 'forward points' on any forward exchange contracts or their equivalent.

2   Gap positions

Gap positions in any currency represent the mismatch in delivery dates between currency flows. A gap position is exposed to movements in forward premiums or discounts between the currency concerned and sterling.

3   Credit risk

There is, in any foreign exchange transaction, a credit risk of 'non-delivery' in exactly the same way as for any other commercial transaction. This is a risk which is of far more significance to the active trader in foreign exchange, rather than perhaps the traditional corporate treasurer who is merely hedging his currency mismatches. It is, nevertheless, an exposure which should not be forgotten. The exposure itself is the risk of default by the counterparty, and the resultant need for the company to 'close out' what is perhaps a loss-making position at new market rates.

4 Exchange control

Many corporates have learnt of the dangers of regulatory intervention in the currency markets through their own unfortunate experiences. The risk of exchange controls being either implemented or amended in some way still exists in relation to many of the world's foreign currencies, and is often extremely difficult to effectively guard against. The utilisation of trade financing arrangements, combined with effective currency hedging techniques, is generally the most satisfactory way of at least minimising the risks in this area. Such procedures are generally well understood in relation to a currency which is familiar to the company and it is, perhaps, the unusual or 'one- off' transaction which tends to present the more serious problem.

The accounting system needs to be able to assist in the management of each of the above risks by providing suitably-formatted reports setting out the group's currency positions and comparing those positions to any pre-established limits. It is likely that overall net position limits will have been established for all currencies, and certainly major trading currencies should also be subject to fairly well defined gap limits. If the treasury operation involves a fairly sizeable currency trading activity then those traders should also be subject to credit limits vis-à-vis their counterparties, whether or not the latter are recognised banks. It is not uncommon for a bank to have to turn away a foreign currency transaction with a corporate because its 'lines' to that corporate are fully utilised. It is far less unusual for the corporate to decide that its exposure towards that particular banking operation is already at such a level that it would be more prudent to complete the transaction with another counterparty. Many banks now establish daily delivery limits in relation to their inter-bank business which encompasses both their money market and foreign exchange trading activities, although such an approach may be impractical and possibly unnecessarily prudent for the majority of corporate participants in the foreign exchange markets.

Operational risks

Many of the operational risks associated with a foreign exchange trading operation are similar to those of any other corporate activity. Because of the size of the transactions, however, and the fact that many of them do not result in a cash movement for some considerable time, the implications of operational errors can be far more serious than, for example, a failure to record a sales transaction. It is also important to recognise that many operational risks within a corporate environment often extend well away from the centralised treasury area into the various operational units of the organisation. This is particularly true when the latter are responsible for committing the organisation to currency exposures – either directly, or indirectly via contract terms or sales invoices, etc.

1   Erroneous recording

The erroneous recording of a currency transaction or exposure can originate from a wide variety of sources, both inside or outside the treasury area. It encompasses problems such as the failure to record a particular exposure, errors in the contract terms, clerical errors in processing or accounting for the transactions and cut-off errors at the end of the day or an accounting period.

Addressing the risk of erroneous recording should be a central control objective of any accounting and processing system. It is, for the reasons already mentioned, particularly critical in the case of foreign currency exposures. The effectiveness of a comprehensive systems solution which satisfactorily addresses the problems of data capture can be torn apart if there are persistent errors in the recording of currency exposures. The sorts of controls that can be imposed to address these risks include the following:

(a)Segregation of duties. It is essential for there to be a proper segregation of duties as between dealers, those responsible for preparing currency contracts, paying and receiving instructions areas and accounting and reporting staff. The extent to which such segregation of duties can be introduced into a corporate treasury function is, of course, related to the overall size of the company in question and the magnitude of its foreign exchange trading. It is also virtually impossible to address the issue in a situation where responsibility for currency management is delegated to individual operating units. There are, however, a number of sensible allocations of tasks which can generally be made in order to enhance the overall control environment.

(b)Reconciliation of positions. In any dealing operation, a central element of control is the regular reconciliation of positions as between the dealers and the accounting system. This is particularly true in a foreign exchange dealing operation where a daily reconciliation of positions at the close of business should be standard practice.

(c)Confirmation checking. Virtually all banks active in the foreign exchange market issue counterparty confirmations. Some corporates now do likewise. A proper checking of inward confirmations against the internal records for each particular transaction is fundamental to the identification of potential errors in the contract terms. It is also important that the receipt of inward confirmations is properly segregated from the dealing area, thereby reducing the risk of dealer interference in the control process.

(d)Bank reconciliations. The timely reconciliation of all bank reconciliations can assist in the identification of clerical errors in processing or accounting. Although it is, by definition, an 'after the event' control it is, nevertheless, fundamental to the timely identification of, for example, errors in spot trading transactions.

(e) Sequential control. Most dealing operations impose a prenumbered sequential control over dealing tickets to address the question of cut-off problems and lost tickets, etc. Although the timely agreement of positions

as between the dealers and the accounting records can sometimes reduce the need for a sequential control of dealing tickets, it is a control which should only be dropped with extreme care.

2   *Revaluation errors*

Errors in the periodic revaluation of currency positions can originate from the use of incorrect data and the application of erroneous rates. There should be proper controls to ensure that the underlying data used for the revaluation is tied back to control totals and ultimately to the same records used for position controls. Any rates used for the revaluation process, although perhaps provided initially by the dealers, should subsequently be checked against published rates in the national press or against third parties such as banks or brokers. A fundamental control in this area is the ability of someone independent of the dealing operation to review the results of the revaluation and relate it to the trading activity for the period in question. Dealer sign-off of the periodic revaluation is essential but this does not reduce the need for an independent review of the results in order to ensure that they can be properly explained by the business activity of the period.

3   *Erroneous payment of funds*

An erroneous payment of funds can, of course, flow directly from the erroneous recording of a transaction. It can, however, also arise as a result of the unauthorised use of automated funds transfer facilities or the provision of unauthorised telex transfer instructions. The controls required to address this risk include proper dual control over the various payment facilities, the prompt reconciliation of bank accounts, the prior advice to correspondent bankers of expected payments or receipts and the regular review of outgoing telexes and other messages. Corporates should insist that their correspondent bankers do not transfer funds without properly authorised instructions and should ensure that all correspondents have an up-to-date summary of authorised signatories.

Many electronic cash management systems have sophisticated control systems governing access to them and provide the treasurer with some degree of assurance regarding their use. Such controls do not generally, however, eliminate the need for the more traditional procedures such as timely reconciliation reviews.

4   *Dealing outside limits*

Foreign exchange trading limits need to be adhered to both during the course of the day and on an overnight basis. Limits might be separately established for intra-day trading as opposed to overnight positions, but this does not obviate the need for a careful monitoring of them. The normal procedure is for intra-day limits to be monitored by a positions clerk and for the overnight position to be controlled through the production of a control report by the accounting system. Such reporting should cover all limits established by management, including overall net positions, gap positions and, where appropriate, counterparty limits. Where 'hold over' reports are used and comprise part of the sequence checks already referred to, a careful review of such reports is necessary to ensure that the effect of the transactions recorded therein does not materially impact the overall position of the company vis-à-vis either profitability or the established position limits.

5   Deal suppression

Dealers might be inclined to suppress deals where they feel that they give rise to a particularly unfavourable trading result or where they wish to trade outside of an established limit. Currency gap exposures can be disguised through the use of false tickets. The receipt of incoming confirmations, including the chasing up of outstanding ones, is critical to identifying this sort of activity. It is, of course, also important, as mentioned previously, to ensure that such confirmations are not received direct by the dealers. There should also be a review of all amended or cancelled deals by someone independent of the dealing activity, particularly those deals which appear to have a 'back value date' impact. Foreign exchange trading losses can easily be disguised by processing a number of erroneous tickets on the last day of the month only to reverse them after the month-end, prior to the real transactions being confirmed by the counterparty.

6   Dealing for personal gain

The risk of foreign exchange traders dealing for personal gain has long existed in the currency market. Management should, in general, ensure that no dealing 'on own account' is permitted and that the dealers are not authorised signatories of the group. Most cases of dealer fraud involve the extraction of funds from the company concerned and the sorts of controls already discussed should ensure that the risk of this is reduced. Another area where management should be concerned is that of 'broker's bribes', whereby a particular money broker encourages a corporate to put all of its business through itself by the provision of gifts or cash to the dealers. This is an extremely difficult problem to identify other than through a review of brokerage payments to ensure that a wide range of brokers is being used. Some companies go out of their way to establish a good understanding with a particular broker but senior management should be properly appraised of the nature of the relationship and understand the benefits perceived by the dealers in developing it.

7   Other

There are various other risks such as the integrity of data files, EDP processing controls, etc – most of which are not peculiar to foreign exchange transactions. The controls required in the foreign exchange area in relation to these risks are essentially similar to those for other business transactions.

ACCOUNTING SYSTEMS

The need for sophisticated accounting systems in a multicurrency accounting environment is driven primarily by the control considerations and information needs already discussed. In order to address the reporting requirements of management in terms of exposure control, profitability evaluation, etc it is necessary to have far more information readily available from the accounting system than might otherwise be the case.

The traditional approach to 'coping' with foreign currency transactions was to establish 'memorandum accounts' which were used to monitor balances denominated in any particular foreign currency. This allowed for a crude evaluation of the size of any currency position and an indication, at the end of the day, as to how a particular currency gain or loss may have

---

Dual currency accounting

Dual currency accounting systems developed from the traditional approach of maintaining memoranda records of foreign currency transactions. The approach initially involves opening a separate ledger account for each balance sheet item where a second currency is required. If, for example, a UK company maintained currency bank accounts in US$ and DM as well as in £, and incurred costs in DM whilst receiving some revenues in US$, it would need to open accounts as follows:

Cash	— £ balance
Cash	— DM balance
Cash	— $ balance
Receivables	— £ amounts
Receivables	— $ amounts
Payables	— £ amounts
Payables	— DM amounts

Each of the non-sterling accounts above would have two balances attaching to them: an underlying currency amount and a sterling equivalent. The sterling equivalents would form part of the overall self-balancing sterling ledger, whereas the currency amounts would be in the nature of memorandum entries.

The rate used to derive the sterling equivalent of any currency amount would be a standard, or 'par', rate which would probably be changed on a periodic (perhaps monthly) basis. Any differences between that rate and the actual rate applying to the transaction would be taken to a currency 'unders and overs' expense account.

At any balance sheet accounting date it is necessary to revalue all of the underlying currency items into sterling at the prevailing balance sheet rate and the net result, taken together with the balance on the 'unders and overs' account will then be taken to P/L as a currency gain or loss. The other side of the entry to P/L will either be held in the balance sheet as a currency suspense account or (if the standard rates are amended to the new rates at the same time) could be allocated against the £ equivalents of the various currency balances.

Advantages of a dual currency accounting system include the maintenance of double entry within a single currency ledger without using a self-balancing 'plug' position account, together with the ease with which consolidated £ balance sheets can be produced. The disadvantages are fairly self-evident and are discussed briefly in the main text.

originated. Such an approach is, however, totally inappropriate as soon as the volume of currency transactions increased beyond a nominal level.

The first organisations to recognise the need for a more sophisticated approach to foreign exchange accounting were the international banks which moved into London during the late sixties and early seventies. Whereas some of the larger institutions tended to simply try to create 'mega memoranda accounts' the smaller organisations experimented with systems (frequently run on visible record computers) which came to be known as dual currency accounting systems. Some international banking packages today still utilise this original concept: essentially a sophisticated development of the earlier memorandum account approach.

As systems analysts became involved in trying to resolve the problem of foreign exchange accounting, at a time when exchange rate volatility demanded a far greater degree of control than might hitherto have been the case, the concept of multicurrency accounting was developed. Multicurrency accounting (or multiple currency accounting, as it is sometimes known) allowed for far more control over currency positions and provided for an easier approach to the periodic revaluation of those positions. The approach also tended to utilise less storage capacity than the dual currency accounting system previously employed.

The majority of accounting systems now used to process foreign currency transactions utilise a multicurrency accounting approach.

Multicurrency accounting overview

In a multicurrency accounting system, there is essentially a completely separate ledger system for each natural currency in which the company wishes to record transactions. Each of these currency ledgers is self-balancing through the use of a 'position account', sometimes referred to as a 'currency buffer account'. There may be any number of such accounts in a particular system, each being used for specific purposes, but the overall concept remains essentially the same.

Currency assets and liabilities are recorded as such in the appropriate currency ledgers, whereas any cross-currency transaction is recorded in the two appropriate ledgers via the position account. If, for example, the company were to purchase a US dollar security in exchange for a payment in sterling, one would record the US dollar asset in the dollar ledger, the reduction in sterling cash would be recorded in the sterling ledger and both ledgers would be made to balance by entries to their respective position accounts.

The concept underlying a multicurrency accounting system is that the position account or accounts should reflect the underlying position in the currency in question, thereby providing a straightforward indication of the size of those positions as well as facilitating the periodic revaluation process. Many systems utilise the fact that the position account is equal and opposite to the net assets and liabilities in that currency, to facilitate a daily spot revaluation. Such an approach reduces the need to revalue all assets and liabilities on a daily basis and can significantly increase the efficiency of such systems.

A multicurrency accounting system continues to embody the idea of double entry but there is generally a need for extremely tight controls over the use of the various position accounts which are, of course, the 'other side' of any currency transaction. Any imbalance in a currency ledger should be treated with extreme caution as it might indicate a one-sided posting within the system.

The general ledger for the company has to be produced by aggregating the various currency balances for each particular ledger account. This involves the application of spot exchangé rates to those currency balances whenever a general ledger run is produced. Although the resulting balance sheet is a product of the accounting system, the balances shown therein are not usually maintained on the system in a separately identifiable form. Arrangements for aggregating balances within the income statement vary from system to system but most require a periodic 'selling off' of accumulated profits or losses in each particular currency. The 'sell-off' is into the base currency (sterling) and results, in itself, in a movement across their respective position accounts.

Where a company has off balance sheet currency commitments it is necessary to control those commitments in a separate ledger. That ledger is used to generate further accounting entries on the ultimate value date of the transactions concerned and, in the meantime, is taken into account by the system for revaluation purposes. The commitment positions need to be aggregated with balance sheet positions for reporting and control purposes. For this reason there is usually a separate position account for forward foreign exchange contracts, which can be aggregated with the rest of the balance sheet for revaluation and position monitoring purposes, but which can be treated as being off balance sheet at other times. With this exception, the forward position accounts operate in essentially the same way as those for the balance sheet. Further ledgers and, where necessary, additional position accounts, are likely to be employed where the company is entering into contingent type arrangements such as currency options. The approach is, however, essentially the same, with the position account acting as a balancing item and a 'cross-currency buffer' in each case. The use of option position accounts can be somewhat more complex than those relating to forward transactions, due to the additional complexity of the product.

Systems selection

This book does not set out to be a guide to selecting an appropriate multicurrency accounting system, because it is recognised that there will be fundamental differences in the requirements of different organisations. It is also important to recognise that the systems solution in any particular case must be driven, as already mentioned, by policy decisions concerning the management of exchange exposures.

A fundamental decision to be taken is whether or not to establish group-wide accounting systems on a multicurrency basis or whether the focus of management's attention on currency exposures should be in the group treasury area. The latter can result in the need for currency data in individual operating units being somewhat more limited. It may, of course, still be necessary to establish detailed currency ledgers for items such as sales, for example, but this need only produce information which then feeds directly into a group-wide treasury accounting system.

The decision as to which system to install for a centralised treasury operation is also far from straightforward. Some corporates opt to employ one of the small international banking packages now available on the market, while others choose, instead, to develop their own in-house solutions, with the advantage of being able to address any particular local requirements. Whatever the approach adopted, the essential prerequisite is to be totally clear on the ultimate objectives of the system and to ensure that it is compatible with the policy decisions already taken by management.

Reference section

INTRODUCTION

A. FOREIGN EXCHANGE PRODUCTS

B. TRANSACTION ACCOUNTING

C. BALANCE SHEET TRANSLATION

D. CONSOLIDATIONS

Introduction

This section of the book has been constructed in such a way as to provide the reader with a ready reference guide to accounting for foreign exchange. It does not attempt to repeat the ground covered in the earlier chapters, but seeks to explain the way in which any particular transaction should generally be accounted for.

In view of the large number of complex hedging products now available, it is not possible to cover every conceivable form of hedging arrangement in the examples set out in this section. The approach is, instead, to discuss, in section A, the more common products currently available, and then to explore, in sections B and C, how these products can be used in different circumstances. Section B addresses the question of transaction accounting and therefore covers the use of various foreign currency products for the purposes of transaction hedging. Section C deals with balance sheet translation and reviews the way in which these hedging products can be applied in the management of currency exposure. Section D contains a detailed example of a multicurrency consolidation which demonstrates the concepts discussed in the text.

This section of the book does not attempt to substantiate the recommended accounting approach, and the reader is referred to earlier chapters for an explanation as to the reason for particular approaches being adopted. In particular, transaction accounting is discussed in chapter 7, balance sheet translation accounting in chapter 8, and consolidations in chapter 9.

Foreign exchange products

Introduction

Chapter 2 discussed the operation of the foreign exchange market and, in particular, the relationship between spot exchange rates and forward rates. The detailed discussion in that chapter is not repeated in this section.

The following pages set out to describe the more common foreign exchange products now available in the market, commenting upon their availability, their pricing characteristics and reviewing some of their potential uses. It should be recognised that there are today a large number of tailor-made currency hedging arrangements available in the market and that it is not possible, in the space available, to attempt to cover anything other than the 'generic' groups of products commonly encountered. In most cases, it is possible to treat any more sophisticated currency hedging arrangement as being a derivative of one or more of the products listed in this section. Careful consideration as to the structure of any such arrangement and the way in which it can be 'broken down' into its constituent parts should ensure that a fairly sound understanding of its nature can be obtained. In any non-standard transaction it is, in the author's view, always essential to ensure that one understands the pricing of the transaction prior to being in a position to account for it.

Apart from the fairly straightforward 'cash-based' foreign exchange products such as spot currency purchases or sales, it is possible to consider most hedging arrangements as fitting into one of three categories: those built around a forward commitment to exchange currency; those involving an option by one party or the other in relation to a particular exchange of currency; and the so-called 'third generation' products which tend to be option-based derivatives of some of the more standard products. Whereas commitment products can generally be used for both transaction hedging and translation hedging, the most common use of option based products is probably in the area of transaction hedging.

A.1 Spot purchase or sale

Spot purchases or sales of a foreign currency, or between two separate foreign currencies, may be effected either automatically, as a result of a standing instruction with the company's bankers, or as a result of a decision made by the company to effect a transfer of funds between separate currency accounts. A similar transaction takes place if a company asks its banker to make a foreign currency payment out of its sterling funds or, for example, to present it with a foreign currency denominated bill of exchange, etc. The rate applicable to the exchange of currency will be based upon the currently prevailing spot rate, but is likely to vary from that rate as a result of the precise nature of the transaction and the actual amounts involved. The buy/sell rates quoted on the foreign exchange market are generally for standard amounts of currency between inter-bank participants, and the rate is generally not quite so favourable in the case of non-standard amounts of currency or where a corporate counterparty is involved.

A pure spot foreign exchange contract requires settlement two business days after the date of the transaction. The form that this settlement takes will depend upon the underlying nature of the transaction itself. Settlement may occur in the home country of the company entering into the transaction, or in some other country or may, as is often the case, be split – with the delivery taking place in one location and the receipt in another.

Most banks issue standard counterparty confirmations for all spot foreign exchange transactions carried out and many corporates now ask that this be done by way of telex. If a company is utilising a comprehensive cash management system (see chapter 4) it is likely that the spot foreign exchange deals will either be carried out automatically or via a computer link between the customer and the bank.

For a more detailed discussion of spot foreign exchange trading, the reader is referred to chapter 2.

A.2   Same-day/next-day spot purchase or sale

Although the spot market operates on a standard two-day settlement basis, it is possible to enter into transactions which involve same-day or 'next-day' settlement. In such cases, the spot rate of exchange prevailing at the time will be adjusted by the bank undertaking the transaction, to take account of the implicit 'interest effect' between the settlement date and the 'two days forward' date.

There is generally little demand for same-day or next-day settlement transactions other than where the currency concerned is particularly illiquid or where there is some reason to suspect that, for example, foreign exchange controls might be imposed within the next two days. Most banks are prepared to consider dealing for same-day or next-day settlement, but generally the customer is unlikely to be any better off than if they were to pay overdraft charges on any shortfall of funds in a particular currency, and offset that cost with the interest on the compensating currency. The adjustment made by the banks for the early settlement often more than offsets the interest differential incurred by the company in running the mismatch position.

COMMITMENT-TYPE PRODUCTS

A.3 Forward transactions

The operation of the forward market and the way in which forward transactions are priced is discussed extensively in chapter 2. The price of a standard inter-bank forward transaction will be a function of the spot price then prevailing and the interest differential between the two currencies concerned over the period of the forward commitment. This adjustment to the forward price is known as the premium or discount applied to the transaction. Most banks are prepared to quote forward exchange rates between the majority of commonly-traded foreign currencies and their own currency, and a good many are prepared to quote rates between two separate foreign currencies.

The extent to which banks trade the forward markets varies substantially, however, and there can be fairly noticeable pricing differentials between a 'market maker' and a bank which is not traditionally active in that particular market.

It should be recognised that if a corporate enters into, say, a Deutschmark/Swiss franc forward transaction with a small UK-based bank, it will be necessary for that bank to enter into a number of transactions in order to hedge out its position. At a minimum it is likely to enter into two separate forward transactions, between Deutschmarks and US dollars and between Swiss francs and US dollars. Furthermore, if the forward cover is for a 'non-standard' period, it is still likely to retain some residual exposure. A large market maker in the forward markets of the currencies concerned is much more likely to be able to off-load the exposure in an efficient way and is, accordingly, going to be more ready to 'find a rate' on the overall transaction.

The forward market tends to discriminate against corporate counterparties and non-standard size transactions in the same way as the spot market. In addition, however, there is generally a discrimination against 'non-standard dates' whenever the forward date of the transaction does not coincide with one of the more normal periods used by the market – eg one month, three months, six months, etc. It is also likely that any cross-currency transactions not involving, for example, sterling or US dollars would be likely to cost a little more than the straightforward arithmetic derivation of the individual currency rates against either sterling or dollars would indicate. All of these differences reflect the greater complexity which will be experienced by the banking counterparty in hedging out the exposure created by the forward transaction.

No premium or fee is generally payable in relation to a forward transaction and the only evidence of the deal tends to be the counterparty confirmation traditionally issued by the bank. Where a corporate chooses to use a broker to effect the transaction, it is likely that it will also receive a statement from the broker setting out the basic details of the transaction.

Settlement will take place on the 'value date' and at the rate specified in the forward transaction. The considerations as to the location of that settlement are the same as in the case of a spot transaction. It is generally not possible to have a value date which is on a non-business day in the location of ultimate settlement, although it is often possible to make special settlement arrangements in particular cases should the need arise. The cost of such arrangements, however, can sometimes be fairly substantial.

No example has been included to demonstrate the pricing of a forward foreign exchange transaction because a detailed example was included in chapter 2. The reader is referred to page 24.

A.4   Long-dated forward transactions

A long-dated forward transaction is any forward deal extending beyond 12 months. Because of the interaction of the euro-currency markets and the forward foreign exchange markets (see chapter 2) it was, until fairly recently, quite difficult to arrange long-dated forward foreign exchange transactions. These are, however, now fairly commonplace in most of the main currencies and are increasingly available in some of the second-tier currencies. The extent to which it is possible to arrange a long-dated contract will generally depend upon the liquidity of the fixed-rate international debt markets in that currency. Although, in some cases, it may be possible for a bank undertaking such a transaction to find a counterparty with an opposite hedging requirement, the most likely way in which it will eliminate its exposure will be through the utilisation of the long-term fixed rate debt markets. The increasing number of currency exchange agreements (see section A.8) now being entered into, has substantially increased the liquidity of the long-dated forward markets, and it now appears that in some currencies the long-dated fixed-rate debt markets, the long-dated forward currency markets and the volume of currency exchange agreements are all growing together and generating increased liquidity in each other.

The pricing of a long-dated forward transaction is similar to that of a forward deal, but needs to take account of the compounding effect of interest. This will, in most cases, be assumed by the pricing of the transaction to arise on at least an annual basis. Some pricing arrangements work on the assumption of a six-monthly interest flow as this is the way in which it is likely that the forward position can be closed out by the banking counterparty.

Most of the issues relating to forward foreign exchange contracts are also of relevance in relation to long-dated forwards. It is far more important to utilise a banking counterparty which is active in the market, and most corporates should generally consider alternative hedging arrangements as a means of verifying the reasonableness of the rate being quoted. It might well, for example, be cheaper to enter into a series of appropriate debt-related transactions than, in effect, to use a bank as an intermediary to do likewise. This can be particularly true in some of the less common currencies.

Pricing long-dated forward transactions

There are numerous ways of pricing a long-dated forward foreign exchange transaction, depending upon the method most likely to be used in hedging the position so created.

The following is one of the more straightforward means of calculating the price of a three-year forward US$/Sw fr exchange transaction.

If we assume a three-year US$ interest rate of 7% and a three-year Sw fr rate of 3%, then, with a current spot rate of, say, 1.5550, the forward rate can be calculated as follows:

	US $	Sw fr
Assumed principal	10,000,000	15,550,000
Interest for 1st year	700,000	466,500
Interest reinvested	49,000	13,995
Interest for 2nd year	700,000	466,500
Available at end of 2nd year	1,449,000	946,995
Interest reinvested	101,430	28,410
Interest for 3rd year	700,000	466,500
Available at end of 3rd year	2,250,430	1,441,905
Total Principal + interest	12,250,430	16,991,905

Dividing one into the other produces the forward rate of 1.3870. When compared with the spot rate of 1.5550 this produces a 'swap rate' (see chapter 2) of 0.1680 or 1680 points.

A.5 Rollover transactions

The term rollover is used in the foreign exchange market to describe an overnight swap. In other words it is a transaction entered into by a bank to 'roll over' a particular currency position into the next day. If, for example, today is Monday, a rollover might be either Monday – Tuesday or Tuesday – Wednesday, the spot date itself being of course Wednesday. The objective of a rollover in this context is the short-term management of day-to-day currency liquidity by the bank using same-day or next-day spot transactions.

The form of rollover found in the corporate sector is totally different and involves a methodology whereby it is sometimes possible to extend the commitment period of a currently outstanding forward transaction into the future. Many banks now refuse to enter into such rollover transactions as they have been used in the past to 'manipulate' corporate results.

If a company has entered into a forward transaction which is due to mature on a particular date, but decides that it wishes to extend the hedge into the future, this can be done in essentially one of two ways. Either the forward transaction can be allowed to mature with the company entering into a spot transaction to close out the position and then undertaking a new forward transaction to reinstate the future commitment date; or, alternatively, it 'rolls over' the forward transaction with the banking counterparty to the new future date desired. When the latter course of action is undertaken, the bank will impose a revised rate on the transaction which will take account of the 'alternative performance' costs of arranging the spot transaction to close out the position and entering into a new forward deal to reopen the commitment period. The costs of the latter two transactions are, in effect, 'rolled into' the pricing of the forward transaction.

This facility has, in the past, been used to advantage by some corporates who have chosen to 'roll over' what are perceived to be loss-making hedging positions into a future accounting period, and then to argue that the hedging arrangement related to a future transaction which has not yet been consummated. If for example, the company traditionally hedges its future receipts of US dollar revenue by way of forward sales of dollars into sterling, it might choose to enter into forward dollar sales on an ongoing basis in order to hedge, perhaps, its next 12 months' expected flows of revenues. If, towards the end of an accounting period, the US dollar strengthens against sterling, the hedged transaction itself will be showing a loss. It is possible, in such circumstances, for the company, for example, to effect a spot sale of its last quarter's US dollar revenue (thereby recording a greater amount of sterling revenue than would otherwise have been the case), whilst at the same time effecting a 'roll over' of the forward transaction into the following accounting period at a rate which was quite clearly penal to the company at that time. As the new foreign exchange contract would bear a trade date towards the end of the current accounting period, and as the company traditionally entered into forward foreign exchange contracts to cover future flows of US dollar revenue, it might be extremely difficult for an outsider, such as an auditor, to identify that the outstanding contract existing at the end of the accounting period actually included certain hedging costs which would more properly have been recognised in that period's income.

Some companies enter into short-term rollovers where they have slightly miscalculated the timing of expected cashflows, and it is frequently cheaper for them to adopt this course of action than to incur the costs of a spot transaction and a new forward. Although such an approach might be acceptable if it does not extend over the end of an accounting period, it does have certain implications for the treatment of the hedge and the way in which any transaction being hedged is subsequently accounted for. This matter is explored further in section B.5 below.

Example of a rollover transaction

A company enters into a three-month forward sale of Deutschmarks against US dollars when the spot rate for the DM is 1.8340. Let us assume that interest rate differentials are such that the three-month forward rate at that time is 1.8235 and that the deal is for DM 10 million.

If, in two months time, the company becomes aware that it will now not be in a position to sell the Deutschmarks for a further three months, then it may decide to 'rollover' its outstanding forward commitment.

Let us examine the arithmetic underlying that transaction assuming that, at the time:

(a) the one month forward rate is 1.8175; and
(b) the three month forward rate is now 1.8125.

	US $	DM
Outstanding commitments at 1.8235	5,483,960	(10,000,000)
Theoretical close-out of Commitment at 1 month forward rate of 1.8175	(5,502,063)	10,000,000
Reinstatement of 3 months forward commitment at 1.8125	5,517,241	(10,000,000)
Effective rate thus	5,499,138	(10,000,000)

The above suggests an effective rate of 1.8185 (10,000,000 divided by 5,499,138) and it is accordingly that rate which would be used for the purposes of the replacement forward deal.

All that has happened in the above is that the bank undertaking the transaction has 'rolled' the loss on closing out the current position into the determination of the rate used for the new transaction.

The resultant rate is an 'off-market rate' which would result in an immediate loss of $18,103 if the company attempted to close it out.

It should be noted that in performing the above calculation the bank would in reality also take account of bid/offer spreads and probably add in a 'fee' for issuing a contract at a non-market rate. For larger amounts or longer periods, one would also take account of the interest cost of any deferred loss.

A.6 Currency futures

Chapter 2 contains a general overview of the development of the world-wide currency futures markets. That chapter notes that currency futures have not, in general, experienced the substantial growth seen in certain other futures markets, largely because of the efficiency of the forward foreign exchange markets. Currency futures are, however, now traded on a variety of exchanges around the world to a greater or lesser extent, and do provide an alternative means of hedging currency exposures. Recent regulatory moves in the US and the UK are likely to result in increasing use being made of the currency futures markets, and the recent growth of composite currency futures, such as the dollar index future, have no direct competition in the forward market. In general, however, currency futures are considered to be less versatile than the forward markets, because they have fixed settlement dates, predetermined contract amounts and, of course, a daily margining requirement. The latter can often result in additional operational complications, as well as requiring considerably more monitoring of exposures than many companies have become accustomed to.

Currency futures traded around the globe

The following are the main currency futures contracts available on the major exchanges around the world at the time of writing. All contracts are against US$ and denominated in the currency concerned unless otherwise stated.

Mid-America Commodity Exchange
£12,500; DM62,500; yen 6.25 m; Sw fr 62,500; C$50,000;

Chicago Mercantile Exchange
£25,000; DM125,000; Sw fr 125,000; ECU125,000; Fr fr 250,000; yen 12.5 m; C$100,000; A$100,000;

Philadelphia Stock Exchange
£12,500; DM62,500; yen 6.25 m; Sw fr 62,500; Fr fr 125,000; C$50,000; ECU62,500; US$ Index;

New York Cotton Exchange
ECU100,000; US$ Index;

London International Financial Futures Exchange
£25,000; yen 12.5 m; DM125,000 (also traded in US$50,000 lots); Sw fr 125,000;

Toronto Futures Exchange
C$ in US$100,000 units;

Sydney Futures Exchange
A$ in US$100,000 units;

New Zealand Futures Exchange
NZ$ in US$50,000 units;

Singapore International Monetary Exchange
yen 12.5 m; DM125,000.

Currency futures are in general traded against the US dollar in fixed amounts of the foreign currency concerned. In some cases trading is against the foreign currency with the US dollar amount being fixed. The exchange on which each particular currency future is traded determines in advance the delivery months and delivery dates in each delivery month, covering a future period of up to approximately 18 months.

In London, the London International Financial Futures Exchange ('LIFFE') has contracts for £25,000, Sw fr 125,000, yen 12.5 m and DM125,000. DM/US$ is also traded in units of US$ 50,000. The standard contract specifies delivery of the currency concerned in the principal financial centre in which that currency is traded. Delivery dates are determined as being the second Wednesday of each delivery month, or the next business day, if that Wednesday is a non-business day in the delivery centre concerned. The delivery months for these contracts are March, June, September and December, with five delivery months being traded at any one point in time. An initial margin is payable for each contract entered into of US$1,500, or the currency equivalent thereof. Variation margin is payable at the close of business each day on the basis of a mark-to-market revaluation of the net profit or loss on all open contracts.

All of the futures exchanges require the prompt payment of variation margins on losses, whereas the processing of profits tends to vary slightly from exchange to exchange. Settlement is usually on a net basis – netting open profits and losses against each other, and most exchanges require that where their members are trading on behalf of a third party, they must also collect margins from those third parties. Although margins are often paid in cash, and are subject to interest, it is also possible to comply with margin calls by depositing either securities or guarantees with the clearing house concerned. The objective of the margining process is to ensure that neither the clearing house nor the other members of the exchange suffer losses in the event of a trader defaulting on a particular transaction.

Dealing on the exchange is generally limited to members, and there is frequently a limitation on the total number of members. On some exchanges this has had the effect of substantially increasing the cost of an exchange seat. All trading is carried out by 'open outcry' on the floor of the exchange and, of course, commission is generally payable by non-member participants to the members operating on their behalf in a broking capacity. Commission rates are now fairly standard for similar-sized transactions, although it is sometimes possible to negotiate a 'bulk discount' depending on trading volumes.

The impact of regulatory changes in the US and the UK in relation to the forward foreign exchange markets should, on balance, make futures transactions marginally more competitive. This will be particularly true in relation to the longer-dated transactions. It remains to be seen whether or not this will increase the use made of futures transactions in the corporate sector, or whether it will encourage the introduction of longer dated contracts on the exchanges.

A.7 Currency·swaps: Introduction

One of the most impressive phenomena in the capital markets over recent years has been the enormous growth in the volume of capital market swaps. The major part of that volume now consists of interest rate swaps, a large percentage of which are cross-currency. The swap market has its origins, however, in the currency swaps entered into during the latter part of the 1970s as an alternative means to effecting what had by then become known as 'back-to-back loans' or 'parallel loans'. These arrangements between international corporates had often been entered into either in order to avoid UK exchange controls, or as a means of getting round what was otherwise seen as the damaging impact of the then US Accounting Standard, SFAS 8.

Although interest rate swaps developed out of currency swaps, they should, in theory, probably have predated them in evolutionary terms. The simplest form of interest rate swap is the coupon swap, which is an exchange of two different forms of interest flows within the same currency. The most obvious example of this is the 'fixed to floating' swaps which developed out of the recognition that different companies had different borrowing strengths in the capital markets. This concept of 'comparative advantage' has become even more pronounced over the last few years as a large number of corporate borrowers have been 'squeezed out' of the fixed rate capital markets by the increasing borrowing requirements of governments and their agencies. The typical fixed to floating interest rate swap involves a 'lesser credit' corporate which finds itself virtually unable to obtain realistically priced long-term fixed rate funds, 'swapping' its obligation to make floating rate payments with a more creditworthy institution (traditionally perhaps a bank) which is better able to gain longer-term fixed rate financing — probably through the bond markets.

There are many other forms of coupon swaps now available in the market, including basis swaps (where there is an exchange, for example, between a LIBOR and a prime based interest flow) or gap swaps (involving flows of interest on mis-matched dates). This book does not hold itself out as being a comprehensive work on capital market swaps and the following sections accordingly concentrate on cross-currency swaps rather than interest rate swaps. For more information on the overall subject of capital market swaps, the reader is referred to the excellent work, *Price & Henderson Currency and Interest Rate Swaps (Butterworths)*.

The nature of the swap market is such that there are now a large number of tailor-made arrangements available – sometimes with extremely complex pricing details and very sophisticated hedging arrangements being arranged by the banking counterparties. Most swaps are now entered into with either banks or security houses, with the latter either temporarily absorbing the exposure, amalgamating it with the rest of their foreign exchange and interest rate exposures, running a self-contained 'swap warehouse', or acting as a temporary holder of the position and seeking an appropriate counterparty either to match or partially match it. Many swaps are carried out between financial institutions in order to 'lay off' exposures

The evolution of currency swaps

Swaps evolved from parallel and back-to-back loans. Those two forms of financing arrangement can best be explained diagrammatically (see below).

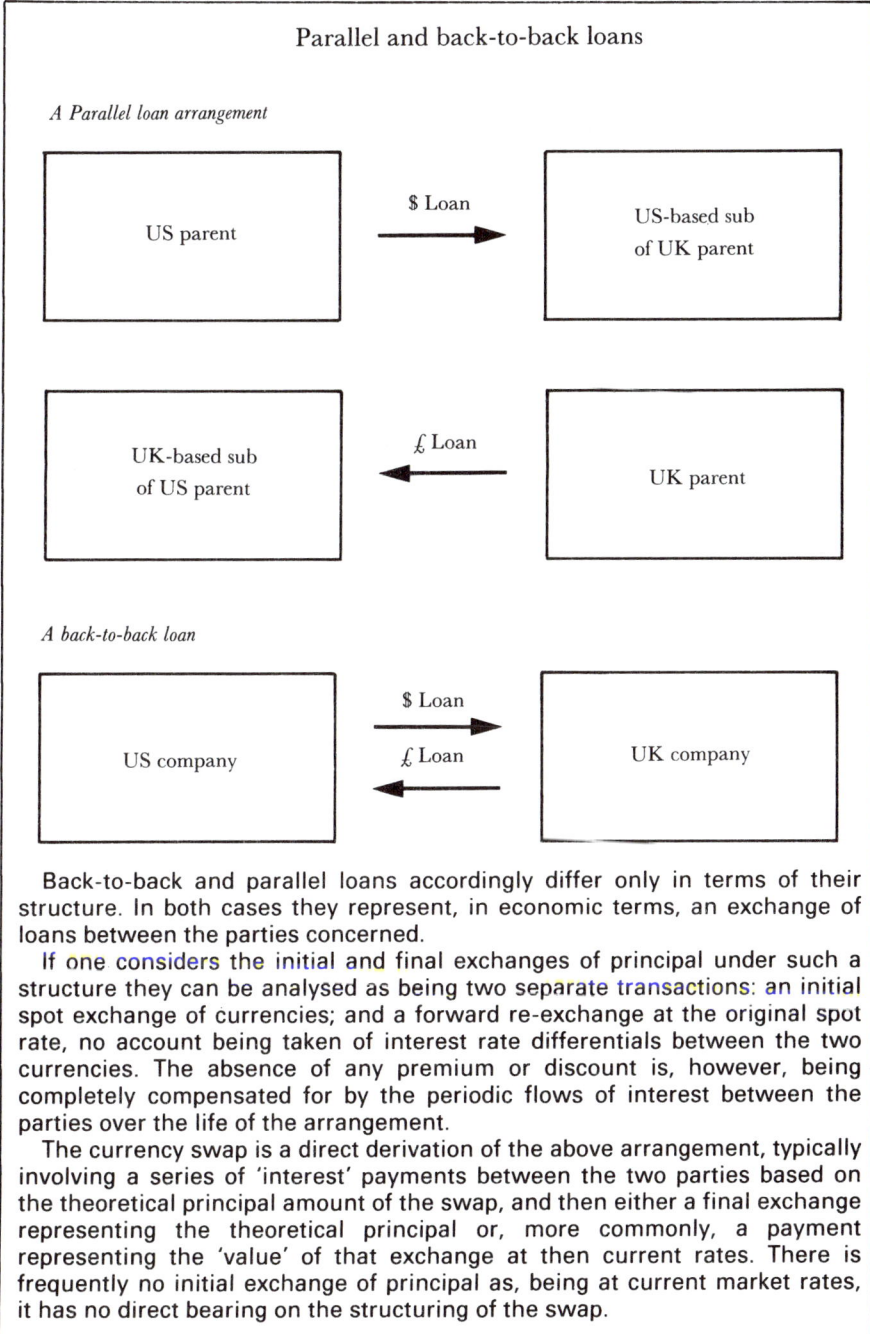

Parallel and back-to-back loans

A Parallel loan arrangement

	$ Loan →	
US parent		US-based sub of UK parent

	← £ Loan	
UK-based sub of US parent		UK parent

A back-to-back loan

	$ Loan →	
US company	£ Loan ←	UK company

Back-to-back and parallel loans accordingly differ only in terms of their structure. In both cases they represent, in economic terms, an exchange of loans between the parties concerned.

If one considers the initial and final exchanges of principal under such a structure they can be analysed as being two separate transactions: an initial spot exchange of currencies; and a forward re-exchange at the original spot rate, no account being taken of interest rate differentials between the two currencies. The absence of any premium or discount is, however, being completely compensated for by the periodic flows of interest between the parties over the life of the arrangement.

The currency swap is a direct derivation of the above arrangement, typically involving a series of 'interest' payments between the two parties based on the theoretical principal amount of the swap, and then either a final exchange representing the theoretical principal or, more commonly, a payment representing the 'value' of that exchange at then current rates. There is frequently no initial exchange of principal as, being at current market rates, it has no direct bearing on the structuring of the swap.

generated in the primary market, and an increasing number of corporates are now involved in 'trading' their swap positions in an effort to optimise their funding arrangements, etc. Some companies have been able to generate fairly substantial revenues as a result of the accounting treatment employed for certain of their swap exposures.

The next three sections briefly examine the three general types of cross-currency swap under the headings of 'fixed to fixed', 'floating to floating', and 'fixed to floating'. The reader should, however, recognise that these are only general groupings of these transactions and that there are, as already mentioned, numerous variations on these general concepts.

A.8   Fixed to fixed cross-currency swaps

The standard textbook scenario for a fixed to fixed cross-currency swap involves the two parties to the transaction having undertaken borrowings in particular currencies which they have now decided are not the currencies in which they would have preferred to have raised the funding. The reasons for their raising the financing in the currencies concerned, however, might have been dictated by the familiarity of their name in those particular capital markets, regulatory considerations, historic reasons or similar factors. The structure of a fixed to fixed cross-currency swap can be depicted as follows:

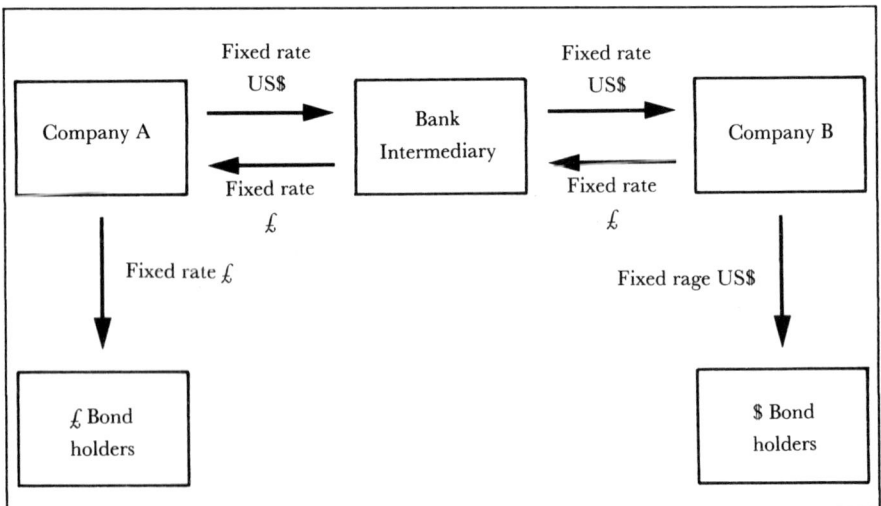

This sort of arrangement is frequently referred to as a currency exchange agreement because the documentation can be structured around a spot exchange of currency, a forward re-exchange of the same amounts of currency and periodic payments over the life of the transaction which take account of the interest differentials between the theoretical principal amounts.

In order to explore the pricing of such a transaction, it is necessary to examine the cashflows arising over the course of the arrangement. For the purposes of illustration, we shall consider a three-year US$/Sw fr fixed rate swap involving annual interest payments and, in the interests of simplicity, ignoring any 'external' transactions, such as the underlying debt, if any, issued by those companies.

Assumed principals: US$10 million and Sw fr 15,550,000.
Current spot rate of exchange: 1.5550.
Assumed interest rates: 7% for US$ and 3% for Sw fr.

	COMPANY A		COMPANY B	
	US$	Sw fr	US$	Sw fr
Initial exchange	(10,000,000)		10,000,000	
		15,550,000		(15,550,000)
End of 1st year	700,000		(700,000)	
		(466,500)		466,500
End of 2nd year	700,000		(700,000)	
		(466,500)		466,500
End of 3rd year	700,000		(700,000)	
		(466,500)		466,500
Re-exchange at end of 3rd year	10,000,000		(10,000,000)	
		(15,550,000)		15,550,000

The cashflow on the initial exchange can be said to have no 'value' to either party to the transaction, in that the exchange is carried at the then current spot rate of exchange. It would, in other words, be possible to dispose of the funds again if not required at no cost. The transactions with value or potential value are, accordingly, the three annual interest flows and the re-exchange at the end of the third year. If one were to show a 'reinvestment profile' of these cashflows using the interest rates applying to the underlying theoretical principal, it would produce exactly the same results as the example in section A.4 on the pricing of a long-dated forward transaction.

If the swap involves assumed interest rates at current market rates, the cashflows inherent in the transaction can be thought of as having no 'value' to either participant. Let us assume, however, that current Sw fr interest rates are at 4%, and compare the cashflows in the 3% swap with those under a 4% swap. Although the US dollar interest flows would remain the same, those for Swiss francs would increase. The position from the standpoint of Company A can be summarised as follows:

	US$	Sw fr at 3%	Sw fr at 4%
End of 1st year	700,000	(466,500)	(622,000)
Investment at 7%/3%/4%	49,000	(13,995)	(24,880)
End of 2nd year	700,000	(466,500)	(622,000)
	1,449,000	(946,995)	(1,268,880)
Investment at 7%/3%/4%	101,430	(28,410)	(50,755)
End of 3rd year	700,000	(466,500)	(622,000)
	2,250,430	(1,441,905)	(1,941,635)
Re-exchange	10,000,000	(15,550,000)	(15,550,000)
	12,250,430	(16,991,905)	(17,491,635)

The first two columns above are, of course, consistent with those shown in the pricing example for a long-dated forward transaction in section A.4, whereas the third column simply recomputes the Swiss franc cumulative interest position, using 4% rather than 3%. The implications of the increase in the Swiss franc interest rate can be seen in terms of either an increase in the value of the future flows of Swiss francs or as an increase in the long-term forward exchange rate from 1.3870 to 1.4278. Continuing to view the position from the standpoint of Company A, if it decided to 'close out' the original swap position at the new level of Sw fr interest rates, it could do so by arranging a new swap which would have opposite cashflows to those shown above. Although the US$ side would net to zero, there would be a net gain of almost Sw fr 500,000 over the life of the swap.

As the Sw fr payer, Company A can accordingly be seen to have a swap position with an inherent value. If it were to sell the rights and obligations arising under that swap to a third party, it could expect to receive some payment for the assignment as a result of that value.

In crude terms, it is possible to calculate the 'value' of a swap position by discounting the future currency flows back to the present day. This is, of course, looking at the cashflows from the opposite direction to that employed above, but nevertheless maintains the same basic concepts. The net present value of the flows of Swiss francs under the original swap at the new discount rate of 4% can be calculated as follows:

	Sw fr	4% Discount Factor	Present value Sw fr
End of year 1	466,500	0.9615	448,540
End of year 2	466,500	0.9246	431,326
End of year 3	466,500	0.8890	414,718
End of year 3	15,550,000	0.8890	13,823,950
			15,118,534

At the spot rate of exchange of 1.5550 this discounted amount is equal to US$9,722,530. As the present value of the stream of US dollar cashflows using a 7% discount factor will be $10 million, this suggests a net positive value of $277,470. This will be, subject to certain other factors discussed below, the sort of payment that Company A could be expected to receive in return for assigning its rights and obligations under the swap to another party.

Swap pricing is an extremely complex subject and in addition to the actual timing of cashflows, the duration of the swap and the extent to which implicit interest rates differ from current market rates, it is also necessary to consider any fees payable and factors such as the identity of the counterparty. A bank will need to take account of capital adequacy requirements and there is always a question of supply and demand, with some forms of swap being more readily available than others. The amount at which swaps are typically 'assigned' to other parties sometimes, therefore, bears little direct relationship to the sort of crude analysis performed above. From a corporate perspective, however, it should be possible to evaluate the majority of swap transactions using this sort of approach, and then apply the results as a test that the transaction is broadly compatible with current market conditions. This can be a valuable step for the accountant who will wish to ensure that he has a complete picture of the transaction before deciding how to account for it. If a cashflow-based analysis does not appear to work, it is possible that there is some other element to the transaction of which he is currently unaware.

A.9 Fixed to floating cross-currency swaps

A fixed to floating cross-currency swap is a combination of the coupon swap and the fixed to fixed cross-currency swap. Although many of these types of swap originate in the banking sector, they are becoming increasingly popular with corporates who may see an opportunity to convert both the currency and the rate profile of parts of their balance sheet at the same time. Many investment products have been created recently using this form of swap to repackage sovereign debt securities into a higher yielding floating rate based asset. The attraction to some investors of obtaining above LIBOR securities guaranteed by an overseas government, and yet denominated in their own currency, is fairly obvious.

In the previous section it was seen how a fixed to fixed currency swap had a 'value' which was dependent upon the market's current yield curve in the two currencies concerned. If long-term fixed interest rates moved in either of the currencies concerned, it could impact the intrinsic value of the swap. From a banker's perspective, there is an interest rate exposure on both sides of the swap. In contrast, a fixed to floating swap has, over the medium term, exposure only on the fixed-rate side. This is because the floating rate side of the transaction yields interest payments which will vary over the life of the swap, depending upon market movements. It is the fixed rate side which gives rise to an interest rate exposure.

Many of the 'sub-LIBOR' funding arrangements now mentioned in the financial press have their origins in a fixed to floating currency swap which capitalises on the borrower's ability to borrow fixed rate funds in another market and then swap them into the floating rate funds of its choice. The ability to achieve sub-LIBOR funding in this way flows directly from the comparative advantage of the borrower in terms of its ability to raise fixed rate funds in certain markets.

The traditional form of fixed to floating cross-currency swap involves the bringing together of two parties, one of which will generally have far better access to fixed rate funds than the other. It is generally the 'stronger credit' of the two which has the comparative advantage in the fixed rate market, with the lesser credit being prepared to swap its floating rate debt for a fixed rate exposure.

The structure of a fixed to floating cross-currency swap might be depicted as follows:

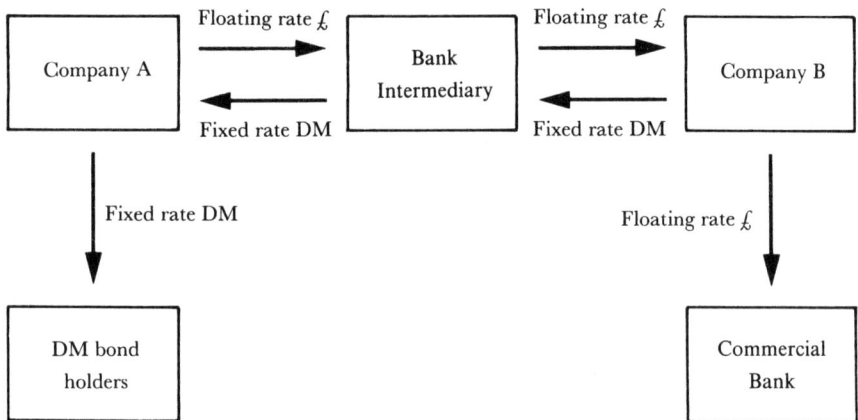

```
                  Floating rate £                    Floating rate £
 ┌──────────┐   ──────────▶    ┌──────────┐   ──────────▶    ┌──────────┐
 │          │                  │   Bank   │                  │          │
 │ Company A│   ◀──────────    │Intermediary│  ◀──────────   │ Company B│
 │          │                  │          │                  │          │
 └────┬─────┘    Fixed rate DM  └──────────┘   Fixed rate DM  └────┬─────┘
      │                                                            │
      │  Fixed rate DM                          Floating rate £    │
      ▼                                                            ▼
 ┌──────────┐                                          ┌──────────┐
 │  DM bond │                                          │Commercial│
 │  holders │                                          │   Bank   │
 └──────────┘                                          └──────────┘
```

Company A in this example is the stronger credit, frequently either a bank or a government agency, whereas Company B is perhaps only able to obtain fixed rate Deutschmarks at a comparatively more expensive rate. This might be the result of its lower credit standing or could, perhaps, simply be due to its lack of access to the German capital markets.

Fixed to floating cross-currency swaps are generally priced using the same sorts of techniques as are applied to the pricing of fixed rate bonds. This is because the nature of the swap is essentially similar to the exchange of two securities — one with a floating rate coupon and the other with a fixed rate. If the floating side of the transaction involves interest payments at market rates, the value of the theoretical security giving rise to the flow of interest payments will approximate par. Most of the 'value' in a fixed to floating swap accordingly derives from the fixed rate side.

In reality, the actual pricing of a swap will be affected by numerous other considerations, such as the nature of the floating rate index, the source of the floating rate quote, payment and rate reset frequencies, actual payment dates, any fees payable and, of course, the extent to which the fixed rate side is in line with market rates.

A.10 Floating to floating cross-currency swaps

This is the least developed end of the swap market and there has, to date, been little in the way of volume. This is, perhaps, hardly surprising if one considers the nature of the arrangement in a little more detail.

Most companies have access to floating rate funds and to the foreign exchange market, and for most currencies, there is reasonable liquidity in the forward foreign exchange markets. A floating to floating cross-currency swap can really only serve a useful purpose if a company's access to floating rate funds in a particular currency is in some way restricted or if, for some reason, it had no access to the forward foreign exchange markets. Such swaps have, accordingly, been arranged where there are regulatory barriers, or in certain circumstances where a company did not wish to be seen to be borrowing floating rate funds in a particular currency. They have also been entered into as an alternative to a forward foreign exchange contract where there is very little liquidity in the forward markets, due, perhaps, to a virtual lack of any active participants. The effect of using a floating to floating swap as an alternative to a forward foreign exchange contract is, however, quite different as one is still, of course, exposed to future interest rate movements. It is, in other words, not possible to lock in the effective forward premium or discount.

A floating to floating cross-currency swap can be depicted as follows:

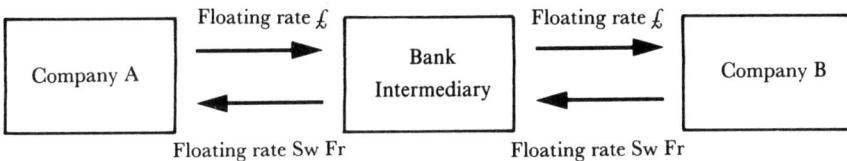

CONTINGENT-TYPE PRODUCTS

A.11   Currency options: Introduction

Many of the more recent 'third generation' products explored later in this section of the book derive, at least in part, from the foreign currency option. The present section briefly explores the development of the currency options markets and reviews in general terms some of the pricing characteristics of the product.

Options have existed in various shapes and forms for many years and, in particular, have been traded on the Chicago Board Options Exchange since 1973. These early options were initially stock options relating to the US equities market although the concept quickly moved into a number of the major commodity markets. Although a handful of large American banks started writing currency options for their corporate customers as early as the mid-1970s, and contracts were launched on the Amsterdam Exchange in 1978, there was extremely limited activity in the product and little, if any, inter-bank trading. The breakthrough occurred in 1982 with the creation of the world's first widely traded currency option on the Philadelphia Stock Exchange. This had an immediate and substantial impact on the liquidity of the market and was rapidly followed by the establishment of currency options contracts on a number of other exchanges around the world.

Currency options are now available in two major forms: the standardised contracts traded on a large number of exchanges world-wide; and the 'over-the-counter' (hereafter referred to as 'OTC') options individually tailored by international banks to meet the particular requirements of either their corporate customers or of other players in the market. Here in the UK it is one of the more highly regulated areas of activity for the foreign exchange dealer with the Bank of England putting a general stop on all options trading by licensed institutions (other than on a case by case basis) until such time as the institution is able to demonstrate that it has sufficient internal controls etc. to be able to cope with the complexities of the product. The UK market has also developed sufficiently for there to be standardised inter-bank product terms, developed by the British Bankers Association and known as 'LICON' terms.

Annual volumes for exchange traded options are now running at in excess of 30 million contracts per year, with about 90% of these being accounted for by Philadelphia and the Chicago Mercantile Exchange. There are no official figures for the OTC market, but annual turnover is now estimated to amount to about US$500 billion.

There are a wide range of uses for currency options, including the specific hedging of contingent exposures, the creation of a 'one-sided hedge', which limits the downside exposure whilst retaining the upside potential for profit, the overall provision of 'insurance' against structural or economic currency exposures and, in a somewhat more productive sense, as a mechanism for enhancing the profitability of established currency relationships. These various uses are examined in greater detail in sections B and C following.

A currency option, however constructed, is a contract between a buyer and a seller which gives the buyer the right, but not the obligation, to buy or sell a specific amount of currency at some time in the future at a predetermined price. The buyer pays a premium to the seller in return for being granted that right. The premium is retained by the seller irrespective of whether or not the option is exercised.

Currency options traded around the globe

The following are the main currency options contracts available on the major exchanges around the world at the time of writing. All contracts are against the US$ and are denominated in the currency concerned unless otherwise stated.

Chicago Mercantile Exchanges
  (Options on futures)
  £25,000; DM125,000; Sw fr 125,000; yen 12.5 m; C$100,000;

Chicago Board Options Exchange
  £25,000; DM125,000; Sw fr 125,000; yen 12.5 m; C$100,000;
  Fr fr 250,000; A$50,000;

Philadelphia Stock Exchange
  £12,500; DM62,500; Sw fr 62,500; yen 6.25 m; C$50,000; Fr fr 125,000;
  ECU62,500; A$50,000;

New York Cotton Exchange
  (Options on futures) US$ Index

London International Financial Futures Exchange
  £25,000; DM in US$50,000 units;

London Stock Exchange
  £12,500; DM62,500;

European Options Exchange
  £100 (against Dutch guilder); £100 (against DM); ECU100 (against US$);
  US $100 (against Dutch guilder);

Montreal Exchange
  C$50,000 (also traded in US$);

Sydney Futures Exchange
  A$ in US$100,000 units.

Notwithstanding the large number of derivative forms of option product examined later in this section, the underlying market essentially provides for two basic forms – the call option and the put option. A call option gives the buyer the right to purchase the currency, whereas a put option gives the buyer the right to sell that currency. The options traded on certain exchanges (see table above) in fact relate to the purchase or sale of a currency future rather than the currency itself.

The terminology in the currency options market has been derived, not unexpectedly in view of the market's history, from the language used in the commodity markets. The seller of an option is frequently known as the 'option writer', the predetermined price at which the option may be exercised is referred to as either the 'exercise price' or the 'strike price', and the trading jargon, both on the floor of the various exchanges and in the inter-bank telephone market, is as mystifying as one would probably expect. A particular area of complexity which needs to be understood is the difference between an 'American' option and a 'European' option. Unfortunately it is not true to say that European options are traded in Europe and American options in America and, to a large extent, the opposite is in fact true. The London Stock Exchange sterling option, for example, is an 'American' option whereas those traded on the Chicago Board Options Exchange are in fact 'European' options. The terminology derived largely from historical factors, with the 'American' option being traded on the first of the American exchanges (the Philadelphia Stock Exchange), and the Chicago Exchange subsequently adopting the format already in fairly common use by certain American banks in Europe – the so-called 'European' option.

To understand the difference between American and European options it is necessary briefly to review the concepts of 'exercise date' and 'settlement date'. Both forms of option include an 'expiration date' which is the latest date on which they can be exercised and, in the case of an exchange traded option, will be one of the four settlement dates each year specified by that particular exchange. In the case of an OTC option the expiration date is the date mutually agreed between the buyer and the seller.

The 'exercise date' is that date on which the option writer accepts valid instructions from the purchaser of the option as to his decision to 'exercise' his rights under the option. In the case of an American option, the option can be exercised at any time up to the expiration date and delivery will then take place two business days after the exercise date. In the case of a European option, although the option can be exercised at any time up to the expiration date, settlement will always take place on the 'settlement date'. Although the settlement date for an American option will be on the second business day following the exercise date, in the case of a European option, the settlement date will always be the second business day immediately following the expiration date. The reason for the adoption of the 'two business days' rule is that this ensures consistency with the spot foreign exchange market.

A.12 Option pricing

The price of an option at the time that it is granted is, by definition, the premium paid by the purchaser to the writer of that option. The determinants of that premium and, for that matter, of the value of the option subsequent to the date of granting, are as follows:

(a) the current spot price between the currencies concerned;
(b) the strike price embodied in the option;
(c) the forward exchange rate applicable to the settlement date (ie the relative interest rates of the two currencies concerned);
(d) the remaining time to expiry of the option; and
(e) the expected volatility of the exchange rate over the remaining life of the option.

It is the last of these factors, expected volatility, which ensures that the pricing of currency options is a far more subjective process than, for example, pricing currency futures. In reality there are usually additional subjective elements in the overall pricing such as market expectations as to future movements in the spot rate.

The value or the price of an option is generally perceived as comprising two separate elements – the intrinsic value and the time value. The intrinsic value is the amount the option would be worth if it were able to be exercised immediately. It is a direct function of the strike price and the prevailing spot price. Time value, on the other hand, is a function of the length of time remaining to expiry and the expected volatility of the underlying exchange rate. Although it declines over the duration of the option, the rate of decline reflects the subjectivity of assessing volatility.

A European option is said to be 'in the money' if the currency forward rate is less favourable than the strike price. It is said to be 'out of the money' if the current forward rate is more favourable than the strike price. An option which is 'at the money' will have a strike price equal to the current forward rate. These definitions are similar in the case of an American option, but the relevant market exchange rate will be the current spot rate rather than the forward rate. If a call option is 'at the money' or 'out of the money' it has no intrinsic value, and any remaining value in the option will accordingly relate to its 'time value'. An option that is 'in the money' will have both time value and intrinsic value.

At this point it is worth exploring a number of observed relationships between the intrinsic value and the time value of a currency option. Diagram 1 following shows the decay over time of the typical time value of an option. The most interesting feature of this graph is that the rate of decrease in the option's time value is not constant, but rather increases as the time remaining until maturity falls. The most rapid decay occurs in the last few weeks before the maturity date. This relationship is not quite the same in the case of an option which very deeply 'in the money', as in that case the time value tends towards zero much earlier.

Diagram 1

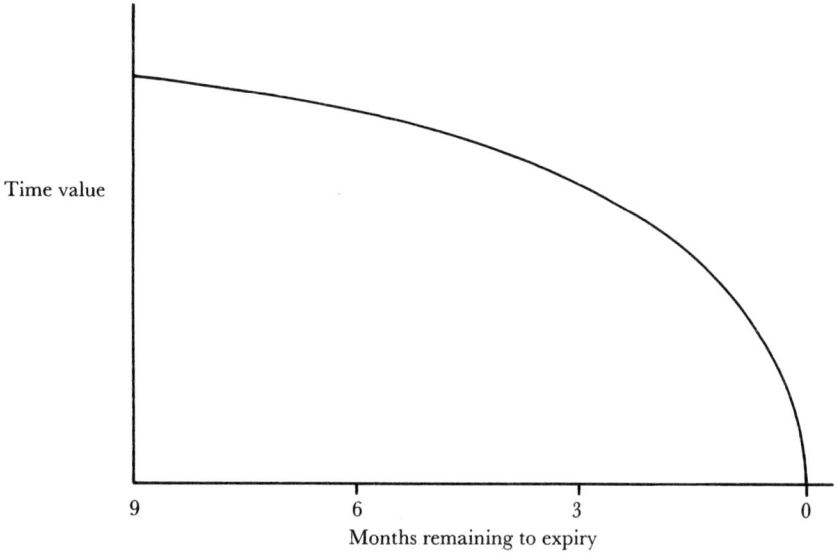

Diagram 2 below shows the typical relationship between the time value and the intrinsic value of a call option. The time value of the option is shown on this graph by the shaded area, from which it can

Diagram 2

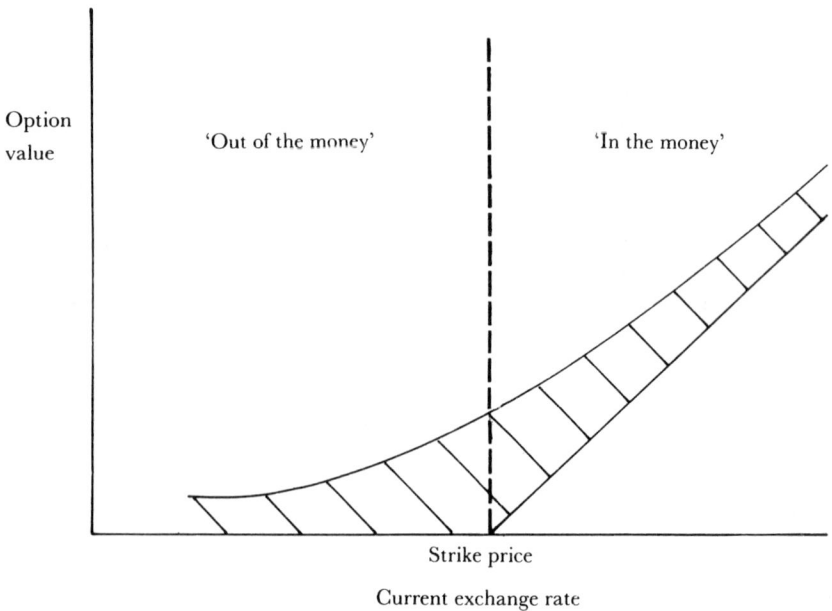

be seen that its maximum value occurs at the point where the option is 'at the money'. Where the option is deep in the money, the time value tends towards zero.

A key feature of Diagram 2 is that the slope of the option pricing curve is 45 degrees at the strike price. The slope of the option pricing curve itself is known as the 'hedging ratio' or 'option delta'. This represents the cash position which would be required to protect the option position against incremental fluctuations in the spot (or current forward) rate of exchange at that particular point. The slope tends towards 0, where it is out of the money, and 1, where it is in the money. The reference to the 'delta' is, of course, borrowed from calculus but can be represented graphically by the traditional option 'S' curve shown in Diagram 3 below. The vertical axis here represents the rate of change in the option price as a function of the rate of change in the spot price.

Diagram 3

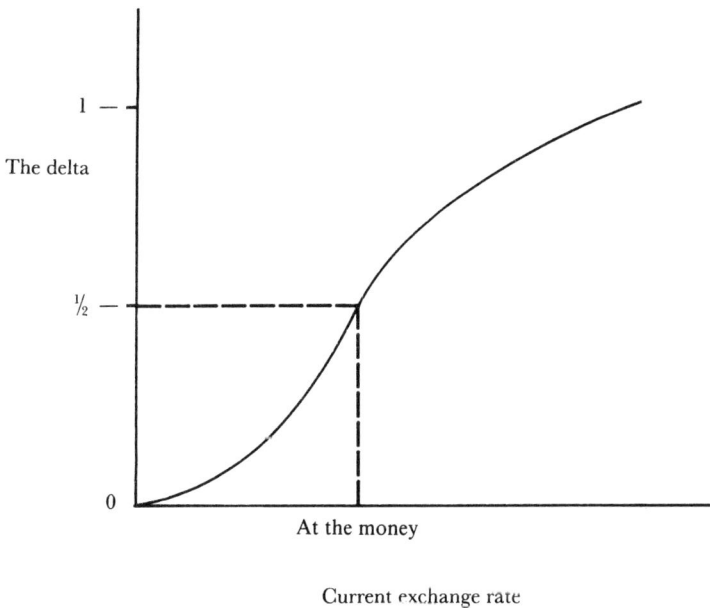

At the money

Current exchange rate

The rate of change in the option price for a given change in the spot price – ie the rate of change in the hedging ratio, is known as the 'gamma' of the option. It can be seen from the graph that this increases as the spot price approaches the strike price and the option moves to becoming 'in the money'. The gamma (in essence the slope of the S curve at any point) may be illustrated by the gamma curve shown in Diagram 4 following.

The importance of the hedging ratio is that it tells the writer of the currency option how much spot currency should be held in order to hedge the risks inherent in the option. The gamma tells the writer how quickly he must adjust this cash position in order to accommodate changes in the underlying spot rate. In order to fully hedge an option at any point in time, it is necessary for the cash held to be of such an amount that it will respond to changes in the spot rate in such a way as to offset resultant changes in the value of the option itself. This is the methodology used by most financial institutions to hedge those options which they write. In practice the hedging is usually carried out using forward foreign exchange contracts, thereby avoiding the need to invest funds in the underlying position. Such a hedging approach can be applied either to a single currency option or to a portfolio of options in a particular currency. It generally entails a fairly sophisticated monitoring of option positions and underlying exchange rates and, unless managed carefully, can very quickly wipe out any premium charged for originally writing the option.

The analysis to date has shown how the intrinsic value is a function of the strike price and the current spot rate, or, where appropriate, the forward rate. The time value, however, is more a function of expected volatility, and it is this factor which is the single most important variable influencing the price of an option. Volatility varies from one currency pair to another and changes over time as the underlying foreign exchange markets develop. The volatility factors fed into option pricing models are usually based on an assessment of historic performance and expected future trends. Indeed, the exchange traded currency option market is essentially a market for trading volatility, because the other factors in the calculation are identical, due to the standard nature of the contracts concerned.

Diagram 4

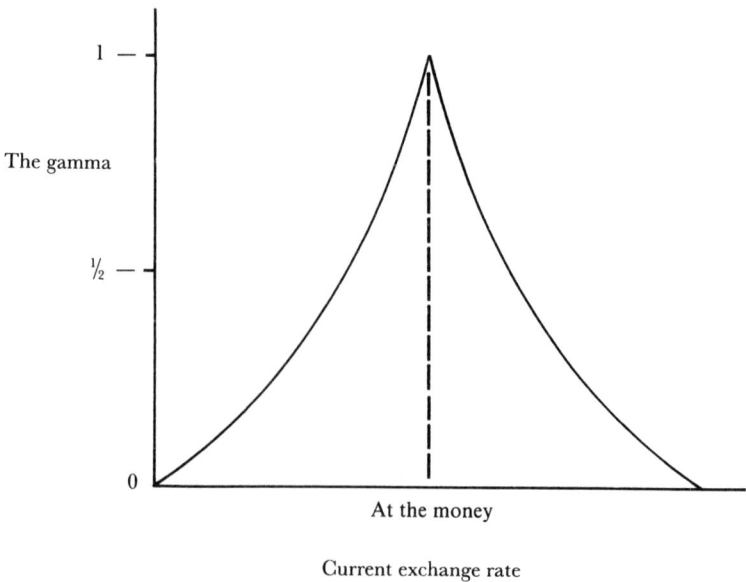

Current exchange rate

It is interesting to note that, in theory at least, an option buyer wishing to speculate on volatility should not buy an option unless he believes that future volatility will be higher than the level assumed in the pricing of that option. If he believes that volatility will in fact be lower, it will in theory be cheaper for him to utilise other markets for the purposes of creating his option hedge.

A.13 Exchange traded vs OTC options

The growth of exchange traded and OTC currency option markets is progressing very much hand in hand. At the moment it is probably still true to say that the vast majority of the users of exchange traded options are banks and other financial institutions active in the currency markets, whereas the majority of OTC options originate from corporate hedging requirements. It is useful to examine the differences between the two available markets because increasingly today the corporate has a choice as to whether or not to use an exchange or go for an OTC option.

The most obvious difference between the two markets is that an exchange traded option is standardised – for a predetermined amount of currency, at a predetermined price and for delivery on a particular date. Whilst substantially increasing the liquidity of the market and therefore substantially enhancing the ability of an option buyer to 'off-load' the option if it is no longer necessary, it does mean that the hedging of any particular position is usually far more complex. In contrast, OTC options can be tailor-made for the specific requirements of the corporate, thereby allowing a perfect hedge of any identified exposure.

Many corporates find the exchanges too remote, partly because they will generally need to use a broker to access them. Furthermore, unless they are properly geared up for such products, the margining required may substantially increase the complexity of their back office procedures. In general corporates tend to use the OTC market unless they are likely to have a fairly substantial volume of options, justifying development of a relationship with a broker and the establishment of a suitable margin control system.

It is logical to expect a tailor-made option created to the needs of a particular corporate to cost more than a standardised product available on an exchange. Actual prices quoted by banks, however, frequently vary quite substantially due to their differing perceptions of future volatility and the extent to which they may already have a compensating position on their books. Although it is very easy to argue that the treasurer should simply 'phone around the market' and then go for the best price, it is a role to which many medium-sized companies are unaccustomed. Exchange traded option prices are generally determined by the interaction of a very large number of buyers and sellers, thereby generally reflecting a 'fair' market price. Another point to be borne in mind when considering the two alternative approaches, is that banks usually quote on a 'net basis' – with no additional commission payable, whereas exchange traded options will need to be dealt via a broker member of the exchange and will probably be subject to a commission of between 3% and 6%, depending on the exchange concerned, the nature of the relationship between the broker and the corporate, and the underlying size of the transaction.

A final factor which should be taken into account in determining how to go about entering into an option will be whether or not the corporate requires a European or an American style option. Many corporates favour European options because the premiums tend to be lower, and they take the view that even if they wish to exercise early, they should be able to sell the option back to the writer to realise both the intrinsic and the time value. Although most banks will now buy back or cancel European options, the price that is effectively charged for doing so tends to be fairly high in real terms, and it is sometimes better for the corporate to write a similar European option itself – thereby nullifying the position.

A.14   Currency warrants

A far more recent form of currency option is the so-called 'naked currency warrant' which has started to appear in the Eurobond market as an attachment to new bond issues. The 'naked' or 'pure' currency warrant is essentially identical to an OTC currency option, in that it gives the holder the right, but not the obligation, to buy a certain amount of a currency within a given exercise period at a specified exchange rate. Although the warrants are generally created for the purposes of being issued jointly with a primary bond, the fact that they are 'naked' allows them to be traded as independent securities away from the host bond.

An interesting phenomenon of the currency warrant market is that they have tended to trade at prices somewhat higher than comparable OTC options. The reasons for this would appear to be that holders attach a certain amount of value to their 'securitised' nature, thereby allowing the holder to dispose of the warrant in the market rather than having to turn to the writer of an OTC option in order to eliminate the position. They accordingly tend to display the liquidity characteristics of an exchange traded option, whilst generally being for periods of between one-and-a-half and five years (periods which are not available on any option exchanges at the present time). The apparent pricing differential also seems to reflect the fact that those purchasing the warrants do not always have particularly good access to the OTC market. Private German investors are, for example, completely barred from dealing in currency options, and many small investors are likely to find the warrants price competitive if their securitised nature is taken into account.

The 'naked' currency warrant has developed from so-called 'double whammies' which entitled holders to buy a fixed or floating rate bond denominated in one currency with a fixed amount of another currency. Whereas those warrants tended to provide investors with the opportunity to play both the interest rate and currency markets at the same time, the 'naked' currency warrant is directly comparable to a traditional currency option.

The majority of currency warrants issued as at the time of writing have tended to be between US$ and Deutschmarks, with a certain amount of dollar/yen and sterling/Deutschmark activity. Both put and call warrants have been issued, often in connection with the same host bond issue, and typically with each warrant being exercisable into either US$500 or £500. The issue sizes to date have tended to be fairly small, averaging between 100,000 and 400,000 warrants.

The extent to which the market will develop from these initial beginnings remains to be seen, although it would seem likely that there will be a gradual reduction in the premium over OTC options as the product becomes more widely available.

A.15 Bearer options

The idea of a fairly small value 'bearer' option originated from the perception of certain banks that there was a demand from smaller speculators for such a product, and that many smaller companies wishing to acquire a negotiable form of option contract had neither the resources nor the systems to be able to justify dealing on one of the recognised options exchanges.

The first form of bearer option, the so-called 'Bero' was introduced by Barclays in 1986 as a standard sterling/dollar currency option with a standard face value of £5,000. No details of volumes are available, so it is extremely difficult to judge the success or otherwise of the product. The only advantage of a bearer option over an OTC option is that its standardised nature enables the issuing bank to post screen prices at which it is prepared to issue or buy back such an option. It seems inconceivable that the market could ever develop to the extent that holders will be able to trade other than through the issuing bank.

A.16 Deferred premium options

The 'deferred premium option', or so-called 'Boston option', is a direct derivative of the standard OTC contract. The only difference is that the option premium is deferred until the maturity of the contract and is paid at the point where it is either exercised or abandoned.

An interesting aspect of the deferred premium option is that it requires the issuing bank to grant a credit line to the holder. In the case of a normal OTC option there is no credit exposure to the issuer – its risk simply relates to the market exposure created by the option. A deferred premium option, on the other hand, does involve a credit exposure for the bank and a credit line will be required in the same way as for normal forward foreign exchange contracts.

THIRD GENERATION PRODUCTS

A.17 Cylinder options

One of the first so-called 'third generation' products was the cylinder option – essentially a combination of two standard option contracts, which were structured in such a way as to provide the client with the downside protection desired, but more cheaply than a normal option by limiting his upside potential.

Cylinder options first emerged in 1985, with Citicorp being credited with their creation. The basic idea of the product is that the client purchases a call option to provide protection against a currency going up but, at the same time, writes a put option in favour of the bank at a lower rate. The company's proceeds from the sale of the put option partially offset the cost of acquiring the call, thereby reducing the overall cost of the transaction. The strike prices of the two options can, if desired, be tailored in such a way as to eliminate the premium entirely or, in certain cases, even to result in a payment being made by the bank to the client.

The result of the transaction is that the customer is left with two currency levels which provide him with an upper and lower limit to his currency exposure. On maturity of the two contracts, if the market price is between the two parameters, neither option will be exercised and the hedger will obtain his foreign exchange on the spot market. If, on the other hand, the rate then prevailing is either above or below the two limits, either the client's or the bank's option will be exercised and the hedger receives his currency at the appropriate strike price.

By way of example, assume that a company wishes to arrange forward cover in relation to a possible receipt of US$500,000 in, say, six months' time. If the current spot price is $1.36 and the company decides that it does not wish to risk sterling rising above $1.40, then it will initially buy an option to sell the dollars at $1.40. Depending on the actual market at the time, that option might cost the company a premium in the order of £8,000. The corporate then writes an option in favour of its bank which allows the latter to call the $500,000 at a rate of, say, $1.30. For the granting of that option the bank is prepared to pay, perhaps, £7,500.

The overall effect of the above is that, for a net premium of only £500, the corporate has acquired his protection at $1.40, but has in return given up any upside potential beyond $1.30. Upon exercise in six months' time he will receive between £357,143 and £384,615 depending on the spot rate then prevailing.

There are numerous variations on the standard form of cylinder option with a particular favourite among treasurers being to structure the transaction in such a way that the put option is granted on only 50% (or some other percentage) of the amount being hedged. To compensate for the reduced premium on the put option, the transaction is often structured in such a way as to grant the bank a higher value option than would otherwise have been necessary. The advantage of such an arrangement is that it maintains the advantage of a reduced or nil premium whilst, at the same time, maintaining a certain amount of upside potential for the corporate.

If we consider the previous example, the company might have been able to grant a put option on $250,000 at, perhaps, $1.35 and still receive a premium of $7,500. The remaining $250,000 would then be protected on the downside, but subject to unlimited profit potential on the upside.

The outcome for the company in six months' time can be compared under the two scenarios as follows:

Proceeds of $500,000 sale

	Traditional cylinder £	Alternative 50% Scenario £
Net premium paid	500	500
Eventual spot rate:		
1.40 and above	357,143	357,143
1.35	370,370	370,370
1.32	378,788	374,579
1.30	384,615	377,493
1.25	384,615	385,185

It can be seen above that by choosing to retain a limited amount of upside potential, the company is agreeing to a lower net receipt of sterling at ranges between approximately 1.35 and 1.25. The lower 'break even' point will of course depend upon the specific market conditions at the time, and the way in which the deal is structured. It is, however, generally possible to manipulate the percentages involved in such a way as to construct the scenario most appropriate to the company's circumstances.

A.18 Range forwards

Range forward contracts, or collars or forward spread contracts as they are sometimes known, are a hybrid product combining the simplicity of a forward foreign exchange contract with the profit potential of an option. They have precisely the same effect as a cylinder option and are, indeed, generally hedged out by those marketing them in the options market.

Range forwards were first seen towards the end of 1985 and Salomon Brothers are credited with having pioneered them. Like cylinder options, however, they are now available from a large number of institutions under a variety of different names. They all provide the holder with a range of forward prices at which the forward purchase or sale of the currency concerned will be effected. The applicable price will be the spot price ruling at the maturity date, if it falls within the range, or the upper or lower end of the range, as appropriate, if the spot price is outside of it.

Range forwards tend to operate in the same way as cylinder options, in that the client usually quotes the end of the range which limits his downside exposure, and the bank then provides the upper end of the range at such a level as to be able to avoid charging the client a premium.

The growth in range forwards has, like the cylinder option, been driven to some extent by the absence of an initial premium. Many corporate treasurers have found it far more acceptable to enter into a contract such as a range forward than to have to pay a premium for the more traditional OTC option.

As with cylinder options, there are a number of derivative forms of range forwards now available, some being specifically tailored to the very particular requirements of individual clients.

A.19 Cancellable forwards

There are a number of different forms of cancellable forward contract now available, generally constructed in such a way as to avoid any form of up-front premium. The best known of these are the 'Break Forward' contracts which Midland Montagu have made available since the middle of 1986. A similar product is the 'Fox' (or forwards with optional exit) which is available from Hambros.

A cancellable forward is, in most cases, a normal forward contract which can be cancelled at the option of the purchaser. There is generally no up-front premium but, in order to allow the issuing bank the capacity to arrange the necessary option hedging of the position, the forward rate embodied in the contract will be some way off the market rates available at inception. Although, from the purchaser's standpoint, it is simply buying a forward contract at a slightly less favourable rate than might otherwise be available, from the issuing bank's standpoint, the arrangement is more akin to the structure created by a cylinder option or a range forward. It is, in other words, possible to determine the range of spot rates ruling on maturity of the transaction at which the corporate will choose to exercise the forward and, by implication, the range of rates which would cause them to 'break' the contract.

There are a variety of ways in which contracts such as break forwards can be structured. The more popular version rolls the entire premium for the option element of the arrangement into the forward rate, so that any 'break' can be effected at the then spot rate of exchange. Alternatively there may be a predetermined 'break rate' at which the deal is unwound in the event of the holder opting for cancellation. The major advantage of this form of arrangement from the standpoint of the corporate is that it can, as with cylinder options or range forwards, eliminate the need for any up-front premium whilst at the same time allowing a degree of upside potential in the event of rates moving in its favour.

Although there are no volume figures available for contracts such as the break forward, there is some evidence to suggest that they are proving extremely popular with corporate treasurers, largely because of their simplicity when compared with similar products which provide a combination of a forward contract and an option. They are generally easier for the treasurer to explain to his board of directors and are conceptually appealing to those companies that are perhaps less familiar with the foreign exchange markets.

A.20 Participating forwards

A participating form of cancellable forward is the so-called participating forward available from Salomon Bros. It comprises a commitment to buy or sell foreign currency above an agreed 'floor' rate of exchange, but with the applicable rate above that floor being weighted in such a way as to 'share' the upside profit between the customer and the issuing bank. The bank's share of that upside potential is used to pay for the cost of establishing the floor.

The client is either able to determine the floor rate to be applied or, alternatively, the participation rate required on any upside movement. For the customer seeking an 80% share of the upside potential, it may be necessary, for example, to forego 4% of the current forward rate.

A.21 Contingent forwards

There are now a variety of products available which have been specifically designed for tender situations where the tenderer wishes to cover its potential exposure against a foreign currency but does not necessarily wish to bear the full cost of a currency option. One of the more interesting of these products is the 'Scout' (shared currency option under tender), available from Midland, which has been specifically designed for situations involving a number of competitive tenderers.

The Scout is available either to a group of independent tendering organisations or to the organisation asking for tenders. The advantage of the arrangement is that it allows for the option premium to be shared amongst the parties choosing to make tenders – thereby resulting in a substantially lower premium than would have been payable had each of them arranged their own option hedges. The bank benefits from the transaction in that it is generally able to charge a slightly higher premium for the option than would normally be the case. Scouts can even be made to work in the case of a multinational tender, in that one can utilise, perhaps, a sterling/ECU Scout in the case of a number of European tenderers for a UK contract. This would leave each individual tenderer with a residual exposure relating to the relationship between its own local currency and the ECU, perhaps a far more manageable exposure than that relating to sterling.

There are a number of other forms of 'tender to contract' cover available, whereby the client fixes the forward rate which will apply to its tender and is obliged to deal at that rate if the tender is successful. In the event of the tender being unsuccessful, the contract is declared null and void. The client pays a premium for this privilege which, from the standpoint of the issuing bank, is treated a little like an option premium. The interesting point about this form of 'insurance' is that the client is able to obtain a guaranteed hedge of its forward exposure with no upside, and no downside, exposure in the event of the contract proving unsuccessful. From the bank's point of view, the 'contingency' attaching to the contract is in fact related to both the success or otherwise of the tender, and the eventual spot rate of exchange ruling at the maturity of the contract.

Tender to contract cover is frequently arranged to coincide with the ultimate cashflows expected under the contract under tender, although the period between making the tender and knowing whether or not the tender has been successful is usually far shorter. If there are provisions in the contract whereby the bank must be informed at the earliest opportunity of the outcome of the tender bid, its real exposure under the contract is limited to the period between the making of the tender and ascertaining the outcome of the bid, thereby allowing it to quote a lower premium than would traditionally be available under a standard OTC option contract.

Another form of protection available in a tender type situation is the 'insurance' type contracts now available, such as the 'Extra' (export tender risk avoidance) obtainable from Hambros. This form of contract provides the client with a right to a compensating payment in the event of his tender being accepted and the value of sterling moving beyond a certain threshold. Extra contracts are available for periods of three, six or 12 months and covering bids up to a maximum of $2.5 million. An interesting facility in the Hambros contract is the fact that if the bid is unsuccessful, the bank will sometimes repay a portion of the client's original fee. This portion is agreed at the outset and is simply taken into account by the bank in terms of its overall pricing and hedging strategy. The competitiveness of this form of contract as opposed to a tender to contract arrangement or, for example, a Scout, will generally depend upon the particular circumstances of the transaction.

It is interesting to note that these kinds of product have, to date, only been seriously marketed to companies active in the export market and have not yet really been taken up in other sectors of the economy. It is possible that the advantages of some of these products could also prove attractive to certain investment organisations or, for example, to international holiday operators. Although they essentially embody the more straightforward characteristics of a currency option, from the point of view of the purchaser they also carry an element of insurance in the more traditional sense. The volume of this form of product is, at the present time, still probably fairly low, largely because the demand has tended to be for extremely large principal amounts over very long periods — both factors which have tended to make the premium rather expensive. If the product can be made more accessible to the smaller operator, it is likely that volumes could increase substantially.

A.22   Compound options

The 'compound option' has been available from Standard Charter since 1986 and similar products are now available from a number of other organisations. It is essentially an option on an option, and can be structured in a variety of ways to provide the client with a lower initial premium than might otherwise apply to a straightforward option.

The compound option can be used in the same way as certain contingent forward type contracts to provide the purchaser with contingent forward cover in such a way that he maintains a certain amount of upside potential. If, for example, a UK company is tendering for a contract which is priced in US dollars and wishes to arrange for an option hedge in the event of it winning the contract, it could enter into a compound option which would provide it with the option to acquire a call option at the point where the outcome of the tender became known in, say, two months' time. There would be a premium payable on entering into the compound option itself, with a further payment required in two months' time if the company chooses to exercise its right to acquire the underlying call option. This arrangement provides the purchaser with a number of alternative outcomes, depending upon the movement in exchange rates over the tender period and, of course, over the subsequent contract period.

Let us assume, by way of example, that the UK company is tendering in the amount of US$5 million and that, if it is successful, it expects to receive the dollars in six months' time. It expects to know the outcome of its tender bid in two months' time.

If the current spot rate of exchange is $1.50 it may wish to ensure that it receives at least that rate for any eventual receipt of dollars. It believes, however, that sterling is likely to depreciate over the next six months and wishes to retain its ability to gain from any such depreciation whilst at the same time limiting its exposure to any appreciation.

It enters into a compound option for a premium of, say, £30,000 which provides it with the option to acquire a call option on $5 million at $1.50 in two months' time for a further premium of, perhaps, £110,000.

In two months' time, the tenderer could be faced with any one of the following scenarios:

(a) *Tender successful and sterling either at a similar or higher level.* In such a situation the company could be expected to exercise the option and thereby protect its ultimate receipt of foreign currency.

(b) *Tender successful but sterling now at much lower levels than previously.* It would now probably be cheaper for the company simply to take out a normal market option at $1.50 than to exercise its rights under the compound option. If it decides that sterling is unlikely to depreciate any further, it might alternatively choose to hedge its position through the forward market.

(c) *Tender unsuccessful and sterling at higher levels.* Depending upon the extent of the sterling appreciation, the company should be able to exercise its rights under the compound option and then close-out its option position at a profit.

(d) *Tender unsuccessful and sterling at lower levels.* The compound option would be abandoned.

The concept of a compound option is, at the time of writing, probably still in its infancy, although the product provides a large number of potential configurations which might suit particular circumstances. The extent to which it becomes more common over the next few years will probably depend upon the success of the banking community in marketing it, and the liquidity of the underlying options markets themselves.

A.23 Hindsight options

A comparatively recent product to join the option menagerie has been the so-called 'hindsight option', which has appeared in a variety of forms, and which allows the purchaser to exercise the contract at the best rate actually experienced over a predetermined period of time. In a typical case the contract might, for example, provide for a commitment to deal at, say, 5% below the best price available.

Alternative structures utilising this kind of arrangement can link a forward contract to the idea of a hindsight option, so that the client knows that it is hedged at either a predetermined rate, or at a fixed percentage below the best rate available over a particular period, if that rate is better than the predetermined forward rate.

These forms of product all require an up-front premium and are generally of interest to the corporate with a desire for forward protection but a wish to maximise any upside potential. They are particularly interesting when the corporate perceives a period of currency instability but has no particular view as to the likely direction of rate movements. Although they are similar to a number of the products examined in earlier sections, they present certain additional complexities in terms of exposure management from the standpoint of those banks selling them.

A.24 Swap derivatives

One of the most interesting developments over the last year or so has been the evolution of swap derivative products, which utilise the characteristics of the forward or option markets and apply them to the kinds of capital market swap discussed in sections A.7 to A.l0. The idea of a 'forward swap' has been around for some time and, as one would expect, essentially involves entering into an agreement to transact a swap on predetermined terms at some fixed date in the future. The swap options or swaption market is a newer phenomenon, where the volume of discussion amongst traders probably far outweighs the underlying volume of actual transactions.

A swaption is essentially a facility which provides the purchaser with the option of entering into a swap at some point in the future on a predetermined basis. In the same way as with any other kind of option, the buyer has the option to execute the swap but not the obligation to do so. Swaptions come in both American and European formats (ie exercisable on any day within the period or upon expiry) and premiums are granted for the issuance of the swaption. The so-called 'extendable swaption' is an arrangement which allows the buyer to extend the maturity of a particular swap at a predetermined rate should he wish to do so. It has been employed where the swap is attached to a callable bond which the issuer may, or may not, wish to call at a particular date. The extendable swaption provides him with the facility of delaying the call should he so wish, while maintaining the financing arrangements inherent in the original issue and attached swap.

Another swap derivative is the contingent currency swap, where a currency swap takes place in the event of certain predetermined events occurring. Typically, for example, a contingent swap will be attached to a warrant issue where the exercise of the warrants will, itself, be dependent upon, for example, future interest rates, currency rates or stock market prices. The contingency attached to the contingent currency swap might accordingly relate to any one or more of these factors.

Because a swap is essentially a 'second generation product' in the same way as a forward transaction or currency option, there is an enormous scope for the development of derivative products utilising the sort of arrangements employed for other third generation products. The development of such hybrid transactions is likely to be constrained only by the willingness of the corporate sector to entertain them, and the ability of the banking market to control their resulting exposures.

Transaction accounting

Introduction

Introduction

Transaction accounting is concerned with the way in which foreign currency transactions are recorded in the base currency accounts of a company. The recommended approach to transaction accounting and the basis for same is dealt with in chapter 7. This section is simply designed as a reference guide to transaction accounting, and no attempt is made to cover the matters discussed in more detail in that chapter.

A foreign currency transaction is defined as being any transaction which either creates or disposes of a foreign currency denominated asset, liability, commitment or contingency. Transaction accounting is concerned primarily with the way in which any non-monetary items originating from a foreign currency transaction are recorded in the base currency accounts. It does not deal with the treatment of monetary items which are subject to periodic revaluation into base currency equivalents. The latter is considered in connection with balance sheet translation in Reference Section C.

Foreign currency monetary items are defined as being foreign currency cash balances and any amounts that are either payable or receivable and are denominated in a foreign currency. As discussed in chapter 7, certain dealing operations involve commodities or securities which, due to the nature of the operation, should generally be treated as monetary items.

B.1 Unhedged purchase or sale

Accounting for an unhedged purchase or sale of a non-monetary item involves determining the base currency equivalent of a foreign currency denominated item. The value of the item in foreign currency terms should be determined by applying the same accounting policies as would be employed in the case of a base currency transaction and can then be converted into a base currency equivalent using the spot rate of exchange prevailing on the transaction date.

The transaction date should be determined having regard to the nature of the transaction, but should not, necessarily, be the date on which the transaction itself is accounted for. Chapter 7 above defines the transaction date as being the date on which the foreign currency commitment relating to the transaction arises. Although, in most cases, this will be the date on which the transaction falls to be accounted for, in certain circumstances it could be an earlier date.

If there are two rates of exchange in relation to the foreign currency concerned (for example a 'commercial' and a 'financial' rate) the rate to be employed in accounting for the transaction should be that at which it is possible to settle any monetary obligations arising from the transaction as at the transaction date.

Once a purchased non-monetary asset has been translated into the base currency it is treated as a base currency item and is not subject to subsequent revaluation. If a non-monetary item is sold for a foreign currency amount, the amount of base currency revenue to be recorded in the accounts is, likewise, fixed in that base currency from the transaction date – irrespective of the way in which the cash settlement of any related monetary position might occur.

B.2   Unhedged costs and revenues

Unhedged foreign currency costs and revenues should be translated into the base currency using the spot rate of exchange ruling on the date on which those costs and revenues arise. The determination of the appropriate transaction date should take account of the underlying nature of the transaction, but should be consistent with the concepts employed in the translation of an unhedged purchase or sale.

Costs which originate over a period of time should generally be translated at the average rate applicable to that period, whereas those, such as taxation, that are directly attributable to a particular flow of income, should be translated at the same rate as is applied to the related income. Revenues that arise as a result of service arrangements and the like should generally be translated at the rates prevailing on the dates on which the revenues are booked in the accounts. In general the approach should be to define the transaction date as being that on which the foreign currency obligation arises. This may, in some cases, be different to the date on which the transaction is actually accounted for.

Although SSAP 20 permits the use of an average rate of exchange for the translation of foreign currency costs and revenues, such an approach should be adopted only as an approximation to the use of actual rates. An attempt should be made to utilise as realistic an average rate as possible – making allowances for variations in the volume of transactions over the period in question. If such variations are substantial, and if the exchange rate fluctuates quite a lot over the period, it is unlikely that the use of an average exchange rate will be a sufficiently accurate approximation to actual rates.

Where more than one exchange rate exists in relation to the foreign currency concerned, the rate to be used should be that at which any related monetary commitment could be settled as of the transaction date.

B.3   Contracted exchange rates

Where a transaction is carried out under the terms of a contract, and where that contract has the effect of defining the exchange rate at which certain foreign currency items will be translated, the transaction itself should be treated as a base currency denominated transaction rather than a foreign currency transaction. In other words, the base currency equivalent of the foreign currency amount is determined by reference to the exchange rate embodied in the contract.

If a contract has the effect of defining what might otherwise be a sterling amount in foreign currency terms, any transactions carried out under that contract should be treated in exactly the same way as any other foreign currency transaction. The exchange rate to be applied to the foreign currency transaction would, under such circumstances, be the spot rate prevailing on the transaction date as described in section B.1 or B.2, as appropriate.

B.4 Transaction hedging: general comments

The objective of a transaction hedge is to fix, in advance of the transaction date, the local currency equivalent of the foreign currency transaction. It is important to differentiate such a transaction hedge from the hedge of a translation exposure (see Reference Section C) which endeavours to protect a monetary exposure from future movements in exchange rates.

For a hedging arrangement to be effective in the context of transaction hedging it will normally be necessary for the hedge to be carried out in the same currency as that relating to the transaction. In the event of a different currency being used to effect the hedge (perhaps due to a lack of liquidity in the currency concerned) it is necessary to show that, in broad terms, the two currencies concerned can be expected to move in parallel. It is not necessary for a transaction hedge to extend up to the date of the transaction itself, but it is not acceptable to have the hedge extending beyond the transaction date. If the hedge *does* extend beyond the transaction date and there is a monetary exposure flowing from the transaction, it is likely that the post-transaction date hedge will relate to that monetary exposure (and accordingly constitute a translation hedge as discussed in Section C). If there is no such monetary exposure subsequent to the transaction date, the latter period of the hedge will essentially comprise an outright position.

Where a hedge matures or is closed out prior to the transaction date, any gain or loss arising on the hedging arrangement should be deferred and then taken into account in recording the subsequent transaction. Where a hedge extends beyond the transaction date it is necessary to identify separately that portion of the hedge relating to the pre-transaction date period. Where a hedge is entered into with the intention of protecting both the transaction and the translation exposure relating to a future transaction, it is necessary either to separate the two component parts of the hedging arrangement and account for each part as appropriate or, as an alternative, to treat the entire hedge as relating to the translation exposure and treat the transaction itself as being unhedged. The latter is suggested in chapter 7 as a suitable 'pragmatic approach' where the duration of the transaction exposure is not overly long, and where the nature of the transaction is essentially a part of the company's trading activity rather than, perhaps, being of a longer-term capital nature. In the event of the transaction exposure becoming longer, the hedged item itself being of a longer term nature, or the amounts involved becoming more significant, it is likely that this approach would *not* be acceptable.

A composite hedging arrangement

In order to demonstrate the way in which a composite hedge of a transaction exposure can be analysed into its separate parts, the following example assumes that the company in question has decided to hedge a future foreign currency transaction, together with the monetary exposure flowing therefrom, using a forward foreign exchange contract.

We assume that the currency transaction involves the acquisition of an asset of $10 million in one month's time, with settlement expected two months after the transaction date. The current spot rate of exchange is 1.5950 and the forward rates for one month and three months are 1.5980 and 1.6050 respectively. The company hedges both its transaction and its translation exposure by entering into a three-month forward contract to purchase $10 million for £6,230,530. How should the transaction be recorded?

The three-month forward premium of 0.1000 translates into £39,062 and this amount, in the case of a pure translation hedge, would then have normally been amortised over the following three months in accordance with the recommendations included in Section C. A portion of this, however, is attributable to the transaction hedge, and that portion should be taken into account in valuing the actual transaction.

As the entire transaction has been hedged, it might be inappropriate simply to capitalise the first month's amortisation and then use it to adjust the spot price ruling on the transaction date. Adopting such an approach could lead to a gain or loss being recorded on the transaction date with a corresponding set-off arising on the closing out of the exposure in three months' time.

The more appropriate treatment is to use the prevailing one month forward rate of 1.5980 (or a rate derived from applying a proportion of the total swap rate if this is considered more meaningful) for the purposes of recording the transaction, and then amortise the residual points differential of 0.0070 over the remaining two months of the contract.

In other words, the asset would be recorded at £6,257,822 ($10 million at 1.5980) and the monetary exposure (the payable) would be fixed at a similar amount. The difference between this amount and the ultimate settlement rate of 1.6050 or £6,230,530 would be taken to income as an adjustment to net interest income/expense over the two months' settlement period. The amortisation would accordingly amount to £13,646 per month.

Chapter 7 extends the concept of transaction hedging to hedges carried out using the company's balance sheet and the idea of global or generalised hedging of future transactions which flow from known structural positions. Such global hedging arrangements might be effected either by using the balance sheet or through the use of off balance sheet transactions. The only additional complication when using the balance sheet to effect a transaction hedge is that it is necessary, in some way, to take account of the implicit interest cost of the funding arrangements either by deferring those costs and then taking them into account when recording the subsequent transaction, or simply by applying the forward rate of exchange prevailing at the inception of the hedge and then accumulating the theoretical premium or discount over its life – taking the amortisation to net interest income or expense, with the accumulated amount as at the end of the hedge then being brought into account in recording the actual transaction.

A global hedging arrangement

Let us assume that a company has a known long-term structural position which involves future anticipated flows of dollars from export sales. Rather than selling those dollar receipts at the rates prevailing when the funds arise, the company chooses to hedge its next three months' sales on a rolling basis by borrowing US dollars and then exchanging the funds received into sterling to fund its working capital requirements. In this way the company seeks to hedge both the transaction exposure on its future sales covering a period two months forward, and the translation exposure arising from the average one month settlement period subsequent to each sale. How should it account for its dollar sales?

Because of the virtual impossibility of matching dollar sales against specific debt hedges, it will be necessary to record all sales at current spot rates of exchange, and then adjust the resulting figures to take account of the hedges. If we assume that the company fixes its dollar borrowing requirement once a month and always borrows fixed three-month funds, the most straightforward approach is probably to identify at each borrowing date the equivalent cost of sterling three-month funds, and then compute (at the outset) the funding difference arising from borrowing dollars.

The easiest way to calculate the funding gain or loss is simply to calculate the difference between the spot and three month forward sterling equivalent of the amount of the proposed dollar borrowing.

If the sales are recorded at spot rates of exchange ruling on the transaction date, and if the interest on the dollar borrowing is taken to interest expense, the only adjustment that will be required will be to treat one-third (one month out of three) of each monthly sterling funding gain or loss as a reclassification between sales and interest expense. This will have the effect of adjusting the sales onto a hedged basis, whilst leaving the remaining two months of the financing adjustment in net interest as required by Reference Section C.

B.5 Hedging with commitment-type products

If a transaction hedge is effected by way of a forward contract or a currency future, and the hedge is kept in place up until the transaction date, the rate to be used in translating the transaction into the base currency will be the rate embodied in the transaction hedge.

If a currency future is used to effect the hedge, it might not have been possible to arrange for a complete matching of dates and it is likely, in any event, that the currency future will be closed out on its expiry date as a separate exercise to the booking of the underlying transaction. If, for example, a UK company arranges a futures hedge of an anticipated US$ sale during a particular futures delivery month, it will need to close out that futures position on the predetermined delivery date, irrespective of the date of the underlying transaction. The sterling base currency equivalent of the US$ sale will be determined by the spot rate of exchange ruling on the date of sale, plus or minus the sterling equivalent of any gain or loss on the closing out of the futures transaction.

The same criteria applies where there is no matching of a forward transaction hedge and the underlying transaction date. The rate to be used when booking the transaction will, in that case, be the spot rate ruling on the transaction date plus or minus any gain or loss arising on the 'close out' of the forward currency deal. The latter would be defined as the difference between the forward rate of exchange embodied in the contract and the spot rate ruling on maturity, irrespective of whether or not the currency was actually converted into sterling on that date.

If a forward foreign exchange contract is 'rolled over', as explained in section A.5, it is necessary to examine whether or not the rollover has been effected merely in order to 'fine tune' the timing of the transaction or whether, in fact, the transaction has been ignored or accounted for in some other way and the hedge is being used for some other purpose. If the rollover has been arranged to fine tune the timing of the transaction, the entire gain or loss on close-out is attributable to the related transaction. If, on the other hand, the contract has been rolled over for some other purpose, then it will be the gain or loss accumulated as at the last rollover date which should be taken into account when recording the foreign currency transaction. The post-rollover costs of the hedge will be attributable to some other transaction or exposure.

B.6 Hedging with contingent-type products

The various forms of option product discussed in sections A.11 to A.16 above are used extensively for transaction hedging in one way or another. Although their most obvious use is when there is some doubt as to whether or not the transaction itself will take place, they are also used when there is some certainty regarding the transaction, but the company concerned wishes to retain a certain amount of upside potential whilst limiting its downside exposure.

Where there is fairly clear evidence to suggest that an option-type product has been used as an effective transaction hedge, the rate to be used in booking the transaction should be the spot rate of exchange ruling on the transaction date, adjusted for any gain or loss arising on the closing out of the option position. The latter should take account of any premiums paid in order to acquire the option position and, in those cases where the option is actually exercised, the gain or loss should be determined by the spot rate of exchange ruling on the exercise date.

If, for example, a UK company wishes to hedge an expected DM1 million sale in four months' time at the current spot rate of DM2.95 it may do so through the purchase of a Deutschmark OTC put option value in four months' time. The cost of that option is, say, £8,500. Let us assume that the transaction actually takes place in just over four months' time, and let us consider two separate scenarios with Deutschmark spot rates of 3.05 and 2.80 on expiry of the option, and of 3.10 and 2.90 respectively on the transaction date.

In the first case the option will be exercised on expiry and, if the Deutschmarks required are then purchased on the spot market, will yield a profit of £11,114 (representing the difference between DM1 million at the option rate of 2.95 and at the spot rate of 3.05). The rate prevailing at the subsequent transaction date is 3.10 and the sale will be recorded as follows:

DM 1 million at spot rate of 3.10	£322,581
Adjustment for profit on option hedge	11,114
Less cost of option	(8,500)
Net value of sale	£325,195

In the second case the option would not be exercised as it would yield a loss. The rate at the subsequent transaction date has moved back to 2.90 so that the sale would be recorded as follows:

DM 1 m at spot rate of 2.90	£344,828
Less cost of option hedge	(8,500)
Net value of sale	£336,328

Some hedging with options is intentionally carried out on a mismatch basis. If, for example, a company wishes to arrange an option hedge for three months forward, it can do so by acquiring a three-month exchange traded option, a six-month traded option or a four-month OTC option. Because of the way in which time value decays over the period of an option (see section A.12) it might be more cost effective to utilise six-month exchange traded options which are then closed out at the four month stage. Such an approach minimises the time decay over the hedge period and thereby maximises the potential gain on close-out.

Whenever there is a mismatch between the period of a required hedge and the length of an exchange traded option used to effect the hedge, it will generally be necessary to purchase more contracts than are required to cover the underlying principal amount. This is because the price sensitivity of the option contract will be such that a full hedge will require in excess of 100% cover. The relationship between the required value of the contracts and the underlying hedged principal is commonly known as the hedge ratio and is available from published option tables based on assumed pricing relationships.

If, for example, a US$-based company wishes to hedge a £1 million payment in three months' time, using six-month exchange traded contracts, it may find that it is necessary to acquire, perhaps, 103 call option contracts of £12,500, with a total value of £1,287,500 rather than the £1 million being hedged. The hedge ratio is approximately 0.7767 (£1,000,000 divided by £1,287,500).

A final point to consider in relation to the use of options for transaction hedging is the extent to which the hedger should feel obliged to pass on the entire cost of the option to the counterparty to the transaction being hedged. It is interesting to note that although an option can provide adequate protection in relation to a particular exchange rate, it does not eliminate all of the upside potential in the event of the exchange rate moving in a favourable direction. Whether or not any hedged tender bid, for example, is actually successful, the option holder will still be able to benefit from any favourable movement in the exchange rate. A certain amount of analysis has been carried out to endeavour to determine the value of that upside potential to the option holder and, in economic terms, it can be argued that it is only the element relating to the downside risk which should in theory be passed on to the client.

B.7   Hedging with third generation products

Using one of the third generation products referred to in sections A.17 to A.24, for the purposes of a transaction hedge typically requires the same sort of approach as that explored in section B.6 in relation to option hedging. The additional complexity tends to be in the structure of the hedging product itself rather than in the way in which it is accounted for.

The overriding rule in the case of any of these products is initially to ascertain whether or not the arrangement represents a bona fide hedge of the transaction in question, and then to evaluate the gain or loss arising on the closing out of the hedge. That gain or loss is then taken into account, together with any hedge premium, in determining the underlying base currency equivalent of the hedged transaction.

Balance sheet translation

Introduction

This section considers the way in which foreign currency monetary items are treated for the purposes of a periodic currency revaluation and examines the extent to which off-balance-sheet items should be taken into account in that process. The detailed approach to balance sheet translation and the basis for same is dealt with in chapter 8 and the present section is designed solely as a reference guide without repetition of the more detailed discussion in that chapter.

Section B summarised the way in which any non-monetary items originating from a foreign currency transaction should be recorded in the base currency accounts. It did not consider the treatment of monetary items deriving from foreign currency transactions which, because of their nature, are not deemed in economic terms to have a fixed base currency amount. For this purpose, foreign currency monetary items are defined as being foreign currency cash balances and any amounts that are either payable or receivable in a foreign currency. As noted elsewhere, certain trading balances involving commodities or securities should, due to the nature of the related trading operation, also generally be treated as monetary items.

Chapter 3 discusses the reasons for translation exposure sometimes being referred to as 'accounting exposure' and why it is occasionally perceived as being an 'artificial' form of exposure. It was pointed out, in this context, that there were perhaps two different forms of translation exposure – that originating from the short-term delays in the settlement of foreign currency transactions, and that deriving from longer-term 'structural' positions or from economic exposures. The approach adopted to balance sheet translation in chapter 8 does not differentiate between these two forms of exposure which are, in accounting terms, essentially similar.

The key to a sound approach to balance sheet translation is to ensure that it includes a comprehensive review of all currency exposures – whether on or off balance sheet. That review should encapsulate all existing hedging arrangements, including any 'implicit hedges' which the company perceives to exist as a result of its current economic exposures. In this context, a foreign currency exposure is generally defined as one existing at the balance sheet date – therefore excluding non-monetary items which may be likely, at some time in the future, to give rise to foreign currency monetary exposures. Such prospective exposures are excluded from the balance sheet currency position on the basis that they relate to what are, in economic terms, future transactions. Any hedges of those prospective exposures are also excluded from the revaluation process and are treated as transaction hedges as discussed in Section B.

C.1   Unhedged monetary items

In general terms, any unhedged foreign currency denominated monetary item should be translated into sterling (or the appropriate base currency) at the closing spot rate of exchange ruling as of the balance sheet date. Where a two-tier exchange rate system exists, the rate to be used for the purpose of that translation should be that which would apply to any transaction which would eliminate the exposure in question. In the case of a trading exposure, the latter is likely to consist of the cash settlement of the exposure, whereas in the context of a longer-term 'capital type' exposure, the appropriate rate could be either that relating to a suitable hedging arrangement or that which would be appropriate in the event of ultimate settlement. Where there are doubts concerning the convertibility of the currency in question then this should be reflected in the exchange rate used for the purposes of translation.

Unhedged monetary items should include, for balance sheet translation purposes, all unhedged off balance sheet commitments and any hedges of off balance sheet contingencies, other than those which are themselves of a contingent nature. The process should exclude, however, any balance sheet or off balance sheet monetary items which are being used to hedge future transactions or known structural positions (see Section B).

Any monetary item, whether on or off balance sheet, should be treated as being hedged only to the extent that it is possible to identify a specific effective hedging arrangement which relates to the exposure in question. To be effective, it is necessary for the hedge to match the exposure in terms of amount and currency, although it need not match the ultimate exposure in terms of its maturity date. In the event of there being any doubt as to whether or not a hedge is effective in the context of a particular exposure, it is generally more appropriate to treat both the exposure and the related hedge as being separate unhedged monetary exposures.

In the event of a forward commitment-type contract being treated as an unhedged monetary item, it will generally be appropriate to revalue the underlying currency position at the then spot rate of exchange, whilst amortising the financing element (eg any premium or discount) over the period of the contract concerned. Any such contracts which represent hedges of future transactions should be excluded from the revaluation process as already mentioned.

C.2   Translation hedging: general comments

The objective of entering into a hedge of an exposed monetary item is not so much to fix the sterling equivalent of that monetary item, as to protect the exposure represented by same from future movements in exchange rates. Irrespective of the nature of the hedging arrangement itself, it is the current spot rate of exchange which is therefore of relevance in terms of any future revaluation of the exposure concerned.

Where a non-cash hedge of an exposure is arranged, it is likely that there will be a financing element (eg a premium or discount) associated with the arrangement, and this should be taken into account over the life of the hedging transaction as an integral part of the company's overall net financing activities. It is, in other words, amortised to income as an adjustment to either interest income or interest expense as appropriate.

Where a trading transaction has been subject to a 'composite hedge' as discussed in section B.4, it will probably be the spot rate ruling on the date on which the monetary item arises which will be of relevance from a translation hedging perspective. Section B.4 discusses in broad terms the way in which one should attempt to de-consolidate a composite hedge into its two separate elements – the transaction hedge and the exposure hedge. As noted in that section, an alternative approach to the handling of a composite hedge is to treat the entire hedge as relating to the translation exposure. Although this more pragmatic approach will result in a different sterling value being attributed to the non-monetary item originating from the transaction, it does not affect the underlying concept of the residual translation hedge being employed to eliminate the exposure to future movements in exchange rates. It is, accordingly, still the spot rate of exchange ruling on the transaction date which is of relevance. Whether or not a composite hedge is de-consolidated for the purposes of transaction accounting, the treatment of any resulting monetary exposure will accordingly be the same. (There will, of course, be an impact on the amount of the financing element amortised to income over the remaining life of the hedging arrangement, thereby impacting upon the classification of net income as between net interest and, for example, cost of sales.)

The impact of hedging a monetary exposure can be thought of in terms of having fixed, in local currency terms, the value of the foreign currency monetary amount. Irrespective of the nature of the hedging arrangement, the 'fixing' in economic terms will always be at the current spot rate of exchange. The only real issue which accordingly needs to be addressed in relation to translation hedging arrangements concerns the way in which any financing element relating to the hedge should subsequently be amortised to income. This amortisation should take account of the nature of the hedging arrangement, and the following three sections examine the particular circumstances of using commitment, contingent and third generation type products to effect the hedge. Section C.6 then explores the special circumstances of a hedged foreign equity investment.

C.3 Hedging with commitment-type products

Forward foreign exchange contracts have long been used as effective hedging vehicles for monetary exposures originating from trading transactions, due largely to their simplicity of construction, their ready availability and the fact that they avoid the company concerned having to worry about managing foreign currency cash balances. Increasingly today many companies are using currency futures to achieve the same result and, where capital type transactions are concerned, the use of currency swaps is now more common.

Where a forward foreign exchange contract is used to hedge a balance sheet exposure, the accounting approach recommended in

Amortising premium/discount on a long-dated forward

The example in section A.4 involved a three-year US$/Sw fr forward transaction with a spot rate of 1.5550 and a forward rate of 1.3870. How should the forward dollar discount of 0.1680 be amortised to income?

By re-ordering the cashflows set out in that example we have the following:

	US$	Sw fr
Assumed principal	10,000,000	15,550,000
Interest for 1st year	700,000	466,500
Cumulative (year 1)	10,700,000	16,016,500
Interest for 2nd year	700,000	466,500
Interest reinvested	49,000	13,995
Cumulative (year 2)	11,449,000	16,496,945
Interest for 3rd year	700,000	466,500
Interest reinvested	101,430	28,410
Cumulative (year 3)	12,250,430	16,991,905

In the same way that we obtained the three-year swap rate of 0.l680 by dividing the Sw fr three-year cumulative total by the US$ cumulative total, it is possible to evaluate the one-year and two-year swap rates as follows:

	Rate	Swap points	Incremental swap points
Spot rate	1.5550	—	—
1 year forward	1.4969	581	581
2 year forward	1.4409	1141	560
3 year forward	1.3870	1680	539
			1680

In this example the swap points attributable to each annual period are reducing over time. This is because the lower nominal valued currency (the US$) has the higher rate of interest. Had the position been the reverse, the points differential would have increased over time.

The total discount on the forward transaction in this example should be amortised to income as follows:

34.6% of the total in year 1 (581 divided by 1680);
33.3% of the total in year 2 (560 divided by 1680);
32.1% of the total in year 3 (539 divided by 1680).

In this particular example a straight line amortisation would not have given a very different result, but in some cases, particularly where the lower nominal valued currency also has the lower interest rate, the impact can be substantial.

this book requires that the underlying exposure be translated at the spot rate of exchange ruling at the date on which the hedge is entered into, with any forward premium or discount between the spot and forward rates of exchange then being amortised to income on a straight line basis over the life of the forward contract. The amortisation should be to interest income or expense, as appropriate, reflecting the underlying commercial nature of the transaction – essentially that of a financing activity. This approach should be adopted irrespective of whether or not there is any matching between the ultimate likely settlement date of the underlying exposure and the maturity date of the forward foreign exchange contract.

Where a long-dated forward exchange contract is used to effect the hedge, the only additional complication concerns the way in which the forward premium or discount inherent in the contract should be amortised to income. As discussed in section A.4, the nature of any long-dated contract is such that one must take account of the way in which the inherent interest in the premium or discount is compounded at the end of each year. In some cases, it is probably more correct to utilise a six-monthly compounding on the basis that this is the way in which the underlying contract will have been priced.

Where a currency future is used to hedge a balance sheet exposure the question of amortisation can become somewhat more complex because the rate at which the future can be exercisable may well be different to the current spot rate of exchange. If a futures transaction does embody the current spot rate, the equivalent of the forward premium or discount on a forward transaction is in effect rolled up into the premium payable by way of original margin on the futures contract. It is, accordingly, that original premium which is then amortised to income over the life of the transaction. Any subsequent variation margin will represent movements in exchange rates over the life of the contract and will offset the movements arising from the spot revaluation of the underlying exposure. If the contract is not closed out until maturity, the original margin should, by then, have been fully amortised and any variation margin incurred over the life of the contract will have offset the impact of the related movements in exchange rates on the underlying exposure. If the underlying exposure is, accordingly, revalued to market rates at each revaluation date, any gain or loss arising on revaluation can be offset against the variation margin paid to date on the futures contract. If the exposure is carried in the accounts at the original spot rate of exchange ruling on inception of the futures contract, then any variation margin should be held in a suspense account pending eventual settlement of the exposure in question.

Where a futures transaction does not utilise the current spot rate of exchange this will be taken into account in the amount of the original margin. In terms of accounting for the hedge and the related exposure, it is necessary to extract that portion of the initial margin which is attributable to any mismatch between the contracted rate and the spot rate and to hold it in suspense in the same way as any subsequent variation margin. The remainder of the initial margin is then amortised over the life of the contract in the normal way. The overall objective of accounting for currency futures in this area should be to achieve the same result as would have been the case had the company instead acquired a comparable forward foreign exchange contract which would have matured on the same date. The amount of initial margin to be amortised should, accordingly, be related to the current forward premium or discount for the maturity period in question.

When a forward contract or a futures transaction is used to hedge a monetary exposure, there is, as already mentioned, no requirement for there to be matching between the expected duration of the exposure and the maturity of the related hedge. This means that the hedge can mature, be reversed or, in the case of a futures transaction, be sold, either before, on the date of, or subsequent to the eventual elimination of the monetary exposure. The monetary item itself may, as already mentioned, be carried in the local currency accounts at either the original spot rate ruling at the point where the hedge was arranged, or at the current spot rate. It is, therefore, necessary to examine the way in which the closing out of any hedged position should be handled in each of these scenarios.

1   Exposure at market value

Where the monetary exposure is being revalued on a regular basis at current exchange rates, it is necessary also to revalue (at spot rates of exchange) the related hedge. With the original premium or discount being amortised over the period of the hedge, any gain or loss on the spot revaluation will offset the related gain or loss on the exposure itself. Both exchange impacts can accordingly be taken to income.

Whether the hedge is removed or eliminated before, on the date of, or subsequent to, the elimination of the exposure, it will not impact the way in which the hedge revaluation is accounted for. In the event of the hedge being closed out or maturing prior to the elimination of the related exposure, the periodic revaluation of the exposure will cease to be offset by the revaluation of the hedge. Income will accordingly reflect the true underlying exchange gain or loss on the position, and the balance sheet carrying value of the monetary item will continue to be at current market rates. There should be no net gain or loss taken to income as a result of closing out the hedge, and any unamortised financing element should, in general, continue to be amortised to income over the original duration of the hedge. The reason for this becomes clear if one views the close-out transaction as essentially comprising a separate speculative-type transaction which does not affect either the original exposure or the hedge.

In the event of the exposure being eliminated prior to the maturity date of the related hedge, any gain or loss arising on the hedge subsequent to that elimination will automatically fall into income as a result of the periodic revaluation process.

2   Exposure carried at original rate of exchange

Where the monetary exposure is being carried at a fixed rate of exchange determined at the point where the hedge was entered into, it will be necessary to ignore the hedge in the periodic revaluation process. The unrecognised gain or loss on the hedge will, in effect, offset the unrecognised gain or loss on the underlying monetary position. Where the unbooked gains or losses do not offset, any mismatch should be taken to income. If the hedge and the monetary exposure are eliminated on the same date, the gain arising on the closing out of one should offset the loss arising on the other. The only complication is where there is no coincidence in the elimination of the two sides of the transaction.

If the monetary exposure is eliminated prior to the maturity date of the hedge, it becomes necessary to effect a mark-to-market valuation of the hedge from then onwards. Because the closing out of the exposure will also have resulted in a realised gain or loss in relation to the original hedged spot rate, it is also necessary to account for the accumulated (but unrecognised) gain or loss on the hedge. There are a variety of ways of handling this scenario, with the most convenient probably being simply to begin bringing the hedge into account in the periodic revaluation as from the date on which the related exposure is removed. This will automatically eliminate the gain or loss arising on the elimination of the exposure and, at the same time, ensure that the hedge is brought into account in any periodic revaluation performed subsequently.

Where the hedge either matures, or is reversed prior to the elimination of the related monetary exposure, it is necessary to ensure that any gain or loss arising as a result of movements in the spot rate of exchange over the period of the hedge are capitalised and deferred until such time as the underlying exposure is eliminated. This can generally be achieved by simply calculating the gain or loss arising on closing out the hedge, although it is important to ensure that an adjustment is made in relation to any unamortised premium or discount (see above). Although the deferred gain or loss on the hedge should, in economic terms, be attributed directly to the related monetary exposure, it is frequently retained in a separate balance sheet account until such time as the exposure itself is eliminated. This is generally necessary where the monetary exposure is of a longer term capital nature, and where the company concerned wishes to avoid periodic fluctuations in the local currency carrying value of the amount in its accounts. It does mean, however, that the local currency equivalent of the foreign currency asset or liability as shown in the accounts is in fact somewhat different to the underlying economic value of the position in question. If the amounts are material, this would generally be covered by way of a note disclosure.

The final form of commitment-type product which needs to be considered is the currency swap, which, as has already been mentioned, is sometimes used to hedge longer-term currency exposures. The implications of using a swap to hedge an exposure are, essentially, similar to using either a forward contract or a futures transaction. A fixed to fixed cross-currency swap (section A.8) is, after all, in economic terms no more than an alternative means of carrying out a long-term forward dated contract. Under such a swap, the future flows of interest and the future exchange rate applied to the re-

Hedging using a fixed to fixed cross-currency swap

Let us consider the example of a UK company which currently has an exposed monetary position of, say, US$100 million as a result of an outstanding bond issue for that amount. The bond has a callable facility in three years' time so the company decides that it wishes to hedge its exposure over the next three years. It decides to do so using a fixed to fixed cross-currency swap, but discovers that it is able to obtain a slightly better rate under the swap if it purchases one which is currently a little out of line with market rates.

We shall assume the following:

(a) a current spot rate of exchange of 1.60;
(b) current three-year fixed-rate US$ funds at 7%;
(c) current three-year fixed-rate £ funds at 10%; and
(d) the US$100 million swap involves rates of 10% for £ and 8% on the $ side, and, because the $ side is out of line with the market, the company agrees to pay a premium of £2 million to the bank providing the swap.

The cashflows under the swap (ignoring any initial exchange) are as follows:

	£000	$000
Initial premium	(2,000)	—
Interest at end of 1st year	(6,250)	8,000
Interest at end of 2nd year	(6,250)	8,000
Interest at end of 3rd year	(6,250)	8,000
Re-exchange at end of 3rd year	(62,500)	100,000

As the interest flows take place each year, one is not faced with the cumulative interest implications of a long-dated forward contract. This is not the case, however, with the initial premium, and this will need to be amortised over the three years in such a way as to reflect the fact that it is an up-front cash payment.

This can be achieved by applying the current 10% fixed-rate of interest and creating an amortisation which takes account of the inherent cost of having made such an up-front payment. To do this we apply the following DCF calculation:

	10% Discount factor	Amortisation of premium
Year 1	0.9091	731
Year 2	0.8264	665
Year 3	0.7513	604
	2.4868	2,000

The above assumes an annual amortisation on the anniversary of the inception of the swap. In accounting terms one would then normally amortise on a straight line basis within each of the transaction years. A more sophisticated calculation can be performed to create a monthly amortisation, or one which simply addresses any predetermined financial accounting periods.

exchange of principal, are both known at the outset, and one can calculate the overall implied forward financing element of the transaction in exactly the same way as in the case of a long-dated forward transaction.

The amortisation of the financing element over the period of the swap does not need to take account of any cumulative interest implications, however, as the swap itself involves fixed rate cashflows over its life. There is, accordingly, simply an amortisation of each annual payment over the year in question. An additional complication here is when the swap has an inherent 'value' on inception because one or other of the fixed rates involved is out of line with the market. The position then becomes similar to buying an 'out-of-the-market' futures transaction. The up-front premium payable or receivable on entering into the swap is an inherent part of the overall financing arrangement and should be capitalised and amortised over the life of the transaction. The amortisation of that premium will not necessarily be on a straight line basis, as unlike the underlying swap payments, it will need to take account of the cumulative interest implications flowing from the swap lasting beyond one year.

The same approach to that employed in the above example can be used to determine the amortisation profile for the initial margin on longer-term futures transactions, or to take account of any non-standard features in the predetermined cashflows of the swap.

The future re-exchange of principal in the last example is at the current spot rate of exchange. Had the re-exchange utilised some other rate, it would have been necessary to adopt the same approach as in the case of an out-of-the-market futures transaction. A portion of the initial premium payment would have been attributable to the difference between the spot and the re-exchange rates, and that part would have been deferred and then taken into account at the end of the transaction.

The position can become extremely complex where both the forward re-exchange and one or more of the implicit interest rates are out of line with current market rates. In some cases these two elements might offset each other sufficiently to eliminate most or all of any up-front payment for the swap.

Whatever the specific details of the transaction, however, it will always be possible to break it down into a series of currency cashflows. By then taking account of any difference between the spot and re-exchange rates, it is possible to calculate the market related flows on both sides of the swap. It is then simply a case of ensuring that the accounting approach adopted results in fixed interest yields on both sides. In general terms, an understanding of the pricing of the transaction (in terms of any up-front premium) will lead directly to the calculations of the inherent yield on the swap. This should then 'drive' the way in which the transaction is recorded in the accounts.

The concepts applied in accounting for fixed to fixed cross-currency swaps are also of relevance when dealing with a swap involving a floating-rate stream of payments. The initial step is to ascertain the extent to which the forward re-exchange is out of line with current spot rates, and then to relate any such mismatch to any fixed stream of interest flows over the life of the transaction and any up-front premium. Reducing the transaction to a sequence of cashflows (even if some of them are, for example LIBOR based) will generally provide sufficient guidance as to how to account for the transaction. The pricing of the deal, in terms of any up-front premium, etc should continue to determine the way in which it is subsequently accounted for.

C.4   Hedging with contingent-type products

The fundamental difference between a commitment-type hedge and a contingent-type hedging arrangement is that in the latter case, it is not really possible to say that the base currency equivalent of the foreign currency monetary item has been 'fixed' in the base currency. This is because the contingent hedge will generally allow for an upside gain on the position whilst eliminating any downside exposure. The monetary position is, accordingly, still exposed to future movements in exchange rates – even though that exposure is limited in either one direction or the other. The present section will only deal with the pure contingent-type products discussed in sections A.11 to A.16 above, with third generation product hedging being considered separately in the following section.

Due to the nature of the currency option product, a mark-to-market of its value can only yield a profit in relation to original cost in those cases where there has been a foreign exchange loss on the underlying monetary exposure. The most convenient way of accounting for the exposure and the hedge is, accordingly, to mark them both to market on a regular basis, taking gains and losses direct to income. This will result in the offsetting in income of the hedge profit or loss and any currency impact on the underlying exposure.

The alternative approach, discussed in section C.3, of maintaining the monetary item giving rise to the exposure at a fixed historic spot rate of exchange ruling at the point where the hedge was entered into, becomes far more complex in the case of a contingent-type hedging arrangement, because it will be necessary to record somewhere in the balance sheet the unrealised gains arising from any increase in the value of the monetary position.

The other issue to be addressed is, of course, the treatment of the initial premium. Unlike the up-front payment on a commitment-type hedge, the premium payable on an option is, in economic terms, more in the nature of an insurance premium to ensure that the value of a particular asset does not fall below a predetermined rate. It is calculated by the writer of the option, based upon factors such as volatility rather than being simply the derivation of a figure using interest rate differentials. The alternative treatments would appear to be either to adjust downwards, as at the inception of the hedge, the base currency equivalent value of the exposed position or, to amortise the premium over the period of the option arrangement. Section A.12 described how the price of an option will be the combination of two separate elements, the intrinsic value and the time value, with the former being related to the difference between the current spot rate of exchange and the exercise rate. In economic terms, that portion of the premium relating to the option's intrinsic value is conceptually similar to the forward premium or discount on a forward transaction, whereas the time value of the option is the 'insurance' element.

Any marking to market of the option over the duration of its life will automatically take account of both the intrinsic value and the time value, with the former moving in relation to fluctuations in the underlying rate of exchange and the latter tending to reduce, as described in section A.12, over the period of the option. The option premium already reflects a mark-to-market of the hedge on acquisition, and any subsequent revaluation of the position will accordingly result in an increase or a decrease in the value of the option itself. If the initial premium is deferred in the balance sheet, any increase or decrease in the option value should be reflected through an increase or decrease in the amount of the deferred asset or liability. It is that movement in value which is taken to income.

If the company decides to 'fix' the base currency equivalent of the monetary exposure at the spot rate of exchange ruling at the point where the option is entered into, it will be necessary to effect memoranda revaluations of both the exposure and the option in order to calculate the unrealised gain or loss on the net position. The latter can then be brought into account by way of a balance sheet sundry asset or liability. If the amount of that balance sheet item becomes significant in relation to the underlying exposure and/or the operations of the company, it would be desirable to disclose the underlying economic nature of the related monetary exposure by way of a note to the accounts.

It is interesting to note that the above approach to option hedge accounting is slightly different to the concepts employed in section C.3 in relation to commitment-type hedging. In the latter case, the financing element of the transaction was deferred and amortised over the period of the hedge, with the position created by the commitment-type arrangement then being subject to a spot revaluation over its duration. A similar treatment of an option hedge would require that the premium be amortised over the duration of the hedge and that the underlying exposure then be eliminated from any revaluation *to the extent that the hedge was in a profitable position.* This is, however, an extremely complex approach and fails to take account of the non-standard way in which the time value of the option amortises over its life (see section A.12). Any closing out of the option in advance of its maturity would, accordingly, be likely to yield a gain or loss in excess of that which had been taken into account to date as a result of the periodic spot revaluation and the amortisation. A more sensible approach is, accordingly, to adopt a comprehensive mark to market policy for both the monetary position and the related option hedge.

It was noted in section C.1 that the definition of an unhedged monetary item should include, for balance sheet translation purposes, any hedge of off balance sheet contingencies other than those which are themselves of a contingent nature. In other words, any contingent hedges of an off balance sheet currency contingency should be excluded from the periodic revaluation of unhedged monetary items.

If the contingent exposure is eliminated, the contingent hedge becomes an unhedged monetary item. If the contingent exposure becomes an actual exposure on the balance sheet, the contingent hedge should be treated in the way already described above.

C.5   Hedging with third generation products

The problem with some of these newer hedging products is that there is frequently little or no liquid market available against which one can easily evaluate the market price. The whole concept of 'marking to market' accordingly becomes far more subjective than might otherwise be the case. Although, in most cases, it is possible to obtain a market value either from the provider of the product or through the recalculation of the price using current exchange and interest rates, lack of liquidity in some areas can result in the available price not always reflecting the true value of the hedge. Most banks will, for example, be prepared to quote on some of these more exotic products at 'off-market' rates in view of their lack of experience in dealing with them, and the fact that the hedging cost of entering into such a transaction is likely to be substantially more than might be the case with one of the larger banks. By quoting an off-market price for a transaction, they are choosing to limit their involvement in the market whilst, at the same time, not having to indicate publicly that they are not prepared to enter into the transaction.

Products such as cylinder options or range forwards can best be accounted for by thinking of them in terms of having 'fixed' the base currency equivalent of the foreign currency monetary item, but as only having done so within a predetermined range. The monetary item is, accordingly, revalued at current spot rates of exchange to the extent that it falls within that range, or at the high/low point of the range if the exchange rate moves outside of it. The only complication here concerns the treatment of any up-front premium which is, of course, essentially similar to an option premium. If it proves impractical to effect a regular mark-to-market of the entire position, it will generally be acceptable to revalue the exposure as already noted and then amortise the premium over the life of the hedge. Although the result will not be the same as if the entire position had been revalued on a periodic basis, the overall result will probably be as good an approximation as any other. In the event of the underlying exposure being eliminated prior to the maturity of the hedge, the hedging arrangement naturally falls to be accounted for as an unhedged monetary item in the same way as for any other unhedged off balance sheet commitment.

Products such as cancellable forwards (section A.19) create, in economic terms, a similar scenario to that which is available under a more traditional option arrangement. Although the premium is less, because of the off-market nature of the forward price, the most sensible approach will generally be to treat the arrangement in the same way as a normal option, as discussed in section C.4. The only point to note, perhaps, is that the intrinsic value in most such arrangements is extremely small, and the time value (or the equivalent thereof) is accordingly much larger. The difference between an amortisation-type approach and a mark to market treatment is accordingly usually far more significant. Although a mark to market concept would be preferable, an amortisation approach may need to be adopted where a proper market valuation of the position is not obtainable. Where the contract extends beyond one year, the amortisation of the premium will need to take account of the compounding of interest impact discussed in section C.3.

Most of the other products discussed in Section A are of more use for transaction hedging than for the management of balance sheet exposure. Where, however, another form of product is used to hedge a balance sheet exposure, it should generally be possible to apply the basic rules already discussed in this section and the two preceding ones to the constituent parts of the hedging transaction. In all cases, a proper understanding of the way in which the hedge has been priced is likely to be required in order to determine the most appropriate accounting treatment.

C.6 Foreign equity investments

SSAP 20 provides for foreign equity investments to be denominated in the currency of the overseas company where the investor has hedged its investment using foreign currency borrowings. The rationale for this approach, its limitation and the need to extend the application to non-debt hedges of the investment, are discussed in detail in chapter 8. That chapter concludes that reserve accounting should be employed to the extent that there is a match between the equity investment and the amount of the hedge (however constructed), but that any mismatch in the position – either in relation to the hedge or the underlying exposure, should be marked to market with any gain or loss being taken to income. The net effect of this approach should be to ensure that any gain or loss taken to reserves in relation to the investment will be exactly offset by any gain or loss arising on the hedge.

The rationale for treating non-debt hedges in exactly the same way as any foreign currency borrowing used to hedge a net investment is apparent if one considers the similarity, in cashflow terms, between a straightforward debt hedging arrangement and the use of, for example, the kind of fixed to fixed cross-currency swap explored in section C.3. In other words, had the company borrowed in its domestic currency but then effected a cross-currency swap, the cashflows connected with the overall transaction and, indeed, the currency exposures associated therewith, would be identical. If one then considers the similarities between a fixed to fixed cross-currency swap and a long-term forward foreign exchange contract, it can very quickly be seen that there is no basis whatever for restricting reserve accounting to those cases where the hedge of the foreign equity investment has been carried out in the cash market.

C.7   Foreign currency share capital

A recent development in the UK has been the arrival of foreign currency capital. It is now established in law that it is possible to capitalise a UK company either in a foreign currency or, for that matter, in a basket of currencies. This facility has recently been grasped by a number of international banking groups in the UK as a means of matching the mix of their foreign currency assets/liabilities and share capital. The particular advantage for a banking group having multicurrency share capital is that it allows it to better protect its capital adequacy ratios from fluctuations in overall balance sheet footings as a result of currency movements. The only well-documented instance of multicurrency capital to date is that of Scandinavian Bank Group plc which, in March, 1987 issued 27.5 million 'capital currency units' comprising fixed proportions of shares – themselves denominated in sterling, US dollars, Swiss francs and Deutschmarks. Each capital currency unit in fact comprises one ordinary share of l0p, one ordinary share of l0c, one share of l0 centimes and one of l0 pfennigs. It is not possible to trade the individual shares in these currencies and they can only be traded in the form of currency units.

Scandinavian Bank does not intend to change the way in which it prepares accounts and will continue to translate everything into sterling. The only difference is, of course, that the sterling equivalent of its share capital will now also fluctuate in line with exchange rates. As at the date of the issue, for example, its share capital consisted of approximately 50% US dollars, 20% sterling, 15% Deutschmarks and 15% Swiss francs. The price of the currency units is quoted in sterling, dividends are paid in sterling and all settlement of share purchases or acquisitions made through The Stock Exchange are also carried out in sterling. An interesting result of the designation of its share capital in these four currencies was that Scandinavian Bank found itself having to allocate its share premium account and reserves to those underlying shares in these same currencies. This has resulted in its entire shareholders' interests being denominated in those four currencies. Future sets of accounts will accordingly show movements in reserves, etc allocated across these currencies.

In addition to ensuring that its capital adequacy ratios are better protected in the future, Scandinavian Bank's multicurrency share capital also constitutes a form of hedge against its balance sheet exposures in these currencies. To the extent that the Bank was fully matched prior to the creation of the multicurrency share capital, it would have been necessary for it to sell sterling assets in exchange for the appropriate mixture of currencies in order to maintain a square position. Another way of looking at it is that the Bank will have created an open position in each of these currencies which is similar in magnitude to the size of the share capital in each currency.

It remains to be seen how popular the idea of multicurrency share capital becomes. It has particular relevance to international banks because of the way in which their multicurrency balance sheets are regulated for prudential purposes by the Bank of England, but has far less relevance to the majority of commercial and manufacturing companies. Its growth will probably be driven by the interest of investors in the concept of a mixed currency exposure rather than one denominated in a particular currency. It provides the investor, for example, with the opportunity of speculating *against* his own domestic currency at the same time as investing in a domestic equity. Perhaps the market would react extremely favourably to the idea of acquiring shares in, say, ICI which incorporated a speculative currency element due to 25% of each share being denominated in, for example, yen?

Consolidations

Introduction

Introduction

As explained in chapter 9, there is essentially only one way of dealing with the consolidation of two separate business entities which have different base currencies, and that is to employ the closing rate/net investment method. The so-called 'temporal method' is not so much a means of consolidation, as a method for translating the accounting records of a company into its base currency in those circumstances where some other currency has initially been used for the recording of transactions.

This section demonstrates, by way of example, the key elements of a multicurrency consolidation that are discussed in chapter 9. This section does not explore the underlying rationale for adopting particular approaches in the consolidation process, and the reader is referred to chapter 9 for a comprehensive discussion of the subject.

The example used in this section involves a theoretical UK company, Tops Ltd, and a French company, Sub Cie, which Tops Ltd acquires. The initial discussion builds up a profile of the two companies and sets out the financial information which is required for the subsequent consolidation.

The example includes a detailed consolidation of the balance sheets at the beginning and end of the year, and of the income and funds flow statements for the year in question. It deals with the particular problems of purchased goodwill, reserve accounting in the subsidiary, goodwill arising on consolidation and the hedging of the parent's net investment through foreign currency borrowings. It shows how inter-company accounts should be treated, addresses the question of unrealised intercompany profits and deals with the issue of third currency borrowings.

The following is a summary of tables used in the example:

Tables

1 Pre-acquisition balance sheets at 31 December 19X1
2 Post-acquisition balance sheets at 1 January 19X2
3 Allocation of purchase consideration
4 Results of operations for 19X2
5 Movements on fixed-asset accounts
6 Movements on inter-company accounts
7 Movements in Deutschmark debt
8 Balance sheets at 31 December 19X2
9 Consolidating balance sheet at 1 January 19X2
10 Consolidating balance sheet at 31 December 19X2
11 Consolidating income statement for 19X2
12 Derivation of funds flow movements
13 Calculation of funds flow exchange rate impact
14 Consolidated statement of source and application of funds for 19X2

D.1   Pre-acquisition

The example involves a UK company, Tops Ltd, and a French company, Sub Cie, which Tops acquires on 1 January 19X2. The following is a summary of the balance sheets of Tops Ltd and Sub Cie immediately prior to the acquisition taking place on 31 December 19X1.

Table 1   Pre-acquisition balance sheets at 31 December 19X1

	Sub Cie *Fr fr 000*	Tops Ltd *£000*
Assets		
Purchased goodwill	15,000	—
Land — at valuation	55,000	—
— at cost	—	10,000
Other fixed assets — at cost	35,000	40,000
— accumulated depreciation	(10,000)	(12,000)
Inventory — at cost	8,000	12,000
Other current assets	2,000	6,000
Liabilities		
Long-term debt (DM6 million)	(20,000)	—
Other liabilities	(2,000)	(4,000)
Net assets	83,000	52,000
Shareholders' funds		
Share capital	50,000	40,000
Revaluation reserve	15,000	—
Retained earnings	18,000	12,000
	83,000	52,000

Sub Cie has Fr fr 15 million of purchased goodwill arising from an earlier acquisition of a local French business. The above figures accordingly represent the consolidated accounts of Sub Cie and its subsidiary. The company is active in a regulated sector of the French economy and is required to revalue its property holdings on an annual basis. It is, however, prohibited from adjusting its accounting records to take account of the market value of any other fixed assets.

D.2   The acquisition of Sub Cie

Tops Ltd acquires Sub Cie on 1 January 19X2 for a total consideration of £12 million. With a then current exchange rate of Fr fr 10 = £1 this reprepresents a cost of £3.7 million in excess of the book value of Sub Cie. Tops Ltd funds its acquisition through a Fr fr 100 million bond issue and a £5 million term loan. It utilises the Fr fr difference between the £15 million raised and the £12 million cost of the investment to provide its newly acquired subsidiary with additional working capital. In addition, in view of Tops' aggressive expansion plans for Sub Cie, it injects a further £2 million out of its own resources. This has accordingly provided Sub Cie with total additional working capital of £5 million. Because it would seem that at least £3 million of this additional funding will be required by Sub Cie for some time, and because Tops Ltd is accordingly prepared to view it as a long-term commitment to its newly acquired subsidiary, £3 million of the additional funding is structured as a Fr fr 30 million long-term loan and the remaining £2 million as an intercompany account advance.

Ignoring the costs of the aforementioned transaction, and assuming that they all take place on 1 January 19X2, the adjusted balance sheets of Tops Ltd and Sub Cie as at the close of business on 1 January are as follows.

Table 2   Post-acquisition balance sheets at 1 January 19X2

	Sub Cie Fr fr 000	Tops Ltd £000
Assets		
Purchase goodwill	15,000	—
Land — at valuation	55,000	—
— at cost	—	10,000
Other fixed assets — at cost	35,000	40,000
— accumulated depreciation	(10,000)	(12,000)
Inventory — at cost	8,000	12,000
Other current assets	52,000	4,000
Liabilities		
Long-term debt (DM6 million)	(20,000)	
Long-term debt (Fr fr 100 million)	—	(10,000)
Long-term debt (£5 million)	—	(5,000)
Other liabilities	(2,000)	(4,000)
Inter company items		
Investment in subsidiary — at cost		12,000
Fr fr loan account	(30,000)	3,000
£ intercompany account	(20,000)	2,000
Net assets	83,000	52,000
Shareholders' funds		
Share capital	50,000	40,000
Revaluation reserve	15,000	—
Retained earnings	18,000	12,000
	83,000	52,000

Tops Ltd performs a detailed review of the underlying net worth of its newly-acquired subsidiary and concludes that the total purchase consideration can be allocated as follows:

Table 3   Allocation of purchase consideration

	Per books	Per valuation	
	Fr fr 000	Fr fr 000	£000
Assets			
Purchased goodwill	15,000	—	—
Land at valuation	55,000	55,000	5,500
Fixed assets — net	25,000	50,000	5,000
Inventory — at cost	8,000	8,000	800
Other current assets	2,000	2,000	200
Liabilities			
Long-term debt	(20,000)	(20,000)	(2,000)
Other liabilities	(2,000)	(2,000)	(200)
Net assets	83,000		
Tangible net assets — at valuation		93,000	9,300
Purchased goodwill		27,000	2,700
Total consideration		120,000	12,000

Because of Sub Cie's involvement in a regulated industry, it is prevented from writing-up its non-land assets in its local books of account. It accordingly retains its original Fr fr costs, and Tops will be required to make an adjustment for the underlying acquisition valuations whenever it performs a consolidation.

D.3   Net investment in the subsidiary

The base currency of Sub Cie is determined to be French francs, with the long-term Deutschmark borrowing simply being the result of an earlier financing arrangement relating to the acquisition of some plant and equipment. Tops Ltd also views Sub Cie as a French franc-based operation and has, indeed, endeavoured partially to hedge its exposure to this new investment through its French franc bond offering. It envisages that the bond will eventually be able to be redeemed out of the flow of dividends from Sub Cie over the course of the next ten years. There is no clear view as to the nature of the extra £5 million of working capital provided to Sub Cie although, as already mentioned, Tops' current plans for that company would suggest that the Fr fr 30 million loan will be required on an ongoing basis. Tops Ltd accordingly concludes that it should treat its French franc loan to its subsidiary as an integral part of its investment in that company, resulting in its net investment for the purposes of any future consolidation being £15 million – or Fr fr 150 million (comprising the Fr fr 120 million cost and the Fr fr 30 million loan).

Chapter 9, however, concluded that it was inappropriate to include purchased goodwill in the definition of the parent company's net investment in its subsidiary, both insofar as the purchased goodwill of the parent was concerned and, for that matter, any purchased goodwill already carried in the subsidiary's accounts. The total net investment of Tops Ltd in its subsidiary for the purposes of the consolidation process should, accordingly, be taken as being £12.3 million (or Fr fr 123 million), representing the total deemed investment of £15 million less the purchased goodwill of £2.7 million. The resultant net investment is, of course, equal to the total underlying value of the acquired assets after adjusting for the injection of the Fr fr 30 million long-term loan.

D.4 Results of operations

The above steps have set the scene as at 1 January 19X2, and it is now necessary to make some assumptions regarding the activities of the two companies during the subsequent year. The next group of tables accordingly set out the results of their operations and the movements in certain key balance sheet accounts.

Initially, however, it is necessary to establish some new exchange rates as at 31 December 19X2. We shall assume for this purpose that sterling weakens over the year as compared with both the French franc and the Deutschmark, resulting in closing spot rates of exchange of Fr fr 8 = £1 and DM2.5 = £. These compare with Fr fr 10 and DM3 as at 1 January 19X2.

The following is a summary of the results of operations for Tops Ltd and Sub Cie for 19X2.

Table 4   Results of operations for 19X2

	Sub Cie Fr fr 000	Tops Ltd £000
Sales		
External	220,000	55,000
Inter-company	—	9,000
Total	220,000	64,000
Cost of sales		
Inventory at 1 January	8,000	12,000
External purchases	120,000	40,000
Inter-company purchases	80,000	—
	208,000	52,000
Inventory at 31 December	(20,000)	(10,000)
Cost of sales	188,000	42,000
Gross profit	32,000	22,000
Depreciation	(10,000)	(8,000)
Foreign exchange losses	(50)	—
Interest and other operating expenses	(9,600)	(7,500)
Operating profit	12,350	6,500
Amortisation of goodwill	(3,000)	—
Revaluation of DM long-term debt	650	—
Revaluation of Fr fr long-term debt	—	(2,500)
Dividends receivable	—	750
Net profit	10,000	4,750
Retained earnings brought forward	18,000	12,000
Dividends payable	(6,000)	—
Retained earnings carried forward	22,000	16,750

D.5   Fixed-asset movements

The revaluation of the land holdings of Sub Cie yields a further increase in value of Fr fr 15 million to Fr fr 70 million. The movements on the other fixed-asset accounts for the two companies during the year are as follows:

Table 5   Movements on fixed-asset accounts

	Sub Cie Fr fr 000	Tops Ltd £000
Other fixed assets — at cost		
Balance as at 1 January	35,000	40,000
Additions	45,000	10,000
Retirements	(4,000)	—
Balance as at 31 December	76,000	50,000
Accumulated depreciation		
Balance as at 1 January	10,000	12,000
Additions	10,000	8,000
Retirements	(2,000)	—
Balance as at 31 December	18,000	20,000

Had the underlying assets of Sub Cie been revalued at 1 January 19X2 by Fr fr 25 million (see Table 3) additional depreciation of Fr fr 5 million would have been charged in the accounts.

D.6   Intercompany transactions

Tops Ltd has made active use of Sub Cie for the purposes of increasing its sales, and this has resulted in a fairly substantial volume of inter-company transactions between the two companies. This has also accounted for a large build-up of inventory on hand in Sub Cie, with 50% of the total inventory on hand as at 31 December originally having been acquired from Tops.

Neither Tops Ltd nor Sub Cie maintain full multicurrency accounting records and the movements on their individual intercompany accounts are accordingly recorded in their respective local currencies. The movements in the two intercompany accounts over the course of the year may be summarised as follows:

Table 6   Movements on intercompany accounts

	Sub Cie Fr fr 000	Tops Ltd £000
£ Intercompany Account		
Balance at 1 January	(20,000)	2,000
Inventory purchases	(80,000)	9,000
Cash settlements	60,000	(6,700)
Balance at 31 December	(40,000)	4,300
Fr fr loan account		
Balance at 1 January	(30,000)	3,000
Dividends payable	6,000	(750)
Cash settlements	2,000	(200)
Balance at 31 December	(22,000)	2,050

The inventory purchases and cash settlements in Table 6 have, in effect, been recorded at composite rates of exchange prevailing over the course of the year. The dividend payable has been booked at the exchange rate of Fr fr 8 ruling at 31 December. Tops Ltd applies a standard 25% mark up on cost to all intercompany sales to Sub Cie, with the result that all intercompany inventory on hand in Sub Cie as at 31 December contains a 20% unrealised profit. The loan account and the intercompany account are both interest free.

D.7   Long-term debt

Sub Cie has repaid 25% of the outstanding balance on its long-term Deutschmark debt, leaving DM4.5 million still outstanding as at 31 December. Because it records the debt in its books of account in French franc terms, and because it has revalued the closing balance to the year-end rate of exchange, the movement on that account over the year may be summarised as follows:

Table 7   Movements in Deutschmark debt

	DM 000	Rate of exchange	Fr fr 000
Balance at 1 January	6,000	3.3333	20,000
Repayment during year	(1,500)	3.3000	(4,950)
Revaluation impact	—		(650)
Balance at 31 December	4,500	3.2000	14,400

The Fr fr 650,000 represents a revaluation gain which has been taken to income in preparing the year end accounts of Sub Cie.

There has been no movement in the outstanding amount of Tops' Fr fr bond issue, although a £500,000 initial repayment has taken place on the £5 million loan.

D.8 Year-end balance sheets

The balance sheets of the two companies as at 31 December, after taking account of all of the aforementioned transactions, are as follows:

Table 8   Balance sheets at 31 December 19X2

	Sub Cie Fr fr 000	Tops Ltd £000
Assets		
Purchased goodwill	12,000	—
Land — at valuation	70,000	—
at cost	—	10,000
Other fixed assets — at cost	76,000	50,000
— accumulated depreciation	(18,000)	(20,000)
Inventory — at cost	20,000	10,000
Other current assets	21,200	7,400
Liabilities		
Long-term debt (DM4.5 million)	(14,400)	—
Long-term debt (Frfr150 million)	—	(12,500)
Long-term debt (£4.5 million)	—	(4,500)
Other liabilities	(2,800)	(2,000)
Intercompany items		
Investment in subsidiary — at cost	—	12,000
Fr fr loan account	(22,000)	2,050
£ intercompany account	(40,000)	4,300
Net assets	102,000	56,750
Shareholders' funds		
Share capital	50,000	40,000
Revaluation reserve	30,000	—
Retained earnings	22,000	16,750
	102,000	56,750

D.9 Consolidating balance sheets and income statement

The above information is sufficient to enable us to prepare the consolidated accounts of Tops Ltd and Sub Cie as at 31 December 19X2. For the purposes of completeness, the following schedules also include a consolidated balance sheet as at 1 January of that year, which we shall then use to derive a funds flow statement for the year.

The consolidating schedules have been set up on a fairly traditional basis, but in the interests of clarity, the acquisition adjustment as at 1 January and the translation adjustment as at 31 December have been separately identified in specific adjustment columns. The Schedules should be read in conjunction with notes (a) through (i) following and each of the adjustments on the schedules have been cross-referenced to the appropriate note reference.

Table 9   Consolidating balance sheet at 1 January 19X2

	Sub Cie Fr fr 000	Translated at 1 Jan rate £000	Tops Ltd £000	Consolidated £000	Acquisition adjustment £000 Note (a)*	Adjusted £000
Assets						
Purchased goodwill	15,000	1,500	—	1,500	1,200	2,700
Land — at valuation	55,000	5,500	—	5,500		5,500
at cost	—	—	10,000	10,000		10,000
Other fixed assets — at cost	35,000	3,500	40,000	43,500	2,500	46,000
— accumulated depreciation	(10,000)	(1,000)	(12,000)	(13,000)		(13,000)
Inventory — at cost	8,000	800	12,000	12,800		12,800
Other current assets	52,000	5,200	4,000	9,200		9,200
Liabilities						
Long-term debt (DM6 million)	(20,000)	(2,000)	—	(2,000)		(2,000)
Long-term debt (Fr fr100 million)	—	—	(10,000)	(10,000)		(10,000)
Long-term debt (£5 million)	—	—	(5,000)	(5,000)		(5,000)
Other liabilities	(2,000)	(200)	(4,000)	(4,200)		(4,200)
Intercompany items						
Investment in subsidiary — at cost	—	—	12,000	12,000	(12,000)	
Fr fr loan account	(30,000)	(3,000)	3,000	—		
£ intercompany account	(20,000)	(2,000)	2,000	—		
Net assets	83,000	8,300	52,000	60,300	(8,300)	52,000
Shareholders' funds						
Share capital	50,000	5,000	40,000	45,000	(5,000)	40,000
Revaluation reserve	15,000	1,500	—	1,500	(1,500)	
Foreign currency investment t anslation reserve						
Retained earnings	18,000	1,800	12,000	13,800	(1,800)	12,000
	83,000	8,300	52,000	60,300	(8,300)	52,000

* Note (a) is on p 264 following.

Table 10   Consolidating balance sheet at 31 December 19X2

	Sub Cie Fr fr 000	Translated at 31 Dec Rate £000	Tops Ltd £000	Consolidated £000	Acquisition adjustment £000 Note (a)*	Translation adjustment £000 Note (b)*	Other adjustments £000	Adjusted £000
Assets								
Purchased goodwill				1,500	1,200	(375)	(c) 105	2,430
Land — at valuation	12,000	1,500	—	8,750				8,750
at cost	70,000	8,750	—	10,000				10,000
Other fixed assets — at cost	76,000	9,500	10,000	59,500	2,500	625		62,625
—accumulated depreciation	(18,000)	(2,250)	50,000	(22,250)			(d) (625)	(22,875)
Inventory — at cost	20,000	2,500	(20,000)	12,500			(e) (250)	12,250
Other current assets	21,200	2,650	10,000	10,050			(i) (750)	9,300
			7,400					
Liabilities								
Long-term debt (DM4.5 million)	(14,400)	(1,800)	—	(1,800)				(1,800)
Long-term debt (Frfr100 million)	—	—	(12,500)	(12,500)				(12,500)
Long-term debt (£4.5 million)	—	—	(4,500)	(4,500)				(4,500)
Other liabilities	(2,800)	(350)	(2,000)	(2,350)			(i) 750	(1,600)
Intercompany items								
Investment in subsidiary — at cost	—	—	12,000	12,000	(12,000)			
Fr fr loan account	(22,000)	(2,750)	2,050	(700)		750	(f) (50)	
£ intercompany account	(40,000)	(5,000)	4,300	(700)			(f) 700	
Net assets	102,000	12,750	56,750	69,500	(8,300)	1,000	(120)	(62,080)
Shareholders' funds								
Share capital	50,000	6,250	40,000	46,250	(5,000)	(1,250)		40,000
Revaluation reserve	30,000	3,750	—	3,750	(1,500)	(375)		1,875
Foreign currency investment translation reserve	—	—	—	—		3,075	(g) (2,500)	575
Retained earnings (Table 11)	22,000	2,750	16,750	19,500	(1,800)	(450)	2,380	19,630
	102,000	12,750	56,750	69,500	(8,300)	1,000	(120)	62,080

* Notes (a)–(i) appear on pp 264–270 following.

Table 11 Consolidating income statement for 19X2

	Sub Cie Fr fr 000	Translated at 31 Dec Rate £000	Tops Ltd £000	Consolidated £000	Acquisition adjustment £000 Note (a)*	Translation adjustment £000 Note (b)*	Other adjustments £000 Note*	Adjusted £000
Sales	220,000	27,500	64,000	91,500	—		(h) (9,000)	82,500
Cost of sales	(188,000)	(23,500)	(42,000)	(65,500)			(h) 10,000	55,500
Gross profit	32,000	4,000	22,000	26,000			1,000	27,000
Depreciation	(10,000)	(1,250)	(8,000)	(9,250)			(d) (625)	(9,875)
Interest & other operating expenses	(9,600)	(1,200)	(7,500)	(8,700)			(e) (250)	(8,950)
	12,400	1,550	6,500	8,050			125	8,175
Foreign exchange gain (loss)								
Revaluation of DM long-term debt	650	81	—	81				81
Revaluation of Fr fr long-term debt	—	—	(2,500)	(2,500)			(g) 2,500	—
Other	(50)	(6)	—	(6)			(f) 650 (h) (1,000)	(356)
Total FX gain (loss)	600	75	(2,500)	(2,425)	—	—	2,150	(275)
Amortisation of goodwill	(3,000)	(375)	—	(375)			(c) 105	(270)
Dividends receivable	—	—	750	750			(i) (750)	—
Net profit	10,000	1,250	4,750	6,000	—	—	1,630	7,630
Retained earnings brought forward	18,000	2,250	12,000	14,250	(1,800)	(450)	—	12,000
Dividends payable	(6,000)	(750)	—	(750)	—	—	(i) 750	—
Retained earnings carried forward	22,000	2,750	16,750	19,500	(1,800)	(450)	2,380	19,630

* Notes (a)–(i) appear on pp 264–270 following.

Note (a) Acquisition adjustments

This adjustment is designed to restate the 1 January 19X2 balance sheet onto a basis consistent with the acquisition method of accounting for the purchase of Sub Cie. The adjustment itself can be calculated from the information already set out in relation to the acquisition, in particular that contained in Table 3.

In addition to eliminating the purchased goodwill of Sub Cie and effecting a restatement of acquired assets to their current market values, the adjustment also establishes the goodwill arising on the acquisition in Tops Ltd. The latter will then be amortised in the consolidated accounts on a straight line basis over ten years (in accordance with Tops Ltd's accounting policy for goodwill).

The adjustment can be summarised as follows:

	£000	£000
Debit Goodwill (net)	1,200	
Fixed assets (uplift in value)	2,500	
Share capital (Fr fr 50 million)	5,000	
Revaluation reserve (Fr fr 15 million)	1,500	
Retained earnings (Fr fr 18 million)	1,800	
Credit investment in subsidiary		12,000

The entry to goodwill represents the net of:
(a) the elimination of £1,500,000 of goodwill of Sub Cie; and
(b) the set-up of Tops' purchased goodwill of £2,700,000.

The remaining numbers have been extracted directly from either Table 2 or Table 3.

Note (b) Translation adjustment

The discussion on page 255 established that the net investment of Tops Ltd in its new subsidiary amounted to £12.3 million or Fr fr 123 million. This comprised:

	£000
Cost of investment	12,000
Fr fr denominated loan	3,000
Less — purchased goodwill of Sub Cie	(2,700)
	£12,300

This was equal to the market value of Sub Cie's underlying tangible net assets, after taking account of the injection of the additional long-term loan of Fr fr 30 million.

The translation adjustment booked at 31 December 19X2 has been calculated as set out in chapter 9, by applying the movement in exchange rates to the identified 'net investment'. This may be summarised as follows:

	£000
Fr fr 123 million at 1 January rate of 10.00	12,300
Fr fr 123 million at 31 December rate of 8.00	15,375
Gain on net investment	3,075

As we wish to account for this gain separately in the foreign currency investment translation reserve, it is necessary to 'strip it out' of those accounts where it currently sits. As the assets and liabilities of the subsidiary have been translated at 31 December at the year-end rate of exchange, the gain is in effect sitting in the related reserve and equity accounts. This can be seen by considering the build-up of the Fr fr 123 million as follows:

	Balances at 1 January	Allocation of gain on net investment
	Fr fr 000	*£000*
Share capital	50,000	1,250
Revaluation reserve	15,000	375
Retained earnings	18,000	450
Fr fr loan account	30,000	750
Write-up of fixed assets	25,000	625
Write-off of goodwill	(15,000)	(375)
	123,000	3,075

The write-up of fixed assets and the write-off of goodwill have been included above because the accounts of Sub Cie were never adjusted for these restatements (for the reasons already discussed). It accordingly becomes necessary to repeat the original acquisition adjustment at 31 December (as per note (a) above) and then, in effect, to revalue those 1 January amounts to the 31 December rates used in Table 10.

The £3,075,000 gain on the net investment has been allocated simply by applying the 1 January and 31 December exchange rates to each of the amounts in turn. It is that resulting allocation which then forms the basis for the translation adjustment in Table 10. That adjustment may be summarised as follows:

		£000	£000
Debit	Share capital	1,250	
	Revaluation reserve	375	
	Retained earnings	450	
	Fr fr loan account	750	
	Fixed assets	625	
	Credit Foreign currency investment translation reserve		3,075
	Purchased goodwill		375

No account has been taken in the above analysis of the fact that the Fr fr 30 million long-term loan was reduced slightly during the year. Apart from a small repayment of Fr fr 2 million, the year-end dividend payable has also been debited in the accounts against the long-term loan (refer to Table 6). SSAP 20 provides no guidance as to whether or not the opening or closing balance is more appropriate in this regard, although a strict interpretation of the concepts underlying the definition of the net investment would probably suggest that the year-end balance is more appropriate.

The opening balance has been used in the present example to demonstrate an inconsistency which arises as a result when considering the question of the group's related intercompany account. This matter is discussed in note (f).

Note (c) Goodwill adjustments

During the course of the year, Sub Cie has amortised Fr fr 3 million of its purchased goodwill. As the acquisition adjustment (note (a) above) has reversed the entire original amount of Fr fr 15 million, it is now necessary to add back to income the amount already amortised in the underlying accounts.

Although the 31 December balances have been translated into sterling in Table 10 using the then current exchange rate, the translation adjustment (note (b) above) has, in effect, restated the resulting £ amount onto a historic rate basis. The assumption underlying that restatement was that the combination of the acquisition adjustment and the translation adjustment would eliminate the historic balance. Although this approach is effective in the case of, for example, share capital, it cannot work where there has been a movement on the account concerned during the year. By reversing the goodwill amortisation, however, we also achieve the objective of eliminating the historic balance.

Because the translation adjustment has restated a theoretical balance on goodwill of Fr fr 15 million, the reversal of the amortised portion can now take place at the current balance sheet rate of 8.00. The Fr fr 3 million accordingly results in an adjustment of £375,000.

The position after this adjustment may be summarised as follows:

	£000
Unamortised portion of goodwill	
— Fr fr 12 million at 8.00	1,500
Reversal of amortised portion	
— Fr fr 3 million at 8.00	375
Elimination of goodwill	
—acquisition adjustment — *note (a)*	(1,500)
Translation impact	
— translation adjustment — *note (b)*	(375)
Remaining balance	—

The final adjustment required to goodwill is that relating to the amortisation of 10% of the goodwill arising on consolidation (as described in note (a) above). The amount involved is accordingly £270,000.

The net impact of these two adjustments to goodwill is shown as a single entry on Tables 10 and 11 as follows:

	£000	£000
Debit Purchased goodwill	105	
Credit Amortisation of goodwill		105

Note (d) Additional depreciation

The combined effect of the acquisition adjustment (note (a) above) and the translation adjustment (note (b) above) has been to reinstate the valuation uplift of the fixed assets of Sub Cie. It is now necessary, however, to book the additional depreciation which needs to be recorded on the valuation uplift. As noted under Table 5, had the revaluation been recorded in the accounts of Sub Cie, it would have resulted in additional depreciation of Fr fr 5 million. At what rate, however, should this be translated when recording it in the sterling consolidation?

The effect of the two adjustments discussed in notes (a) and (b) has been to reinstate the original valuation gain, and then restate the sterling equivalent of same onto a current rate basis. It follows that any depreciation of that uplift must now also be recorded at current rates. The Fr fr 5 million accordingly translates into £625,000 and the required adjustment is as follows:

	£000	£000
Debit Depreciation	625	
Credit Accumulated depreciation		625

Note (e) Unrealised inter-company profit

It was noted earlier in the example that 50% of inventory on hand at 31 December in Sub Cie had been acquired from Tops Ltd and that the latter's mark-up on inter-company sales amounted to 25%.

Inventory on hand (at cost) in Sub Cie at 31 December was Fr fr 20 million (Table 4), suggesting that Fr fr 10 million had been acquired from Tops Ltd. With a 25% mark-up on sales, the unrealised inter-company profit included in the cost of inventory is Fr fr 2 million. Translating this at the year-end rate of 8.00 results in an adjustment of £25,000 as follows:

	£000	*£000*
Debit Other expenses	250	
Credit Inventory		250

The unrealised profit would more normally have been debited to sales, but other expenses have been used in this example to maintain clarity on Table 11.

It is important to note that, because of the way in which inventory purchases are recorded in Sub Cie (see Table 6), it is likely that a part of the £250,000 is, in effect, attributable to movements in exchange rates. There will in most cases, however, be little justification in trying to identify the precise effect.

Note (f) Inter company accounts

It will be apparent from Table 6 that the intercompany accounts will not eliminate on consolidation due to the way in which movements during the year have been recorded.

In the case of the Fr fr loan account, the underlying asset in Tops' books should be denominated in French francs. It is, accordingly, the Fr fr 22 million recorded in the accounts of Sub Cie which is of relevance – rather than the 'derived' balance of of £2,050,000 in the books of Tops Ltd. The current sterling equivalent of the French franc balance is £2,750,000, suggesting that Tops Ltd needs to adjust its books by recording a gain of £700,000.

In the event, Tops Ltd has chosen to treat the original loan of Fr fr 30 million as part of its net investment in its subsidiary, and has accordingly already processed a consolidation adjustment (note (b) above) for £750,000 (representing the impact of the exchange rate movement on the full Fr fr 30 million). In order to balance the two intercompany accounts it is accordingly necessary, in fact, to book a loss of £50,000 to square the position.

The problem arises from the fact that there has been a movement over the period which has been recorded at a rate other than that ruling at the year-end. Although the dividend has been recorded at the current rate, the Fr fr 2 million repayment has been recorded at the 1 January rate of 10. The £50,000 loss which now needs to be booked is in fact the impact of the exchange rate movement applied to that Fr fr 2 million.

As discussed in note (b), this raises the question as to whether or not one can justify including the entire Fr fr 30 million in the definition of Tops' net investment in Sub Cie. Should the amount taken to reserves by way of the translation adjustment not be restricted in some way to the amount actually arising on the individual parts of the 'net investment'? In the current example the £50,000 has been taken to foreign exchange P/L in the income statement.

There is a further problem in the group's inter company accounts relating to the £ account. Table 6 shows how Sub Cie has recorded a balance of Fr fr 40 million against Tops' sterling receivable of £4,300,000. At the year-end exchange rate, this would suggest that Sub is overstating its liability by Fr fr 5,600,000. As can be seen from Table 6, this has come about as a result of the fairly high level of 'throughput' on the account over the year at various rates of exchange. The net impact at the end of the day is in fact very significant in relation to the operations of Sub Cie.

As Table 10 has already converted the year-end balances at the year-end rate, the adjustment required (in effect within the books of Sub Cie) of Fr fr 5,600,000 is also translated at that year-end rate. The result is a gain of £700,000.

The net effect of the aforementioned adjustments is processed as a single entry in the consolidation as follows:

	£000	£000
Debit £ intercompany account	700	
Credit Fr fr loan account		50
Foreign exchange gain		650

Note (g) Hedge of net investment

As already noted, Tops Ltd perceives its Fr fr 100 million bond issue as a partial hedge of its net investment in Sub Cie. It accordingly wishes to offset the gain or loss arising on that hedge against the gain or loss on the underlying net investment. We have already ascertained (note (b) above) that the latter consists of a gain of £3,075,000 and have taken that amount to the foreign currency investment translation reserve.

The offsetting loss on the bond holding can now also be taken to the translation reserve and is calculated as follows:

	£000
Fr fr 100 million at 1 January rate of 10.00	10,000
Fr fr 100 million at 31 December rate of 8.00	12,500
Loss on debt hedge	2,500

The entry processed in the consolidation is accordingly:

		£000	£000
Debit	Foreign currency investment translation reserve	2,500	
	Credit Revaluation of Fr fr long-term debt		2,500

Note (h) Intercompany sales

Table 4 identifies the fact that inter company sales by Tops Ltd during the year have amounted to £9 million. There have been no sales by Sub Cie to its parent. These sales have been recorded in the accounts of Sub Cie at a local French franc cost of Fr fr 80 million.

As the income statement has been translated on Table 11 at the year-end rate of exchange, any elimination of intercompany sales must also be made at that rate. The Fr fr 80 million of purchases translates on that basis into £10 million of sales by Tops. The difference of £1 million consists of exchange differences originating from Sub Cie having to record its purchases in the local currency.

The apparent loss of £1 million is, of course, largely offset by the gain of £700,000 recorded as a result of the reconciliation of inter-company balances (note (f) above). In other words, the apparent loss on the inventory purchases is in fact largely the mirror image of the gain arising from the way in which the settlement of those purchases has been recorded.

The adjustment required to correct sales, cost of sales and the foreign exchange impact is as follows:

		£000	£000
Debit	Sales	9,000	
	Foreign exchange loss	1,000	
	Credit Cost of sales		10,000

Note (i) Reclassification of dividends receivable

The final adjustment to be made to the consolidating income statement is the elimination of the inter company dividend. As this was recorded in Sub Cie at the year-end rate of exchange, it is simply a question of reclassifying the amounts payable and receivable as follows:

		£000	£000
Debit	Other liabilities	750	
	Dividends receivable		750
	Credit Other assets		750
	Dividends payable		750

D.10 Consolidated statement of source and application of funds

Table 12 shows the derivation of the consolidated funds flow statement using the 'net' approach recommended in chapter 9. Under this approach, the balance sheet movements are shown net of any exchange rate impact. Table 13 derives the exchange rate adjustments that are processed on Table 12 by translating the 1 January balance sheet of Sub Cie at both the 1 January and the 31 December rates of exchange. The differences originating from using those two separate rates of exchange are adjusted on Table 13 for the translation adjustment as at 31 December, the effect of the third currency borrowing (Deutschmarks) and the required adjustment in the books of Sub Cie to the £ inter company account. The notes following Table 13 discuss these latter two adjustments in more detail.

The net balance sheet movements on Table 12 are used to derive the funds flow statement itself after taking account of the debt hedge of Tops' net investment in its subsidiary. For completeness, a proforma derived statement of source and application of funds has been included as Table 14.

Table 12 Derivation of funds flow movements

£000	Consolidated balance sheet 1 Jan	31 Dec	Movement	Exchange rate impact (Table 13)	Net movement	Land revaluation	Debt hedge	Group profit	Appl'n of funds	Working capital
Assets										
Purchased goodwill	2,700	2,430	(270)		(270)			270		
Land — at valuation	5,500	8,750	3,250	1,375	1,875	(1,875)				
at cost	10,000	10,000	—							
Other fixed assets — at cost	46,000	62,625	16,625	1,500	15,125				(15,125)	
— accumulated depreciation	(13,000)	(22,875)	(9,875)	(250)	(9,625)			9,625		
Inventory — at cost	12,800	12,250	(550)	200	(750)					750
Other current assets	9,200	9,300	100	1,300	(1,200)					1,200
Liabilities										
Long-term debt (DM6 million)	(2,000)	(1,800)	200	(400)	600				(600)	
Long-term debt (Fr fr 150 million)	(10,000)	(12,500)	(2,500)		(2,500)		2,500			
Long-term debt (£5 million)	(5,000)	(4,500)	500		500				(500)	
Other liabilities	(4,200)	(1,600)	2,600	(50)	2,650					(2,650)
Net assets	52,000	62,080	10,080	3,675	6,405					
Shareholders' funds										
Share capital	40,000	40,000	—		—					
Revaluation reserve	—	1,875	1,875		1,875	1,875				
Foreign currency investment translation reserve	—	575	575	3,075	(2,500)		(2,500)			
Retained earnings	12,000	19,630	7,630	600	7,030			7,030		
	52,000	62,080	10,080	3,675	6,405	—	—	16,925	(16,225)	(700)

Table 13   Calculation of funds flow exchange rate impact

	Fr fr 000	Exchange rate of 10 £000	Exchange rate of 8 £000	Differences £000	Translation adjustment £000 Note (b)	Other adjustments £000	Exchange rate impact £000 Table 12
Assets							
Purchased goodwill	15,000	1,500	1,875	375	(375)		1,375
Land — at valuation	55,000	5,500	6,875	1,375	625		1,500
Other fixed assets — at cost	35,000	3,500	4,375	875			
— accumulated depreciation	(10,000)	(1,000)	(1,250)	(250)			(250)
Inventory — at cost	8,000	800	1,000	200			200
Other current assets	52,000	5,200	6,500	1,300			1,300
Liabilities							
Long-term debt (DM6 million)	(20,000)	(2,000)	(2,500)	(500)		100 (j)	(400)
Other liabilities	(2,000)	(200)	(250)	(50)			(50)
Inter-company items							
Fr fr loan account	(30,000)	(3,000)	(3,750)	(750)	750		
£ inter company account	(20,000)	(2,000)	(2,500)	(500)		500 (k)	
Net assets	83,000	8,300	10,375	2,075	1,000	600	3,675
Shareholders' funds							
Share capital	50,000	5,000	6,250	1,250	(1,250)		
Revaluation reserve	15,000	1,500	1,875	375	(375)		
Foreign currency investment translation reserve	—	—	—	—	3,075		3,075
Retained earnings	18,000	1,800	2,250	450	(450)	600 (j)+(k)	600
	83,000	8,300	10,375	2,075	1,000	600	3,675

* Notes (j) and (k) appear on pp 274–275 following.

*Table 14   Consolidated statement of source and application of funds
for 19X2 — net basis*

£000

Sources of funds

Group profit *(Table 11)*   7,630

Adjustments for items not involving the movement of funds —
    depreciation, net   9,625
    amortisation of goodwill   270
    gain on £ intercompany account   (500)
    gain on DM-denominated debt   (100)
Generated from operations   16,925

Application of funds

Purchase of fixed assets, net   (15,125)
Repayment of DM debt   (600)
Repayment of £ debt   (500)
Increase in working capital   700

Increase (decrease) in working capital

Inventory   (750)
Other current assets   (1,200)
Other liabilities   2,650
                                                             700

Note (j) Translation of third-currency borrowings

The long-term Deutschmark debt shown as Fr fr 20 million as at 1
January has been translated on Table 13 at the 1 January and 31
December rates of exchange. Such an approach assumes, however,
that the item is a French franc-denominated asset, which is clearly
not the case.

If one had taken the underlying DM6 million and translated it using
the 1 January and 31 December rates of exchange the result would
have been as follows:

	£000
DM6 million at DM3	2,000
DM6 million at DM2.5	2,400
Sterling exchange loss	400

This compares with the £500,000 loss shown as a net movement on Table 13 above.

In order to derive the underlying movement in this account in sterling terms it is necessary to adjust for the exchange impact of £400,000 rather than £500,000 and adjustment (j) accordingly reclassifies £100,000 of the movement to net income.

In economic terms the £100,000 represents the exchange gain arising in Sub Cie as a result of the movement in the DM/Fr fr rate over the period in question. This can be shown as follows:

	Fr fr 000
DM6 million at 3.3333	20,000
DM6 million at 3,2000	19,200
Fr fr exchange gain	800

This Fr fr 800,000 (or £100,000) accordingly represents a non-cash profit in the accounts of Sub Cie and is treated as such in the consolidated funds flow statement on Table 14. The amount differs from the Fr fr 650,000 (£81,000) shown in Table 7, due to the way in which the part-repayment during the year has been recorded.

Note (k) Sterling intercompany account

The intercompany account used for inventory purchases from Tops Ltd is denominated in sterling and the consolidation adjustments (note (f) above) have already taken account of the year-end mismatch between the underlying £ balance and the Fr fr amount recorded in the books of Sub Cie.

The £500,000 exchange movement arising on Table 13 against this heading has already been taken into account in the consolidation process, and is, in fact, a part of the £700,000 adjustment referred to in note (f). The amount is, in other words, already included in the calculation of group profit and this movement is therefore the non-cash adjustment to that profit to be made in the statement of source and application of funds.

The amount is accordingly reclassified on Table 13 to net income by way of adjustment (k), and has been separately identified on Table 14 as a non-cash movement.

Note (l) Movement on fixed assets

The movement in the fixed-asset accounts used for the purposes of preparing the statement of source and application of funds may be summarised as follows:

	Sub Cie		Tops Ltd	Adjust-ment Note (d)*	Total
	Fr fr 000	£000	£000	£000	£000
Additions	45,000	5,625	10,000	—	15,625
Retirements	(4,000)	(500)	—	—	(500)
Net additions	41,000	5,125	10,000	—	15,125
Depreciation	(8,000)	(1,000)	(8,000)	(625)	(9,625)
Net movement	33,000	4,125	2,000	(625)	5,500

* Note (d) is on page 267 above.

All of the above numbers are available from Table 5.

Note (m) Revaluation of land

The gross movement in the land revaluation in Table 12 amounts to £3,250,000, but this is actually a combination of a gain of £1,375,000 on exchange and £1,875,000 in underlying currency terms. The consolidation process adopted has ensured that it is only the latter balance which has been credited to the revaluation reserve, with the £1,375,000 exchange impact being included in the amount taken to the foreign currency investment translation reserve.

This approach is consistent with that advocated in chapter 9.

Appendices

Statement of Standard Accounting Practice (SSAP 20): Foreign Currency Translation

Foreign currency translation

(Issued April 1983)

The provisions of this statement of standard accounting practice should be read in conjunction with the Explanatory Foreword to Accounting Standards *and need not be applied to immaterial items. The provisions apply to financial statements prepared under either the historical cost convention or the current cost convention.*

This statement sets out the standard accounting practice for foreign currency translation, but does not deal with the method of calculating profits or losses arising from a company's normal currency dealing operations; neither does it deal specifically with the determination of distributable profits.

PART 1 EXPLANATORY NOTE

Background

1　A company may engage in foreign currency operations in two main ways:

(a)　Firstly, it may enter directly into business transactions which are denominated in foreign currencies; the results of these transactions will need to be translated into the currency in which the company reports.

(b)　Secondly, foreign operations may be conducted through a foreign enterprise which maintains its accounting records in a currency other than that of the investing company; in order to prepare consolidated financial statements it will be necessary to translate the complete financial statements of the foreign enterprise into the currency used for reporting purposes by the investing company.

Objectives of translation

2　The translation of foreign currency transactions and financial statements should produce results which are generally compatible with the effects of rate changes on a company's cash flows and its equity and should ensure that the financial statements present a true and fair view of the results of management actions. Consolidated statements should reflect the financial results and relationships as measured in the foreign currency financial statements prior to translation.

Procedures

3　In this statement the procedures which should be adopted when accounting for foreign operations are considered in two stages, namely:

(a)　the preparation of the financial statements of an individual company; and

(b)　the preparation of consolidated financial statements.

The individual company stage

4 During an accounting period, a company may enter into transactions which are denominated in a foreign currency. The result of each transaction should normally be translated into the company's local currency using the exchange rate in operation on the date on which the transaction occurred; however, if the rates do not fluctuate significantly, an average rate for a period may be used as an approximation. Where the transaction is to be settled at a contract rate, that rate should be used; where a trading transaction is covered by a related or matching forward contract, the rate of exchange specified in that contract may be used.

5 Once non-monetary assets, e g plant, machinery and equity investments, have been translated and recorded they should be carried in the company's local currency. Subject to the provisions of paragraph 29 (below) concerning the treatment of foreign equity investments financed by foreign currency borrowings, no subsequent translations of these assets will normally need to be made.

6 At the balance sheet date monetary assets and liabilities denominated in a foreign currency, e g cash and bank balances, loans and amounts receivable and payable, should be translated by using the rate of exchange ruling at that date, or, where appropriate, the rates of exchange fixed under the terms of the relevant transactions. Where there are related or matching forward contracts in respect of trading transactions, the rates of exchange specified in those contracts may be used.

7 An exchange gain or loss will result during an accounting period if a business transaction is settled at an exchange rate which differs from that used when the transaction was initially recorded, or, where appropriate, that used at the last balance sheet date. An exchange gain or loss will also arise on unsettled transactions if the rate of exchange used at the balance sheet date differs from that used previously.

8 Exchange gains or losses arising on settled transactions in the context of an individual company's operations have already been reflected in cash flows, since a change in the exchange rate increases or decreases the local currency equivalent of amounts paid or received in cash settlement. Similarly, it is reasonably certain that exchange gains or losses on unsettled short-term monetary items will soon be reflected in cash flows. Therefore, it is normally appropriate, because of the cash flow effects, to recognise such gains and losses as part of the profit or loss for the year; they should be included in profit or loss from ordinary activities unless they arise from events which themselves would fall to be treated as extraordinary items, in which case they should be included as part of such items.

9 When dealing with long-term monetary items, additional considerations apply. Although it is not easy to predict what the exchange rate will be when a long-term liability or asset matures, it is necessary, when stating

the liability or the asset in terms of the reporting currency, to make the best estimate possible in the light of the information available at the time; generally speaking translation at the year-end rate will provide the best estimate, particularly when the currency concerned is freely dealt in on the spot and forward exchange markets.

10   In order to give a true and fair view of results, exchange gains and losses on long-term monetary items should normally be reported as part of the profit or loss for the period in accordance with the accruals concept of accounting; treatment of these items on a simple cash movements basis would be inconsistent with that concept. Exchange gains on unsettled transactions can be determined at the balance sheet date no less objectively than exchange losses; deferring the gains whilst recognising the losses would not only be illogical by denying in effect that any favourable movement in exchange rates had occurred but would also inhibit fair measurement of the performance of the enterprise in the year. In particular, this symmetry of treatment recognises that there will probably be some interaction between currency movements and interest rates and reflects more accurately in the profit and loss account the true results of currency involvement.

11   For the special reasons outlined above, both exchange gains and losses on long-term monetary items should be recognised in the profit and loss account. However, it is necessary to consider on the grounds of prudence whether the amount of the gain, or the amount by which exchange gains exceed past exchange losses on the same items, to be recognised in the profit and loss account should be restricted in the exceptional cases where there are doubts as to the convertibility or marketability of the currency in question.

12   Gains or losses on exchange arising from transactions between a holding company and its subsidiaries, or from transactions between fellow subsidiaries, should normally be reported in the individual company's financial statements as part of the profit or loss for the year in the same way as gains or losses arising from transactions with third parties.

The consolidated financial statements stage

13   The method used to translate financial statements for consolidation purposes should reflect the financial and other operational relationships which exist between an investing company and its foreign enterprises.

14   In most circumstances the closing rate/net investment method, described in paragraphs 15 to 20 (below), should be used and exchange differences accounted for on a net investment basis. However, in certain specified circumstances (see paragraphs 21 to 24 below) the temporal method should be used.

The closing rate/net investment method

15   This method recognises that the investment of a company is in the net worth of its foreign enterprise rather than a direct investment in the individual assets and liabilities of that enterprise. The foreign enterprise will normally have net current assets and fixed assets which may be financed partly by local currency borrowings. In its day-to-day operations the foreign enterprise is not normally dependent on the reporting currency of the investing company. The investing company may look forward to a stream of dividends but the net investment will remain until the business is liquidated or the investment disposed of.

16   Under this method the amounts in the balance sheet of a foreign enterprise should be translated into the reporting currency of the investing company using the rate of exchange ruling at the balance sheet date. Exchange differences will arise if this rate differs from that ruling at the previous balance sheet date or at the date of any subsequent capital injection (or reduction).

17   Amounts in the profit and loss account of a foreign enterprise should be translated at the closing rate or at an average rate for the accounting period. The use of the closing rate is more likely to achieve the objective of translation, stated in paragraph 2, of reflecting the financial results and relationships as measured in the foreign currency financial statements prior to translation. However, it can be argued that an average rate reflects more fairly the profits or losses and cash flows as they arise to the group throughout an accounting period. The use of either method is therefore permitted, provided that the one selected is applied consistently from period to period.

18   No definite method of calculating the average rate has been prescribed, since the appropriate method may justifiably vary as between individual companies. Factors that will need to be considered include the company's internal accounting procedures and the extent of seasonal trade variations; the use of a weighting procedure will in most cases be desirable. Where the average rate used differs from the closing rate, a difference will arise which should be dealt with in reserves.

19   The results of the operations of a foreign enterprise are best reflected in the group profit and loss account by consolidating the net profit or loss shown in its local currency financial statements without adjustment (other than for normal consolidation adjustments). If exchange differences arising from the retranslation of a company's net investment in its foreign enterprise were introduced into the profit and loss account, the results from trading operations, as shown in the local currency financial statements, would be distorted. Such differences may result from many factors unrelated to the trading performance or financing operations of the foreign enterprise: in particular, they do not represent or measure changes in actual or prospective cash flows. It is therefore inappropriate to regard them as profits or losses and they should be dealt with as adjustments to reserves.

20   Although equity investments in foreign enterprises will normally be made by the purchase of shares, investments may also be made by means of long-term loans and inter-company deferred trading balances. Where financing by such means is intended to be, for all practical purposes, as permanent as equity, such loans and inter-company balances should be treated as part of the investing company's net investment in the foreign enterprise; hence exchange differences arising on such loans and inter-company balances should be dealt with as adjustments to reserves.

The temporal method

21   For most investing companies in the UK and Ireland foreign operations are normally carried out through foreign enterprises which operate as separate or quasi-independent entities rather than as direct extensions of the trade of the investing company.

22   However, there are some cases in which the affairs of a foreign enterprise are so closely interlinked with those of the investing company that its results may be regarded as being more dependent on the economic environment of the investing company's currency than on that of its own reporting currency. In such a case the financial statements of the foreign enterprise should be included in the consolidated financial statements as if all its transactions had been entered into by the investing company itself in its own currency. For this purpose the temporal method of translation should be used; the mechanics of this method are identical with those used in preparing the accounts of an individual company, as stated in paragraphs 4 to 12 (above).

23   It is not possible to select one factor which of itself will lead a company to conclude that the temporal method should be adopted. All the available evidence should be considered in determining whether the currency of the investing company is the dominant currency in the economic environment in which the foreign enterprise operates. Amongst the factors to be taken into account will be:

(a)   the extent to which the cash flows of the enterprise have a direct impact upon those of the investing company;
(b)   the extent to which the functioning of the enterprise is dependent directly upon the investing company;
(c)   the currency in which the majority of the trading transactions are denominated;
(d)   the major currency to which the operation is exposed in its financing structure.

24   Examples of situations where the temporal method may be appropriate are where the foreign enterprise:

(a)   acts as a selling agency receiving stocks of goods from the investing company and remitting the proceeds back to the company;

(b)   produces a raw material or manufactures parts or sub-assemblies which are then shipped to the investing company for inclusion in its own products;

(c)   is located overseas for tax, exchange control or similar reasons to act as a means of raising finance for other companies in the group.

The treatment of foreign branches

25   For the purpose of this statement, foreign operations which are conducted through a foreign branch should be accounted for in accordance with the nature of the business operations concerned. Where such a branch operates as a separate business with local finance, it should be accounted for using the closing rate/net investment method. Where the foreign branch operates as an extension of the company's trade and its cash flows have a direct impact upon those of the company, the temporal method should be used.

Areas of hyper-inflation

26   Where a foreign enterprise operates in a country in which a very high rate of inflation exists it may not be possible to present fairly in historical cost accounts the financial position of a foreign enterprise simply by a translation process. In such circumstances the local currency financial statements should be adjusted where possible to reflect current price levels before the translation process is undertaken.

The special case of equity investment financed by foreign borrowings

27   Under the procedures set out in this statement, exchange gains or losses on foreign currency borrowings taken up by an investing company or foreign enterprise would normally be reported as part of that company's profit or loss from ordinary activities and would flow through into the consolidated profit and loss account.

28   Where an individual company has used borrowings in currencies other than its own to finance foreign equity investments, or where the purpose of such borrowings is to provide a hedge against the exchange risk associated with existing equity investments, the company may be covered in economic terms against any movement in exchange rates. It would be inappropriate in such cases to record an accounting profit or loss when exchange rates change.

29   Therefore, provided the conditions set out in this paragraph apply, the company may denominate its foreign equity investments in the appropriate foreign currencies and translate the carrying amounts at the end of each accounting period at the closing rates of exchange. Where investments are treated in this way, any resulting exchange differences should be taken direct to reserves and the exchange gains or losses on the borrowings should then

be offset, as a reserve movement, against these exchange differences. The conditions which must apply are as follows:

(a) in any accounting period, exchange gains or losses arising on the borrowings may be offset only to the extent of exchange differences arising on the equity investments;
(b) the foreign currency borrowings, whose exchange gains or losses are used in the offset process, should not exceed, in the aggregate, the total amount of cash that the investments are expected to be able to generate, whether from profits or otherwise; and
(c) the accounting treatment adopted should be applied consistently from period to period.

30 Similarly, within a group, foreign borrowings may have been used to finance group investments in foreign enterprises or to provide a hedge against the exchange risk associated with similar existing investments. Any increase or decrease in the amount outstanding on the borrowings arising from exchange movements will probably be covered by corresponding changes in the carrying amount of the net assets underlying the net investments (which would be reflected in reserves). Since in this case the group will be covered in economic terms against any movement in exchange rates, it would be inappropriate to record an accounting profit or loss when exchange rates change.

31 In the consolidated financial statements, therefore, subject to certain conditions, the exchange gains or losses on such foreign currency borrowings, which would otherwise have been taken to the group profit and loss account, may be offset as reserve movements against exchange differences on the retranslation of the net investments. The conditions which must apply are as follows:

(a) the relationship between the investing company and the foreign enterprises concerned should be such as to justify the use of the closing rate method for consolidation purposes;
(b) in any accounting period, exchange gains or losses arising on foreign currency borrowings may be offset only to the extent of the exchange differences arising on the net investments in foreign enterprises;
(c) the foreign currency borrowings, whose exchange gains or losses are used in the offset process, should not exceed, in the aggregate, the total amount of cash that the net investments are expected to be able to generate, whether from profits or otherwise; and
(d) the accounting treatment adopted should be applied consistently from period to period.

32 Where the provisions of paragraph 29 (above) have been applied in the investing company's financial statements to a foreign equity investment which is neither a subsidiary nor an associated company, the same offset procedure may be applied in the consolidated financial statements.

PART 2 DEFINITION OF TERMS

33   *Financial statements* are balance sheets, profit and loss accounts, statements of source and application of funds, notes and other statements, which collectively are intended to give a true and fair view of the financial position and profit or loss.

34   *Company* includes any enterprise which comes within the scope of statements of standard accounting practice

35   An *exempt company* is one which:

(a)   is registered in Great Britain and does not prepare its accounts in accordance with either Sections 149 and 152 of the Companies Act 1948; or
(b)   is registered in Northern Ireland and is exempted from full disclosure by Part 3 of Schedule 6A to the Companies Act (Northern Ireland) 1960 as amended by the Companies (Northern Ireland) Order 1982; or
(c)   is registered in the Republic of Ireland and is exempted from full disclosure by Part 3 of Schedule 6 to the Companies Act 1963.

36   A *foreign enterprise* is a subsidiary, associated company or branch whose operations are based in a country other than that of the investing company or whose assets and liabilities are denominated mainly in a foreign currency.

37   A *foreign branch* is either a legally constituted enterprise located overseas or a group of assets and liabilities which are accounted for in foreign currencies.

38   *Translation* is the process whereby financial data denominated in one currency are expressed in terms of another currency. It includes both the expression of individual transactions in terms of another currency and the expression of a complete set of financial statements prepared in one currency in terms of another currency.

39   A company's *local currency* is the currency of the primary economic environment in which it operates and generates net cash flows.

40   An *exchange rate* is a rate at which two currencies may be exchanged for each other at a particular point in time; different rates apply for spot and forward transactions.

41   The *closing rate* is the exchange rate for spot transactions ruling at the balance sheet date and is the mean of the buying and selling rates at the close of business on the day for which the rate is to be ascertained.

42   A *forward contract* is an agreement to exchange different currencies at a specified future date and at a specified rate. The difference between the specified rate and the spot rate ruling on the date the contract was entered into is the discount or premium on the forward contract.

43   The *net investment* which a company has in a foreign enterprise is its effective equity stake and comprises its proportion of such foreign enterprise's net assets; in appropriate circumstances, intra-group loans and other deferred balances may be regarded as part of the effective equity stake.

44   *Monetary items* are money held and amounts to be received or paid in money and, where a company is not an exempt company, should be categorised as either short-term or long-term. Short-term monetary items are those which fall due within one year of the balance sheet date.

PART 3 STANDARD ACCOUNTING PRACTICE

45   When preparing the financial statements of an individual company the procedures set out in paragraphs 46 to 51 (below) should be followed. When preparing consolidated financial statements, the procedures set out in paragraphs 52 to 58 (below) should be followed.

Individual companies

46   Subject to the provisions of paragraphs 48 and 51 (below) each asset, liability, revenue or cost arising from a transaction denominated in a foreign currency should be translated into the local currency at the exchange rate in operation on the date on which the transaction occurred; if the rates do not fluctuate significantly, an average rate for a period may be used as an approximation. Where the transaction is to be settled at a contracted rate, that rate should be used. Where a trading transaction is covered by a related or matching forward contract, the rate of exchange specified in that contract may be used.

47   Subject to the special provisions of paragraph 51 (below), which relate to the treatment of foreign equity investments financed by foreign currency borrowings, no subsequent translations should normally be made once non-monetary assets have been translated and recorded.

48   At each balance sheet date, monetary assets and liabilities denominated in a foreign currency should be translated by using the closing rate or, where appropriate, the rates of exchange fixed under the terms of the relevant transactions. Where there are related or matching forward contracts in respect of trading transactions, the rates of exchange specified in those contracts may be used.

49   All exchange gains or losses on settled transactions and unsettled short-term monetary items should be reported as part of the profit or loss for

the year from ordinary activities (unless they result from transactions which themselves would fall to be treated as extraordinary items, in which case the exchange gains or losses should be included as part of such items).

50   Exchange gains and losses on long-term monetary items should also be recognised in the profit and loss account; however, it is necessary to consider on the grounds of prudence whether, in the exceptional cases outlined in paragraph 11 (above), the amount of the gain, or the amount by which exchange gains exceed past exchange losses on the same items to be recognised in the profit and loss account, should be restricted.

51   Where a company has used foreign currency borrowings to finance, or provide a hedge against, its foreign equity investments and the conditions set out in this paragraph apply, the equity investments may be denominated in the appropriate foreign currencies and the carrying amounts translated at the end of each accounting period at closing rates for inclusion in the investing company's financial statements. Where investments are treated in this way, any exchange differences arising should be taken to reserves and the exchange gains or losses on the foreign currency borrowings should then be offset, as a reserve movement, against these exchange differences. The conditions which must apply are as follows:

(a)   in any accounting period, exchange gains or losses arising on the borrowings may be offset only to the extent of exchange differences arising on the equity investments;

(b)   the foreign currency borrowings, whose exchange gains or losses are used in the offset process, should not exceed, in the aggregate, the total amount of cash that the investments are expected to be able to generate, whether from profits or otherwise; and

(c)   the accounting treatment adopted should be applied consistently from period to period.

Consolidated financial statements

52   When preparing group accounts for a company and its foreign enterprises, which includes the incorporation of the results of associated companies or foreign branches into those of an investing company, the closing rate/net investment method of translating the local currency financial statements should normally be used.

53   Exchange differences arising from the retranslation of the opening net investment in a foreign enterprise at the closing rate should be recorded as a movement on reserves.

54   The profit and loss account of a foreign enterprise accounted for under the closing rate/net investment method should be translated at the closing rate or at an average rate for the period. Where an average rate is used,

the difference between the profit and loss account translated at an average rate and at the closing rate should be recorded as a movement on reserves. The average rate should be calculated by the method considered most appropriate for the circumstances of the foreign enterprise.

55   In those circumstances where the trade of the foreign enterprise is more dependent on the economic environment of the investing company's currency than that of its own reporting currency, the temporal method should be used.

56   The method used for translating the financial statements of each foreign enterprise should be applied consistently from period to period unless its financial and other operational relationships with the investing company change.

57   Where foreign currency borrowings have been used to finance, or provide a hedge against, group equity investments in foreign enterprises, exchange gains or losses on the borrowings, which would otherwise have been taken to the profit and loss account, may be offset as reserve movements against exchange differences arising on the retranslation of the net investments provided that:

(a)   the relationships between the investing company and the foreign enterprises concerned justify the use of the closing rate method for consolidation purposes;
(b)   in any accounting period, the exchange gains and losses arising on foreign currency borrowings are offset only to the extent of the exchange differences arising on the net investments in foreign enterprises;
(c)   the foreign currency borrowings, whose exchange gains or losses are used in the offset process, should not exceed, in the aggregate, the total amount of cash that the net investments are expected to be able to generate, whether from profits or otherwise; and
(d)   the accounting treatment is applied consistently from period to period.

58   Where the provisions of paragraph 51 (above) have been applied in the investing company's financial statements to a foreign equity investment which is neither a subsidiary nor an associated company, the same offset procedure may be applied in the consolidated financial statements.

Disclosure

59   The methods used in the translation of the financial statements of foreign enterprises and the treatment accorded to exchange differences should be disclosed in the financial statements.

60   The following information should also be disclosed in the financial statements:

(a)   for all companies, or groups of companies, which are not exempt companies, the net amount of exchange gains and losses on foreign currency borrowings less deposits, identifying separately:
   (i)   the amount offset in reserves under the provisions of paragraphs 51, 57 and 58; and
   (ii)   the net amount charged/credited to the profit and loss account;
(b)   for all companies, or groups of companies, the net movement on reserves arising from exchange differences.

Date from which effective

61   The accounting and disclosure requirements set out in this statement should be adopted as soon as possible. They should be regarded as standard in respect of financial statements relating to accounting periods beginning on or after 1 April 1983.

PART 4 LEGAL REQUIREMENTS IN UK AND IRELAND

62   Paragraphs 63 to 69 below apply to companies preparing accounts in compliance with Sections 249 and 152 of the Companies Act 1948 or with Sections 143 and 146 of the Companies Act (Northern Ireland) 1960. The references to the Schedule which follow are to Schedule 8 to the Companies Act 1948 (as inserted by Section 1 of the Companies Act 1981). References to the Schedule will also be to Schedule 6 to the Companies Act (Northern Ireland) 1960, as inserted by Article 3 of the Companies (Northern Ireland) Order 1982, when this is brought into operation on 1 July 1983.

63   Paragraph 12 of the Schedule requires that the amount of any item shall be determined on a prudent basis and, in particular, that only profits realised at the balance sheet date shall be included in the profit and loss account. (Paragraph 90 of the Schedule defines realised profits in relation to a company's accounts as 'such profits of the company as fall to be treated as realised profits for the purposes of those accounts in accordance with principles generally accepted with respect to the determination for accounting purposes of realised profits at the time when those accounts are prepared.')

64   Paragraph 15 of the Schedule permits a departure from paragraph 12 of the Schedule if it appears to the directors that there are special reasons for such a departure. Particulars of any departure, the reasons for it and its effect must be given in a note to the accounts.

65   For companies other than exempt companies, all exchange gains taken through the profit and loss account, other than those arising on unsettled long-term monetary items, are realised. For such companies the application of paragraph 50 of this statement may result in unrealised exchange gains on unsettled long-term monetary items being taken to the profit and loss

account. In this statement the need to show a true and fair view of results, referred to in paragraph 10 above, is considered to constitute a special reason for departure from the principle under paragraph 15 of the Schedule.

66 This statement is based on the assumption that the process of translation at closing rates for the purposes of this statement does not constitute a departure from the historical cost rules under Section C of the Schedule nor does it give rise to a diminution in value of an asset under Section B of the Schedule.

67 Paragraph 58(1) of the Schedule requires that, where sums originally denominated in foreign currencies are brought into the balance sheet or profit and loss account, the basis on which those sums have been translated into sterling shall be stated.

68 Part I of the Schedule lays down the choice of formats permitted for the presentation of accounts. Distinction is drawn between operating and other income and expense. For this reason it is necessary to consider the nature of each foreign exchange gain or loss and to allocate each accordingly. Gains or losses arising from trading transactions should normally be included under 'Other operating income or expense' while those arising from arrangements which may be considered as financing should be disclosed separately as part of 'Other interest receivable/payable and similar income/expense'. Exchange gains or losses which arise from events which themselves fall to be treated as extraordinary items should be included as part of such items.

69 Paragraph 46 of the Schedule requires the following information to be disclosed about movements on any reserve:

(a) the amount of the reserve at the date of the beginning of the financial year and as at the balance sheet date respectively;
(b) any amounts transferred to or from the reserve during that year; and
(c) the source and application respectively of any amounts so transferred.

70 Paragraphs 1 and 2 of Schedule 2 to the Companies Act 1981 permit certain companies to prepare accounts in compliance with Sections 149A and 152A of and Schedule 8A to the Companies Act 1948 instead of Sections 149 and 152 and Schedule 8. Paragraph 11(9) of Schedule 8A requires disclosure of the basis on which foreign currencies have been converted into sterling. Schedule 2 to the Companies (Northern Ireland) Order 1982 will permit similar companies registered in Northern Ireland to prepare accounts in accordance with Sections 143A and 146A of and Schedule 6A to the Companies Act (Northern Ireland) 1960 which require the same disclosure.

71 Similar legal requirements are expected to be enacted in the Republic of Ireland.

PART 5 COMPLIANCE WITH INTERNATIONAL ACCOUNTING STANDARD NO 21: 'ACCOUNTING FOR THE EFFECTS OF CHANGES IN FOREIGN EXCHANGE RATES'

72 Compliance with the requirements of Statement of Standard Accounting Practice No 20 'Foreign currency translation' will automatically ensure compliance with International Accounting Standard No 21 'Accounting for the effects of changes in foreign exchange rates'.

Foreign exchange advisory services

The following is an extremely brief summary of some of the better-known foreign exchange advisory services. The summary has been prepared based on information currently available and apologies are made in relation to any services which have been omitted or any information which is now out of date. The list has been divided between those services that are direct banking offshoots and those that are independent operations. Most recent addresses and telephone numbers have been included at the end of the listing.

1 BANKING OFFSHOOTS

(i)Chase Econometrics. Chase has been a long-standing provider of forecasting services based on econometric models.

(ii)Chemical Bank. Chemical has tended to concentrate on technical analysis and is able to provide advice on a day-by-day basis using its in-house models.

(iii)Goldman Sachs. A more recent service which tends to be based on economic fundamentals over the longer term. Technical analysis is used for short-term projections.

(iv)International Treasury Management. This was originally a partnership between Marine Midland and Hong Kong Bank Ltd and is now marketed by the latter. It provides a custom-made approach to forex consultancy, offering a fairly continuous monitoring of currency exposures.

(v)Others. Most of the other banks are able to provide consultancy services on either a structured or an informal basis. They do not necessarily, however, promote those services in quite the same way as the above organisations.

2 INDEPENDENT OPERATIONS

(i)Barnes & Co Financial. A Chicago-based organisation using chart analysis to recommend hedging approaches relating to futures or options.

(ii)Best & Associates Sarl. A long-standing forecasting service providing custom made advice. Based in Paris.

(iii)A G Bisset & Co Inc. Another well-known US adviser using technical analysis.

(iv)Commodity Management Service Corpn. Another Chicago-based organisation specialising in the commodity markets.

(v)Chemfico. Probably one of the largest independent advisers, used by a large number of banks in Europe and the Middle East. This is a sophisticated service run from Brussels in eight different languages.

(vi)Compucom Research Inc. A newer consultant operating from New York and using both technical models and fundamental analysis.

(vii)Forexia (UK) Ltd. A more limited service run from the UK and covering, primarily, sterling, Deutschmarks, yen and the dollar.

(viii)Friedberg Commodity Management Inc. Another specialised commodity operation, run this time from Toronto.

(ix)FX Concepts. A smaller New York-based consultancy using a number of interrelated trend models.

(x)Hanseatic Group. Both fundamental analysis and technical models are available covering a large number of currencies. Operating from New Mexico.

(xi)Henley Centre for Forecasting. Chartist and other technical methods are used to produce three-month forecasts with fundamental economic analysis being used for longer-term projections. Henley's main output consists of a number of publications which include their foreign exchange forecasts, although advice is available on a case-by-case basis to individual clients.

(xii)Interfinance SA. A more recent consultancy using technical analysis and covering the major currencies. Based in Brussels.

(xiii)International Treasury Consulting Inc. Technical models covering a large number of currencies run from New York.

(xiv)Investment Research. A small, Cambridge-based adviser, using technical models and also providing individual telephone consultancy.

(xv)Brian Marber & Co. Another small, but fairly long-standing, adviser providing a sophisticated one-to-one consultancy service, Brian Marber uses a private Reuters page and is based in London.

(xvi)Multinational Computer Models Inc. Technical analysis provided from New York, primarily for foreign exchange dealers.

(xvii)Predex. Technical models covering a large number of currencies and run from New York.

(xviii)Preview Economics Inc. Providing a 'daily currency report', containing position recommendations based on short-term technical analysis. Based in Virginia.

(xix)Stoll Momentum System. A longer-standing consultancy using technical models for both trading and long-term hedging purposes. Based in Toronto.

(xx)Valuta Economics. A Danish-based service using both technical models and fundamental analysis.

(xxi)Waldner & Co. A long-standing Illinois firm providing direct management exposure and general advisory services.

Addresses and telephone numbers

Banking offshoots

Chase Econometrics
 52 Avenue des Arts
 1040 Brussels
 Belgium
 Tel: (322) 511-1144

Chemical Bank
 20 Pine Street
 New York
 N.Y.10005
 Tel: (212) 310 4730

Goldman Sachs
 5 Old Bailey
 London EC2
 Tel: (01) 248-6464

International Treasury Management
 Hong Kong Bank Ltd
 Wardley House
 7 Devonshire Square
 London EC2M 4HN
 Tel: (01) 626-0566

Independent operations

Barnes and Co Financial
 Board of Trade Building
 141 West Jackson Boulevard
 Suite 1240 A
 Chicago 60604
 Illinois
 USA
 Tel: (312) 341-4500

Best & Associates Sarl
46 Rue de Provence
75004 Paris
France
Tel: Paris 45.26.81.79

A G Bissett & Co Inc
Five Mile Landing
71 Rowayton Avenue
Rowayton, CT 06853
USA
Tel: (203) 866-3540

Commodity Management Service Corporation
327 South LaSalle Street
Suite 800
Chicago, 60604
Illinois
USA
Tel: (312) 922-3662

Chemfico
Avenue des Arts/Kunstlaan 46
B 1040 Brussels
Tel: (322) 512-3647

Compucom Research Inc
60 Madison Avenue
Suite 1217
New York
N.Y. 10010
USA
Tel: (212) 889-5890

Forexia (UK) Ltd
46 Limerston Street
London SW10 0HH
Tel: (01) 351-0350

Friedberg Commodity Management Inc
347 Bay Street
Suite 207
Toronto
Ontario
MH5 2R7
Tel: (416) 364-1171

FX Concepts
    26 Broadway
    New York
    N.Y. 10004
    USA
    Tel: (212) 269-4440

Hanseatic Group
    1110 Pennsylvania NE
    Albuquerque
    New Mexico 87110
    Tel: (505) 262-1981

Henley Centre for Forecasting
    2 Tudor Street
    London EC4

Interfinance SA
    222 Avenue de Terueren
    Box 2
    1150 Brussels
    Tel: (322) 763-0960

International Treasury Consulting Inc
    26 Broadway
    New York
    N.Y. 10004
    USA
    Tel: (212) 809-1400

Investment Research
    28 Panton Street
    Cambridge
    CB2 1DH
    Tel: (0223) 356251

Brian Marber & Co
    16 Charles II Street
    London, SW1Y 4QU
    Tel: (01) 930-8352

Multinational Computer Models Inc
    605 Bloomfield Avenue
    Montclair
    New Jersey 07042
    USA
    Tel: (201) 746-5060

Predex
      3 East 54 Street
      New York
      N.Y. 10022-3108
      USA
      Tel: (212) 319 5400

Preview Economics Inc
      6623 Deer Gap Court
      Alexandria
      Virginia 22310
      USA
      Tel: (703) 97104736

Stoll Momentum System
      50 Teddington Park Avenue
      Toronto
      Ontario
      M4N 2C6
      Canada
      Tel: (416) 488-2181

Valuta Economics
      Hojleddet 12
      DK2840 Holte
      Copenhagen
      Denmark
      Tel: (02) 804151

Waldner & Co
      2301 West 22 Street
      Suite 201
      Oak Brook
      Illinois 60521
      USA
      Tel: (312) 574-0770

Index